AF478468

International Political Economy Series

General Editor: **Timothy M. Shaw**, Professor of Commonwealth Governance and Development, and Director of the Institute of Commonwealth Studies, School of Advanced Study, University of London

Titles include:

Leslie Elliott Armijo (*editor*)
FINANCIAL GLOBALIZATION AND DEMOCRACY IN EMERGING MARKETS

Robert Boardman
THE POLITICAL ECONOMY OF NATURE
Environmental Debates and the Social Sciences

Jörn Brömmelhörster and Wolf-Christian Paes (*editors*)
THE MILITARY AS AN ECONOMIC ACTOR
Soldiers in Business

Gordon Crawford
FOREIGN AID AND POLITICAL REFORM
A Comparative Analysis of Democracy Assistance and Political Conditionality

Matt Davies
INTERNATIONAL POLITICAL ECONOMY AND MASS COMMUNICATION
IN CHILE
National Intellectuals and Transnational Hegemony

Martin Doornbos
INSTITUTIONALIZING DEVELOPMENT POLICIES AND RESOURCE
STRATEGIES IN EASTERN AFRICA AND INDIA
Developing Winners and Losers

Fred P. Gale
THE TROPICAL TIMBER TRADE REGIME

Meric S. Gertler and David A. Wolfe
INNOVATION AND SOCIAL LEARNING
Institutional Adaptation in an Era of Technological Change

Mary Ann Haley
FREEDOM AND FINANCE
Democratization and Institutional Investors in Developing Countries

Keith M. Henderson and O. P. Dwivedi (*editors*)
BUREAUCRACY AND THE ALTERNATIVES IN WORLD PERSPECTIVES

Jomo K.S. and Shyamala Nagaraj (*editors*)
GLOBALIZATION VERSUS DEVELOPMENT

Angela W. Little
LABOURING TO LEARN
Towards a Political Economy of Plantations, People and Education
in Sri Lanka

John Loxley (*editor*)
INTERDEPENDENCE, DISEQUILIBRIUM AND GROWTH
Reflections on the Political Economy of North–South Relations at the
Turn of the Century

Don D. Marshall
CARIBBEAN POLITICAL ECONOMY AT THE CROSSROADS
NAFTA and Regional Developmentalism

Susan M. McMillan
FOREIGN DIRECT INVESTMENT IN THREE REGIONS OF THE SOUTH AT
THE END OF THE TWENTIETH CENTURY

James H. Mittelman and Mustapha Pasha (*editors*)
OUT FROM UNDERDEVELOPMENT
Prospects for the Third World (Second Edition)

Lars Rudebeck, Olle Törnquist and Virgilio Rojas (*editors*)
DEMOCRATIZATION IN THE THIRD WORLD
Concrete Cases in Comparative and Theoretical Perspective

Benu Schneider (*editor*)
THE ROAD TO INTERNATIONAL FINANCIAL STABILITY
Are Key Financial Standards the Answer?

Howard Stein (*editor*)
ASIAN INDUSTRIALIZATION AND AFRICA
Studies in Policy Alternatives to Structural Adjustment

International Political Economy Series
Series Standing Order ISBN 0–333–71708–2 hardback
Series Standing Order ISBN 0–333–71110–6 paperback
(*outside North America only*)

You can receive future titles in this series as they are published by placing a standing order. Please contact your bookseller or, in case of difficulty, write to us at the address below with your name and address, the title of the series and one of the ISBNs quoted above.

Customer Services Department, Macmillan Distribution Ltd, Houndmills, Basingstoke, Hampshire RG21 6XS, England

The Road to International Financial Stability

Are Key Financial Standards the Answer?

Edited by

Benu Schneider

 in association with 

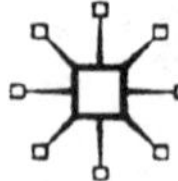

First published 2003 by
PALGRAVE MACMILLAN
Houndmills, Basingstoke, Hampshire RG21 6XS and
175 Fifth Avenue, New York, N.Y. 10010
Companies and representatives throughout the world

PALGRAVE MACMILLAN is the global academic imprint of the Palgrave
Macmillan division of St. Martin's Press, LLC and of Palgrave Macmillan Ltd.
Macmillan® is a registered trademark in the United States, United Kingdom
and other countries. Palgrave is a registered trademark in the European
Union and other countries.

ISBN 1–4039–1587–3 hardback

This book is printed on paper suitable for recycling and made from fully
managed and sustained forest sources.

A catalogue record for this book is available from the British Library.

Library of Congress Cataloging-in-Publication Data
    The road to international financial stability: are key financial standards
    the answer?/edited by Benu Schneider.
        p. cm. – (International political economy series)
    Includes bibliographical references and index.
    ISBN 1–4039–1587–3 (cloth)
    1. International finance. 2. Economic stabilization. 3. Finance –
Developing countries. I. Schneider, Benu, 1955– II. Series.
HG3881.R575 2003
332′.042—dc21   2003054761

10   9   8   7   6   5   4   3   2   1
12   11   10   09   08   07   06   05   04   03

Printed and bound in Great Britain by
Antony Rowe Ltd, Chippenham and Eastbourne

Contents

Part III Private-sector Perspectives

Part IV Invited Commentary

List of Tables, Figures and Boxes

Tables

Figures

Boxes

Acknowledgements

I take this opportunity to express my gratitude and thanks to the UK Department for International Development (DFID) for its financial support for the conference on 'International Standards and Codes: The Developing Country Perspective' and the publication of this volume. DFID supports policies, programmes and projects to promote international development, and provided funds for this study as part of that objective; however, the views and opinions expressed are those of the authors alone. A special thanks to Winston Cox, Deputy Secretary-General, Commonwealth Secretariat and his team for facilitating and providing additional financial support for the meeting on which this volume is based. My gratitude and thanks also go to Yilmaz Akyuz, Chief, Globalisation and Development Strategies Division, and Kamran Kousari, Officer-in-Charge, Debt and Development Finance Branch, United Nations Conference on Trade and Development (UNCTAD) for giving me time to organise the conference and work on this volume, a project that was started prior to my move to UNCTAD. The opinions expressed are those of the authors and do not necessarily reflect the views of UNCTAD. Thanks also to Giorgio Gualberti and Grace Juhn, who assisted with Chapter 2, and to Margaret Cornell who read painstakingly through the manuscript, made editorial changes and compiled the index, Angela O'Callaghan and Tony Traub for providing excellent assistance for the meeting, and Roo Griffiths for co-ordinating the book's publication. Last, but not least, I wish to thank Simon Maxwell, Director, Overseas Development Institute for his continuing support for the project, and the contributors to this volume for their co-operation and ideas, without which the volume would not have been possible.

BENU SCHNEIDER

List of Abbreviations

ADR	American Deposit Receipt
AML	Anti-money laundering
APEG	Asia/Pacific Group on Money Laundering
BCBS	Basle Committee on Banking Supervision
BIS	Bank for International Settlements
BoP	Balance of Payments
BoT	Bank of Thailand
BWI	Bretton Woods institutions
CAPS	Capital Augmented Preference Shares
CARs	Capital adequacy ratios
CCL	Contingency credit lines
CFT	Combating the financing of terrorism
CPLG	Core Principles Liaison Group
CPSS	Committee on Payment and Settlement Systems
DEAR	Daily earnings ratio
DFID	Department for International Development
DR	Depository Receipt
EFT	Electronic funds transfer
EME	Emerging market economy
FATF	Financial Action Task Force
FDIC	Federal Deposit Insurance Corporation
FIRST	Financial Sector Reform and Strengthening
FLC	'Forward-looking criteria' for loan classification
FSA	Financial Services Authority
FSAP	Financial Sector Assessment Programme
FSF	Financial Stability Forum
FSSA	Financial System Stability Assessment
GAAP	Generally Accepted Accounting Principles
GAFI	Groupe d'Action Financière sur le Blanchiment de Capitaux
GDDS	General Data Dissemination System
GDP	Gross Domestic Product
GDR	Global Depository Receipts
HLIs	Highly leveraged institutions
IAIS	International Association of Insurance Supervisors
IASB	International Accounting Standards Board
IASC	International Accounting Standards Committee

IFAC	International Federation of Accountants
IFI	International financial institutions
IMF	International Monetary Fund
IMFC	International Monetary and Financial Committee
IOSCO	International Organization of Securities Commissions
IRB	Internal risk based
KIEP	Korea Institute for International Economic Policy
LTCM	Long-Term Capital Management
MoF	Ministry of Finance
NASDAQ	National Association of Securities Dealers Automated Quotations (USA)
NPLs	Non-performing loans
NYSE	New York Stock Exchange
ODI	Overseas Development Institute
OECD	Organisation for Economic Co-operation and Development
OFC	Offshore financial centre
RBI	Reserve Bank of India
ROSC	Reports on Standards and Codes
RTGS	Real time gross settlement system
S&C	Standards and Codes
SDDS	Special Data Dissemination Standard
SEBI	Securities and Exchange Board of India
SEC	Securities and Exchange Commission
SLIPS	Staple Limited Interest Preferred Shares
SRO	Self-regulatory organisation
UNCTAD	United Nations Conference on Trade and Development

Notes on the Contributors

T. C. A. Anant is Professor of Economics at the Delhi School of Economics, University of Delhi. His research interests are in law and economics, with special focus on the problems of developing countries. In this connection he has been a consultant to the Government of India, the Reserve Bank of India and multilateral agencies. Most recently he has been assisting the Standing Committee of International Financial Standards and Codes in India.

Michael Bates joined Oxford Analytica in 1998. A graduate of Wadham College, University of Oxford (MBA, 1998), and with twelve years in the UK financial services industry, he was elected in 1992 to the UK Parliament, serving for five years as a Member and three years as a Minister (Government Whip, Lord Commissioner of HM Treasury and HM Paymaster General). He is a non-executive director of estandardsforum. com Inc. in the USA, and Congregational and General plc in the UK.

Alastair Clark read Mathematics at Cambridge and Economics at the London School of Economic and joined the Bank of England in the early 1970s. He has worked as Personal Assistant to the Deputy Governor, Alternate UK Executive Director at the IMF in Washington, and Alternate Director of the European Investment Bank. He was appointed Executive Director, Financial Stability, at the Bank of England in March 1997.

Andrew Cornford was until the spring of 2003 a long-serving Senior Economic Affairs Officer at UNCTAD working on international financial issues, his special interests being financial services and their regulation. He is now a Fellow of the Financial Markets Center, where his responsibilities will continue to be financial regulation and closely related policy issues.

Javier Guzmán studied Economics at the National University of Mexico, and did his graduate studies at the University of Louvain and Yale University. He is currently Director of International Affairs at the Bank of Mexico.

David Lubin was educated at Oxford University, where he received a bachelor's degree in Philosophy, Politics and Economics; and at the

Fletcher School, Tufts University, where he received a master's degree specialising in International Economics. He joined the HSBC group in 1989, and represented the Midland Bank in 'Brady plan' negotiations with Argentina, Brazil and Bulgaria. Since 1993 he has been responsible for HSBC's emerging markets research.

Michael Metcalfe is a senior strategist at State Street Bank and Trust Company. A Cambridge Economics graduate, he has spent seven years working as a financial market analyst, specialising more recently in aspects in investor behaviour.

Aziz Ali Mohammed, a Pakistani economist, is currently the G-24 Deputy for his country. He is a former Alternate Executive Director at the IMF, and a member of its senior staff, including heading its External Relations Department. He has also served as Adviser to the Governor of the Saudi Arabian Monetary Agency, and Economic Adviser, Ministry of Finance, Government of Pakistan.

Axel Nawrath is Managing Director, Policy, Communication and Legal, Deustche Börse. He studied Law and Political Sciences at the Universities of Frankfurt and Montpellier, and holds a Doctorate in Law. He has worked for the German Federal Ministry of Finance, NATO and the German Federal Court of Audit. He is a member of the Supervisory Board of Deusche Postbank AG and Hermes Kreditversicherungs AG.

Avinash Persaud is Managing Director and Global Head of Research at State Street Bank and Trust Company. He holds the Mercer School Memorial Chair in Commerce at Gresham College and sits on a number of main boards or governing councils of major public institutions, including the London School of Economics and Political Science, the Overseas Development Institute, the Global Association of Risk Professionals and the World Quality Council for Corporate Governance.

Lionel Price is Chief Economist at Fitch Sovereign Ratings. Before joining IBCA (one of the rating agencies that have merged to form Fitch) in 1997, he was Director of Central Banking Studies at the Bank of England, where he worked for nearly thirty years. From 1979 to 1981 he was the Alternate Executive Director for the United Kingdom at the International Monetary Fund.

Y. Venugopal Reddy is Executive Director for India, Sri Lanka, Bangladesh and Bhutan at the International Monetary Fund. Prior to this, he was Deputy Governor, Reserve Bank of India, responsible for economic analysis and policy, monetary policy, development of financial markets, and external sector management. Formerly, he was Secretary, Ministry of Finance, and Additional Secretary, Ministry of Commerce, in the Government of India. He has been associated closely with several academic institutions in teaching and research capacities. He has written several articles and published a number of books. He also chaired the Standing Committee on International Financial Standards and Codes set up by the Reserve Bank of India in December 1999.

Benu Schneider is a respected expert in international finance, currently based in the Globalisation and Development Strategies Division at UNCTAD. Previous positions have included Research Fellow at the Overseas Development Institute, professorial position at ICRIER, and adviser and consultant to the Reserve Bank of India. She holds a Doctorate in Economics from the University of Kiel, Germany, and is the author of *Capital flight from Developing Countries* (1991), regarded as a seminal work in this area. Dr Schneider has combined academic and consultancy with hand-on policy advice on macroeconomic polices and domestic financial sector reforms. She has also authored an influential policy paper for the Narasimham Committee on Banking Reforms (1998) in India.

Andrew Walter has a doctorate and is Senior Lecturer in International Relations at the London School of Economics, specialising in the political economy of international money and finance. He is currently working on a book about the implementation of international financial regulatory standards in East Asia since the crisis.

1
Introduction

Benu Schneider

The frequency of crises in emerging markets in recent years has set in motion new initiatives to reform the global economy. The establishment of the Financial Stability Forum[1] (FSF) in February 1999 by the G-7 finance ministers and central bank governors was an initiative in response to the East Asian financial crisis and reflects a broad consensus reached by them about the importance of co-ordinating globally certain aspects of domestic financial and regulatory policy and institutions, under the rubric of Standards and Codes (S&C).[2] Recent experience has demonstrated that, as developing countries integrate themselves into the global economy, their national economic and financial policies become a matter of greater concern to other members of the international 'club', who want reassurance that everyone is playing by broadly the same rules, or at least is not exposing the 'club' to unreasonable risks.

Furthermore, the recent history of emerging-market financial crises provides circumstantial evidence that shortcomings in financial regulation and supervision, transparency and market integrity have contributed to the incidence and severity of such crises. The condition of the balance sheets of all segments of the economy is now seen as a factor in explaining crises; thus the S&C exercise is seen as a way of systematising the lessons from past experience. The principal aim of the S&C exercise is the attainment of global financial stability by means of better information and improved governance of financial and non-financial corporate systems. It is an attempt to develop an international rules-based system for crucial areas of domestic policy and institutions, in recognition of the linkages between national and international regulatory arrangements, and between markets and international institutions. Table 1.1 lists the key areas for S&Cs as identified by the Financial Stability Forum,

Table 1.1 Key standards for financial systems[*]

Subject area	Key standard	Issuing body
Macroeconomic policy and data transparency		
Monetary and financial[a]	Code of Good Practices on Transparency in Monetary and Financial Policies	IMF
Fiscal policy transparency[b]	Code of Good Practices in Fiscal Transparency	IMF
Data dissemination[b]	Special Data Dissemination Standard (SDDS)	IMF
	General Data Dissemination System (GDDS)[c]	
Institutional and market infrastructure		
Insolvency[d]	Principles and Guidelines on Effective Insolvency Systems[e]	World Bank
Corporate governance[d]	Principles of Corporate Governance	OECD
Accounting[d]	International Accounting Standards (IAS)[f]	IASC[g]
Auditing[d]	International Standards on Auditing (ISA)	IFAC[g]
Payment and settlement[a]	Core Principles for Systemically Important Payment Systems	CPSS
Market integrity	The Forty Recommendations of the Financial Action Task Force on Money Laundering and eight special recommendations in the aftermath of 11 September 2001	FATF
Financial regulation and supervision		
Banking supervision[a]	Core Principles for Effective Banking Supervision	BCBS
Securities regulation[a]	Objectives and Principles of Securities Regulation	IOSCO
Insurance supervision[a]	Insurance Supervisory Principles	IAIS

Notes

[*] All these 12 key areas have now been incorporated into the operational work of the IMF and World Bank.

[a] ROSC modules in these areas are mostly derived as by-products from a parallel Bank–Fund Financial Sector Assessment Programme (FSAP), although banking supervision, and monetary and financial policy transparency, lie within the Fund's direct operational focus.

[b] The Fund takes the lead in preparing ROSC modules in these areas.

[c] Economies that have, or might seek, access to international capital markets are encouraged to subscribe to the more stringent SDDS, and all other economies are encouraged to adopt the GDDS.

[d] The World Bank takes the lead in preparing ROSC modules in these areas.

[e] The World Bank is co-ordinating a broad-based effort to develop these principles and guidelines. The United Nations Commission on International Trade Law (UNCITRAL), which adopted the Model Law on Cross-Border Insolvency in 1997, will help facilitate implementation.

[f] The BCBS has reviewed relevant IAS, and a joint BCBS–IASC group is further considering bank-related issues in specific IAS. IOSCO has reviewed and recommended use of 30 IAS in cross-border listings and offerings, supplemented, where necessary, to address issues at a national or regional level.

[g] The International Accounting Standards Committee (IASC) and the International Federation of Accountants (IFAC) are distinct from other standard-setting bodies in that they are private sector bodies.

Source: Compiled from FSF and IMF websites.

which are suggested as representing minimum requirements for good practice.[3]

However, there are several elements of the S&C process that raise serious issues from the perspective of developing countries. Standard-setting in many areas appears to be the unique preserve of industrial countries, and at best a minority of developing countries. This lack of representation has led to the aphorism 'no harmonisation without representation'. As against the view that banking is no different in developing countries from developed countries and can therefore be subject to uniform rules, a contradictory voice questions the wisdom of applying globally financial standards that have not prevented crises in the developed countries. Similar issues arise with the codes on corporate governance drawn from the practice of advanced countries that current events have shown to be less than effective in preventing widespread abuse. However, the S&C cover a number of areas where the debate is less acrimonious. Many emerging markets have undertaken reforms in order to reduce their vulnerability to crisis by improving the transparency of their economies and financial sectors. The issue of implementation costs (monetary/human resources) in the developing countries should not be underestimated, but should be considered alongside the costs of failure – leading to a delicately balanced equation.

A conference in London on 'International Standards and Codes: The Developing Country Perspective' on 21 June 2002,[4] organised with support from the UK Department for International Development and the Commonwealth Secretariat, aimed to highlight policy issues both at a global level and for individual developing countries in implementing international S&C. Participants discussed how the process could be adapted to meet the needs of both developing and developed economies more effectively, while at the same time contributing to the overall objective of global financial stability. The conference brought together policy-makers from a wide range of governments, central banks and international organisations, plus economists from research institutes, universities and non-governmental organisations, as well as representatives from the private sector involved in the S&C debate.

This volume reflects the views of policy-makers, private market participants, including credit rating agencies, and academia. Following an overview of the issues, it is divided into four parts: developing country perspectives and experiences; developed country perspectives; private-sector perspectives; plus an invited commentary on the volume which includes comments on emerging issues. An Appendix covers the broad workings of the S&C debate to date. An outline of the issues dealt with can be summarised as follows:

- the rationale for a globally co-ordinated set of codes for domestic financial and regulatory policy and institutions;
- the present level of compliance and the incentive structure for compliance in both developed and developing countries;
- policy ownership, the 'one-size-fits-all' dilemma and the challenge of sequencing;
- resource constraints in implementation and the role of technical assistance;
- issues in monitoring standards and codes by the Bretton Woods institutions: are there other alternatives?
- should standards and codes be a part of conditionality?
- the adherence to standards and codes and its impact on credit rating and access to private capital flows; and
- the role of information in crisis prevention and the information-generation process.

Developing country perspectives and experience

Benu Schneider opens this section by setting out in Chapter 2 the issues involved in defining universally accepted standards in areas crucial for the maintenance of international financial stability, while taking into consideration institutional and legal structures, and the different stages of economic development across regions and countries. The chapter queries whether global financial stability can indeed be secured if countries that are of systemic importance in the international marketplace do not comply with some of the codes, as is the case with some of the G-7 countries. Schneider explains the asymmetric incentive structure between developed and developing countries in implementing the codes. In addition, developing-country perspectives with respect to the issues of ownership, prioritisation, appropriateness and sequencing are taken up. Two further themes are explored: the limitations intrinsic to the codes and the lack of use of the codes by private sector actors. This illustrates the lack of economic evidence for the S&C process. Limitations intrinsic to the implementation process are discussed, using selected codes as illustrations. The chapter argues that it may be better to work with principles rather than more specific rules. It also argues against making the implementation of codes and standards a part of conditionality in accessing funds from the IMF, and makes a case for self-assessments combined with a peer review process co-ordinated by the Bretton Woods institutions as a better way forward than the BWIs themselves acting as global monitors. The chapter opens up the policy debate by highlighting the open issues with this initiative.

In Chapter 3, Aziz Ali Mohammed discusses the institutional aspects of implementing standards and codes through the Bretton Woods institutions. The chapter proceeds from a recognition of the usefulness of S&C as one component of a set of financial crisis prevention tools that the international community is deploying, through the Bretton Woods institutions (BWIs), to strengthen the stability of the international financial system and to help developing countries integrate better into the global capital market. S&C are also seen as a means for these countries to evaluate their own systems against international benchmarks, to identify vulnerabilities and gaps in regulatory structures and practices, and to indicate medium-term development needs and priorities.

Following a description of BWI activity, it summarises the evolution of developing-countries' thinking on the subject of standards, as indicated by ministerial statements made in the context of the Group of Twenty-Four (G-24) communiqués. It discusses some issues arising out of the implementation of the Reports on the Observance of Standards and Codes initiative through the BWIs, and the appropriateness of using them as the main means for monitoring compliance on the part of their developing-country members. The incompatibility between assisting financial reform and providing information on compliance with a single template for the entire membership, and the incompatibility of trying to get market participants interested in the work of the BWIs, might be seen as seeking to impose market discipline in addition to their own discipline.

Two case studies, on India and Mexico, follow. India has been an active participant from the outset in the process of building a new international financial architecture. Financial sector reforms in India did not originate with standards and codes, rather the S&C self-assessment grew out of a reform programme in the 1990s. Recognising the importance of this initiative, and in order to examine the status and guide the implementation of these S&Cs in India, the Reserve Bank of India established in December 1999 a 'Standing Committee on International Financial Standards and Codes'. This Committee then set up ten Advisory Groups encompassing the twelve key areas prescribed by the Financial Stability Forum. Their reports provide a valuable internal assessment of a developing country's perspective on S&Cs.

Chapter 4, by T. C. A. Anant, offers a brief review of the advisory group reports, examining the issue of assessing compliance with the S&Cs and the implications for policy, and drawing upon the reports to highlight the interrelated and dynamic character of the process. It concludes with some lessons that reinforce the traditional position India has taken *vis-à-vis* these S&Cs. This experience indicates that the modalities of consensus building, and the processes of implementation, need to be adjusted to each context. While uniformity is possible for the standards on economic and financial transparency, and to a certain degree for banking supervision and regulation, a more flexible approach is needed for questions of institutional and market infrastructure.

Javier Guzman's chapter (Chapter 5) on the Mexican experience has two objectives. The first is to describe Mexico's experience with international codes and standards, including an explanation of the benefits derived from the assessments carried out, and an analysis of the extent to which concerns frequently heard among developing countries have been relevant in the Mexican case. The second is to evaluate the progress made to date with this initiative at the international level and the main challenges ahead. Mexico has been an active player in the S&C process. The Mexican authorities subscribed formally to the Special Data Dissemination Standard (SDDS) in 1996, a decision that was influenced considerably by the 1994–5 crisis. More recently, a Financial Sector Assessment Programme (FSAP) was carried out for Mexico, which included S&C assessments in five different areas. Furthermore, following the successful completion of this exercise, two additional assessments have been requested.

Notwithstanding these positive developments, the chapter suggests that Mexico is still far from meeting the objectives set for this initiative. In fact, Guzman is of the view that Mexico may have reached a point where further progress, in what is considered by some as the most prominent and ambitious item on the architectural agenda, will be increasingly complicated.

International standards and codes are supposed to play a leading role in transforming financial regulatory governance in post-crisis East Asia. In Chapter 6, Andrew Walter argues that the main problem with this reform strategy is that it underestimates the likelihood of implementation failure in the reforming countries. He shows that, contrary to the intention of the standards and codes, regulatory forbearance remains chronic in a number of East Asian countries. The result is that standards of prudential regulation lag behind the process of financial liberalisation. This 'perverse sequencing' creates ongoing financial vulnerabilities for these countries. Since, as Walter argues, the reasons for implementation failure are deeply ingrained in the domestic political economies, this casts doubt not only on the role of the international financial institutions and capital markets as 'enforcers' of standards and codes, but also on the wisdom of the S&C exercise in general.

Developed-country perspectives

Alastair Clark discusses in Chapter 7 why setting out international best practices has moved up the agenda in recent years. It goes on to discuss the issues in the G-7 economies, and in this context takes up the issues of formulation, monitoring and implementation. The chapter concludes with the value added by the S&C exercise to the international financial architecture.

Axel Nawrath comments in Chapter 8 on external assessments in the standards and codes exercise versus self-assessments, and considers who should review them. His chapter makes a case for the further updating of S&C, prioritisation of standards and the response of market participants.

Private-sector perspectives

Lionel Price introduces Part III by looking, in Chapter 9, for evidence of any impact of the various standards and codes on sovereign credit ratings, and on the ability of emerging-market governments to borrow on international markets. The standards with the greatest potential to enhance the creditworthiness of sovereign governments are those on data, fiscal transparency, banking supervision, and transparency in monetary and financial policies. While issues such as corporate governance are important, this is considered less likely to be the proximate cause of a default. Awareness of the standards does not seem to be widespread among market participants, so they may not yet be having much effect on market incentives. Emerging-market borrowers that were wholly or partly shut out of the market in 1998 are the most likely to have published reports on their implementation of the standards and codes, but it is difficult to find evidence that these have had any favourable effect on their borrowing costs. Yet, since 1998 there has been a strong statistical relationship between upgrades and downgrades of sovereign ratings and the numbers of reports countries have agreed to publish. This suggests that the combined effect of working to improve implementation of the S&C and publishing information about this can strengthen a country's credit rating, although so far there is no conclusive evidence that the resulting upgrades in country rating assessments have led to lower spreads on bond issues. The chapter points out, however, that governments undertaking reforms without permitting the publication of reports risk losing the potential beneficial impact on perceptions of their creditworthiness.

Following the crises in Asia and Argentina, and more recently the weakness in global equity markets following the US accounting scandals, there would appear to be a stronger-than-ever case for better standards regarding the quality and disclosure of information. Yet this assumption is based on the notion that these market failures are caused by lack of information, and that improvement in the quality and dissemination of information will therefore help to avoid future crises. However, taking a long-run perspective, the evidence that better information would reduce the incidence of crises is minimal. While there can be little doubt that access to information improved over the course of the twentieth century, the incidence of crises has not fallen; quite the reverse is the case, in fact.

Considering a variety of recent crisis episodes, Michael Metcalfe and Avinash Persaud in Chapter 10 find three principal reasons why better disclosure alone is not the panacea it is often assumed to be: first, they find market myopia with specific reference to the Asian and NASDAQ crises, where information was available but the market chose to focus on other variables; and second, the provision of 'bad news'. It is important to remember that improved delivery and clarity of information provide no guarantee that investment flows will become less volatile. Using State Street's proprietary database, Metcalfe and Persaud find no statistical relationship between the publication of Reports on the Observance of Standards and Codes, and the volatility of cross-border equity flows into a range of emerging markets since the end of the 1990s. Finally, they consider that the release of some forms of information may in fact make some markets, with specific reference to Latin America, more volatile, if the information contributes to the tendency of investors to herd. The chapter concludes that improved information flows are a necessary, but not a sufficient, condition to prevent crises.

While the information from the Bretton Woods institutions on compliance with standards and codes suffers from lack of global coverage, especially of countries that are important systemically in global financial markets, a private sector initiative has stepped in to fill the information gap. Michael Bates explains this initiative in Chapter 11; the eStandardsForum is a private-sector organisation which identifies, aggregates and interprets third-party assessments in order to provide a single source of information on standards implementation. In Bates's view, the private sector can provide the vehicle for conveying large amounts of complex information in a user-friendly form, but it cannot on its own fill the information gap. Ultimately, it is only through a commitment to transparency and disclosure on the part of governments that information on implementation of S&C can be made more widely available.

In Chapter 12, David Lubin examines the reasons for the lack of interest by the private sector in standards and codes, and in this context discusses some underlying problems with the initiative. The chapter further examines other areas where steps need to be taken as a means of crisis prevention.

Conclusions

The final chapter is an invited commentary on the volume from a developing country perspective. Dr Y. V. Reddy examines the papers critically and recommends issues for future research and debate.

Key financial standards – a guide

The chapter by Andrew Cornford is in the form of an appendix that serves as a useful guide to key financial standards. It covers the recent initiatives aimed at strengthening the international financial architecture, many of which are directed at agreement on and implementation of standards for major areas of economic policy. The key financial standards dealt with in this chapter cover macroeconomic policy, disclosure, the financial sector and financial transactions. The standards on data dissemination and macroeconomic, financial and fiscal policies are concerned with procedures and good governance rather than policy rules. The standards on institutional and market infrastructure cover a number of specific subjects. Concerning many of these, there have been long-standing international initiatives, but they are included in the set of key financial standards because of their potential not only for improving practice at the microeconomic level but also for contributing to systemic stability. These standards deal with insolvency rules, corporate governance, accounting, auditing, payments and settlement, and money laundering and terrorist financing. The last three standards concern rules for the regulation and supervision of banking, securities markets and the insurance sector. The contents of those standards, now embodied in agreed sets of rules, often required difficult and lengthy negotiations to reconcile differing points of view concerning complex issues, and in the case of some of the standards these negotiations are still continuing. Moreover, both rules and negotiations can be subject to the need for revision or extension, because of the unfolding of events such as the bankruptcy of ENRON, which is already having an effect on the standards for accounting, auditing and possibly corporate governance, and will continue to do so for some time to come; and the terrorist attack on New York on 11 September 2001, which has already led to a major extension of initiatives on money laundering.

The summary below picks up the main points made by the papers:

- Financial stability is a global concern, and there are problems regarding its attainment in both rich and poor countries.
- Standards and codes are useful as a way of benchmarking progress in the reform of financial systems.
- There is evidence that adoption of S&C does lead to improved country credit ratings, especially when standard assessments are allowed to be published, though not necessarily to access to international capital markets on more favourable terms.
- However, S&C are not a solution on their own, and may, in some circumstances, contribute to herding behaviour and greater volatility.
- S&C do need to be developed jointly, and owned by all countries, through a consensual process.
- Especially for developing countries, the adoption of S&C is costly and time-consuming, so that a graduated and gradual approach is required.
- Progress in adoption needs to be tracked, of course, but over-dependence on quantitative indicators should be avoided, in favour of an approach incorporating qualitative as well as quantitative information.
- Monitoring of S&C by the Bretton Woods institutions, as at present, is a source of potential difficulties, and a self-assessment procedure, backed up by peer review, would be better.
- The latter approach would also help to avoid inclusion of S&C in IMF and World Bank conditionality, a step concerning which there is probably no consensus at present.

The chapters in this volume take some initial steps in throwing light on some of the issues involved in the development and application of standards and codes. By no means do they address all the relevant questions, however. Rather, they attempt to point to the complexity of a process that will take years to implement. Despite these features of the process, surveillance of standards has already become a part of IMF Article IV consultations, and the publication of ROSCs a consideration in developing countries reaching agreements with the IMF. To the extent that the private sector has also incorporated compliance with key standards in its decision-making processes, additional barriers to developing country access to finance might have been put in place unintentionally. The demand for simplified and easily summarised information by the private sector overlooks the length of time required for successful implementation of S&C. The OECD countries after all took nearly forty years to comply with the Codes of Liberalisation.

Two conflicting elements of the S&C debate are thus becoming apparent. At the multilateral level, there is a growing belief that through ROSCs, and emphasis on compliance with the codes, developing countries can be assisted in financial-sector reform. At the level of the private sector response, after the criticisms made of its lending and investment decisions before the recent financial crises, compliance with S&Cs may be taken into account increasingly as an additional factor in the evaluation of developing countries. However, this may precede adequate understanding of the meaning and significance of standards and codes, and requirements for their successful implementation. Clarification is still needed concerning the objectivity of the codes and further elaboration of the required incentive structures. It is hoped that this volume will go some way towards increasing understanding of the issues raised, and will stimulate researchers, private-sector participants and official policy-makers to undertake the further analytical and policy work that is still needed.

Notes

1 The Financial Stability Forum (FSF) was convened in April 1999 to promote international financial stability through information exchange and international co-operation in financial supervision and surveillance. The Forum brings together on a regular basis national authorities responsible for financial stability in significant international financial centres, international financial institutions, sector-specific international groupings of regulators and supervisors, and committees of central bank experts. The FSF seeks to co-ordinate the efforts of these various bodies in order to promote international financial stability, improve the functioning of markets, and reduce systemic risk (FSF website).

2 In this book, standards and codes denote global rules, principles and regulations defined by the FSF and intended to promote international financial stability. The Reports on the Observance of Standards and Codes (ROSCs) by the International Monetary Fund (IMF) summarise the extent to which countries observe certain internationally recognised standards and codes. The IMF has recognised eleven areas and associated standards as being useful for the operational work of the Fund and the World Bank. These comprise: data; monetary and financial policy transparency; fiscal transparency; banking supervision;

securities; insurance; payments systems; corporate governance; accounting; auditing; and insolvency and creditor rights. Some ROSCs are derived from the joint World Bank and IMF Financial Sector Assessment Programme (FSAP). On the basis of division of labour between the two institutions, some ROSCs derive exclusively from the World Bank's work (for example, in such areas as corporate governance, insolvency regimes, accounting and auditing). Reports summarising countries' observance of these standards are prepared and published at the request of the member country. Short updates are produced regularly, and new reports are produced every few years (IMF website).

3   The FSF identified seventy-three standards, twelve of which were selected as key standards in the three areas of macroeconomic policy transparency and accurate and timely data dissemination; institutional market infrastructure; and financial regulation and supervision. The nature of these standards differs for each area. For example, in terms of macro policy and data transparency, the standards are not about the substance of policy *per se*, but about information provision and disclosure procedures. As far as market institutions are concerned, the standards are more prescriptive, but in terms of broad principles. For the regulation of payments systems, for example, there is a mixture: there are broad principles but few specifics on implementation. Adherence to S&C in these three areas is seen by many to be a fundamental step in reforming the international financial architecture.

4   This volume is based partly on the papers presented at this meeting. Three additional papers were invited: to cover the East Asian experience (Andrew Walter), industrialised country perspectives (Axel Nawrath) and private sector perspectives (David Lubin). Dr Reddy was invited to write an overall commentary, and this is published as the concluding chapter to the book.

Part I

Developing-country Perspectives and Experience

2
Implications of Implementing Standards and Codes: A Developing-country Perspective

Benu Schneider[1]

Introduction

> And I have become convinced that it is in the interests of stability – and of preventing crises in developing countries and emerging market economies – that we seek a new rule-based system: a reformed system of economic government under which each country, rich and poor, adopts agreed codes and standards for fiscal and monetary policy and for corporate governance ... over time – the implementation of the codes should be a condition of IMF and World Bank support. (Gordon Brown, UK Chancellor of the Exchequer, speech to the Federal Reserve Board, New York, 16 November 2001.)

The intention of the architects of the new global financial architecture is to maintain international financial stability. The international initiative consists of defining rules for transparency, financial supervision and regulation. The purpose is to ensure that only countries that accept these globally defined rules gain access to international support – for example, in times of crisis. This process of defining rules has for the most part been undertaken by the industrialised world, along with some of the 'emerging block' countries. Developing countries are expected to comply with the new rule-based system if they are to have access to international finance.

The idea of global rules is very appealing. For the first time, the linkages between national and international regulatory bodies, the market and international financial institutions are recognised explicitly.

Common standards are being attempted to facilitate international comparisons and to avoid confused signals from an individual country. It is also believed that such rules will enhance the role of market discipline, because countries that want to improve their access to international finance will have the incentive to enforce the standards.

Despite the intuitive appeal of a globally defined set of rules, there is a need for caution, because there is a danger of producing a system that is too inflexible and that does not allow for the differences in institutional development, legislative framework, and the various stages of development. The generally accepted rules and principles under which the financial and corporate sectors operate in the industrialised world have evolved over time. Introducing rules that are imported from other parts of the world may not therefore have the desired outcomes. Research to investigate the likely implications is needed. Investigation into the impact of the proposed global rules on the efficiency of financial systems and domestic financial stability is particularly urgent. Other critical research areas include the limitations of the new initiatives, requirements for implementation, and structuring of transition periods. These issues should be discussed and researched from both a developed and a developing country perspective. Furthermore, the urgency of the subject arose against the backdrop of the 1997–8 East Asian crisis, yet problems of compliance with these rules are a global phenomenon, which has often been ignored in recent debate and frequently is regarded as a developing-country or emerging-market issue. What is more, rules alone will not help to prevent a crisis or contagion. Rules of corporate governance in the United States did not help to avert the ENRON disaster, and Argentina has found itself in crisis despite substantial compliance with transparency codes.

This chapter aims to facilitate a discussion about the issues involved in defining universally accepted standards in areas crucial for the maintenance of international financial stability, while taking into consideration institutional and legal structures and the different stages of economic development across regions and countries. Although the implementation of standards is an issue affecting all countries, this chapter devotes more attention to developing-country issues. It is organised as follows: the second section provides the background for the present discussion; and the third section examines some of the general issues arising from the policy initiative from the perspective of developing countries. Two themes run through the fourth section: the limitations intrinsic to the codes are outlined by using a few codes as an illustration, and selected examples are used to illustrate some limitations that also arise in the implementation process and the limits of that process. The fifth and final section throws open the debate with some issues for discussion.

Background

In the aftermath of the East Asian crisis the international community has been engaged in reforming the international financial architecture to deal with some of the dangers inherent in globalisation. The dynamic growth in capital markets following the liberalisation of financial markets in many countries occurred without taking fully into account domestic, economic and financial weaknesses, and regulatory and supervisory frameworks. A vital lesson that has been learnt is that the health of both internal and external balance sheets is important in all sectors of the economy, be it the central bank, the government or the private sector. Another important lesson concerns the role of information in the smooth functioning of international financial markets, a lack of which often leads to contagion and herding by international investors. The crisis also highlighted the lack of transparency on the part of international institutional investors, and the inability of the international financial architecture to prevent and manage financial crises. The post-crisis international emphasis has been on strengthening players, through stronger risk management, more prudent standards and improved transparency.

The establishment of the Financial Stability Forum (FSF) in February 1999 by the G-7 finance ministers and Central Bank governors[2] was a new initiative in direct response to the East Asian crisis, and it reflects the importance given to globally co-ordinated financial and regulatory aspects of domestic policy and the need to rethink those regulations grouped together under the heading of standards and codes (S&C). The Forum supports the belief that financial stability can be promoted by the improved exchange of information, and co-operation with regard to financial supervision and surveillance. This is the first attempt to develop a single set of international rules and principles for crucial areas of domestic policy in the financial and monetary spheres.

Identifying standards is a complex task. Moreover, the dynamic nature of these markets and their increasing sophistication means that these standards will have to be flexible enough to incorporate this process of change. The FSF has identified over sixty standards; and twelve of these standards and codes (see Table 1.1) in the three areas of macro policy and data transparency, institutional market infrastructure, and financial regulation and supervision, have been endorsed by the

G-7 countries and the multilateral institutions as being essential for financial stability. In practice, the classification of the standards and codes into three categories is not very distinct. For example, macroeconomic policy can have a crucial effect on the more sectoral dimensions of financial stability through its impact on the values of financial firms' assets and liabilities (and thus on the context in which financial regulation and supervision are conducted), as well as on the functioning of the payments and settlement system (which is at the heart of the infrastructure of financial markets). Effective financial regulation and supervision are related inextricably to accounting, auditing and insolvency procedures. Insurance products are frequently incorporated into, or sold in close conjunction with, investment products, thus increasing the channels through which disturbances affecting the market for one financial service can be transmitted between markets. And even such an apparently self-contained issue as money laundering has on occasion threatened the stability of financial firms (UNCTAD, 2001).

The codes provide a body of 'best practice' pooled from different international standard-setting bodies and regulatory frameworks related to the legal, regulatory and institutional framework for any financial system. Many of them are intended to serve as guidelines, but some, such as the standard on data dissemination, can be detailed and precise (see Table 1.1).

International standards are not a new concept. The international standard-setting bodies have existed for a long time, but each has developed its rules in isolation. Various international standard-setting bodies have raised awareness about standards of soundness and risk in financial systems.[3] The implementation of these has, until now, been voluntary and differed across countries and firms.

In order to discuss implementation of international best practice relating to the legal, regulatory and institutional framework underpinning a financial system, a global overview of the present situation with regard to compliance is desirable, but not readily available. There are three possible sources of information about the implementation of standards and codes: the Reports on the Observance of Standards and Codes (ROSCs) prepared by the IMF, countries' own self-assessments, and the information provided by a specific private-sector initiative. The preparation of ROSCs started in 1999 assessments, and publication is voluntary. Some of the ROSCs are part of the Financial Sector Assessment Programme, run jointly by the IMF and the World Bank.

ROSCs are currently (as at March 2003) available for seventy-five countries, twenty of which are OECD member countries.[4] There are no modules for one-third of the OECD countries, and among them, for two of the G-7 countries (Germany and the USA).[5] The information available from ROSCs is very limited because of the heterogeneity of both the codes and the country coverage, as well as the uncertain timing of publication. The ROSC modules are not standardised: some contain only a short analysis, while others are very detailed: some take compliance with one standard into account, others with several.

Self-assessments are not collected systematically by any international organisation, and information about them is sometimes difficult to obtain. Private initiatives, such as the eStandardsForum website (http://www.estandardsforum.com), provide information on the implementation of S&C for a large number of countries in a more user-friendly format, but the information is under copyright, and access to the website is not free. Market participants prefer information in a simple format that can easily be quantified or used in a classification system that can be incorporated in tick boxes. However, implementation of S&C is a process, and is not designed to meet fixed target deadlines for compliance, or to provide pass/fail tests. Such a process necessarily requires qualitative assessments. Simplistic quantification and classification risk producing scoring systems capable of creating one-way expectations and bandwagon effects in the market. If market participants are left to make their own discretionary judgements on a country's level of compliance, there is a better chance of a more reasoned assessment.

It is generally assumed that OECD countries are largely compliant with the codes.[6] However, although the information from the private-sector initiative cannot be presented here for copyright reasons, the information obtained from the cross-checking of ROSCs, self-assessments and the eStandardsForum clearly indicates that, despite the fact that the impetus for an international set of codes came from the G-7 countries, compliance with the twelve codes in this group is not complete, and there are varying degrees of compliance with the other standards. In the other OECD countries as well, compliance is weaker and deviations are numerous. Although the East Asian crisis was the trigger in highlighting problems with transparency and central-bank balance sheets, the banking system and the corporate sector, implementation of international financial codes is a global issue.

Issues in defining and implementing standards and codes: developing-country perspectives

It was a challenge to define standards. It is an even greater challenge to gain global acceptance for the defined standards in order to ensure implementation. Standards and codes can only be effective as a tool of financial stability and crisis prevention if they are implemented extensively. Issues that arise in ensuring compliance with the codes in developing countries, such as ownership, appropriateness, incentives and voluntariness, are examined in this section. Other issues discussed are those relating to resources and transition periods.

The linkages between ownership, appropriateness, representation and incentives in implementing standards

The effectiveness of standards and codes as a tool of global financial stability depends on the number of countries adopting them and the extent to which they are implemented. The latter is closely related to the way in which S&C are incorporated into the norms of business practice. In order to achieve effective implementation, country 'ownership' of these policies is crucial. In the case of developing countries, 'ownership' is not possible without representation and positive incentives for implementation. The most constructive incentive for implementation is the appropriateness and meaningfulness of standards in the national interest. 'Ownership' of reforms in domestic financial architecture cannot be achieved while the membership of the FSF[7] and other international organisations[8] involved in standard-setting is dominated so heavily by the industrialised nations. Although developing countries were well represented in the formulation of some of the codes, such as those on transparency, their participation and representation have been limited with respect to others. The Financial Stability Forum is a very important initiative: including members from developing countries as full members and not just a few in working groups will enhance its legitimacy and increase commitment. It is important that their concerns and subject areas are represented: involvement brings commitment. 'Ownership' is meaningless without representation. Appropriateness of the standards is another issue to ensure implementation. The 'ownership' principle cannot work if national governments are not convinced about the appropriateness of some standards. This is the 'one size fits all' dilemma. In discussing the appropriateness of the selected standards, Rodrik (2000) points out that many rich countries have prospered by following different paths in corporate governance (where insiders and stakeholders have played a much more significant role) and in finance (where close links between governments have often been the rule rather than the exception). The Reserve Bank of India, perhaps the only country that evaluates the appropriateness and implementation issues and posts the information in the public domain, makes similar points.[9] Recognition by the standard-setters that different countries are at different stages of economic development with varying institutional capacities does not offer any clues as to how this difficulty will be resolved in practice. The resolution of the 'one size fits all' dilemma is complex, but increasing developing-country representation and participation, and including subject areas of interest to them will be the first step. Appropriateness is a question of participation and involvement, and may not be achieved by providing economic proof alone.[10]

In the absence of appropriate institutions, developing countries' commitment to embracing standards and codes is not likely to lead to the desired goals. Pistor (2000) examines this aspect with regard to legal rules, and argues that historical evidence supports the proposition that imported legal systems have in most cases not produced very efficient outcomes. The content of the rules is not as important as the existence of constituencies that demand these rules and the compatibility of the imported norms with pre-existing legal norms as well as pre-existing economic and political conditions. Voluntary compliance is important. Hence standardised rules are unlikely to be effective in countries where complementary laws exist only in part or not at all. For example, commercial law is a necessary prerequisite for the International Organisation of Securities Commission (IOSCO) standards, and an independent judiciary is a prerequisite for defining and bringing into practice the code on insolvency.

The issue of 'ownership' is also related closely to the 'incentives' a country has to implement standards. The FSF Task Force on the Implementation of Standards, established in September 1999, identified a blend of market and official incentives to encourage the implementation of standards and codes; these were examined in September 2000 by the FSF follow-up group. Compliance thus rests either on countries being convinced of the usefulness of compliance and voluntary co-operation, or on pressures from the markets for their observance. Compliance can therefore be based in principle either on positive incentives or negative ones (compulsions). The present study catalogues market[11] and official incentives, laying emphasis on the former.[12] If the market does not assimilate the information generated by a publicly-led approach to ensure the financial stability that enables market incentives to work, will some of the negative official incentives mentioned here (but for the most part not recommended) become the norm to be imposed by international organisations and by individual countries, or some groups of countries?

The first item in the incentive list (see Box 2.1) from the official sector – making IMF funds contingent on compliance – is among the actions already taken.[13] In the case of the IMF's Contingency Credit Line (CCL), the conditions include a positive assessment during the most recent IMF Article IV consultation on the country's progress in adhering to internationally accepted standards. No country has yet made use of the CCL. It remains to be seen whether a public statement of the intent to comply, or actual compliance, will gain access to this facility.

IMF country programmes include particular steps to implement specific standards. Banking supervision in the home country is already a condition in several countries for market access to foreign financial firms. The disadvantage of this line of approach is that, despite implementation of S&C being a global issue, the pressures for implementation become restricted to countries that seek funds from the IMF. There is also the danger that moves towards conditionality may lead to negative retaliation by developing countries to restrict market access to countries which themselves have not achieved full compliance with international standards. Negative incentives may therefore have the undesirable consequence that issues of financial stability may be lost because such incentives work in

---

Box 2.1   Incentives to implement standards and codes

Positive incentives

- National interest
- Technical assistance
- Policy advice

Incentives that could be applied directly by IFIs

- Making the access to IMF funds contingent on compliance in standards and codes[a] including implementation of certain S&Cs in the conditions of an IMF adjustment programme[b]
- Making implementation of S&Cs a condition for membership in international groupings[c]
- Obligating countries that do not implement S&Cs to pay higher charges for the utilisation of IMF funds is not under active consideration but remains one of the possible future steps[d]

Incentives from the 'market side'

- Disseminating information on compliance
- Encouraging private institutions to be concerned about compliance, and including this information in their risk assessment[e]

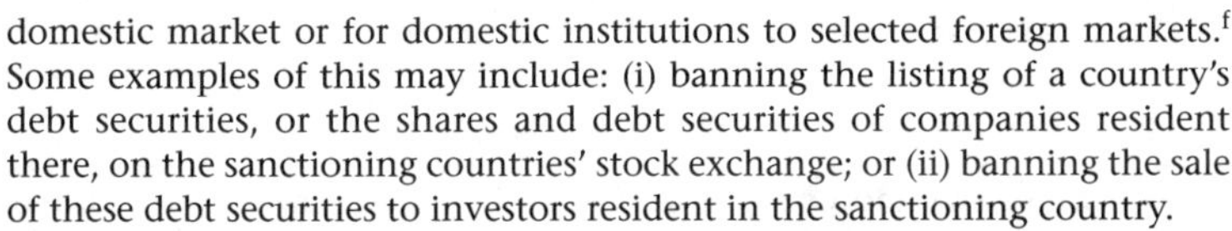

domestic market or for domestic institutions to selected foreign markets.[f]
Some examples of this may include: (i) banning the listing of a country's
debt securities, or the shares and debt securities of companies resident
there, on the sanctioning countries' stock exchange; or (ii) banning the sale
of these debt securities to investors resident in the sanctioning country.

Notes

[a] Access to the CCL (contingency-credit lines) is subject to the adherence of, at least: (i)
subscription to and use of the IMF's Special Data Dissemination Standards, which guide
countries making economic and financial data available to the public; (ii) compliance
with the Basle Core Principles for Banking Supervision; (iii) use of the IMF-designed code
on fiscal transparency; and (iv) use of the IMF-designed code on transparency in monetary
and financial policies. A more comprehensive analysis of adherence would be possible
where a Report on Observance of Standards and Codes (ROSC) has been prepared. ROSCs
include assessment of adherence to seven other sets of standards and codes, (IMF
Executive Board Meeting, 17 November 2000).

[b] Conditionality in the Fund-Supported Programmes-Policy Issues (IMF, 2001: 38).

[c] FSF, 2000.

[d] Ibid.

[e] 'The Group believes that, in addition to the continued encouragement to governments
and congresses, implementation of standards could be promoted effectively by leverag-
ing the private sector within EMEs, especially borrowers and recipients of foreign
investment' (FSF, 2000).

[f] '(i) A *host* jurisdiction in deciding whether, and if so under what conditions, it will
allow a foreign institution to operate in its markets, could take into account the degree
to which that institution's home jurisdiction observes relevant standards. (ii) Where
regulatory approval is required, a *home* jurisdiction could place restrictions on its
domestic financial institutions' operations in foreign jurisdictions with material gaps in
observance of relevant standards' (FSF, 2000).

the case of only a few countries (those that seek IMF funding and
undertake negative retaliation against some of these pressures).

Implementation of codes is of interest to a country only if it intends to
borrow from the private financial market or from bilateral or multilateral
official sources (see Box 2.2). The official incentives are not valid for the
G-7/G-10 countries, as they no longer borrow from multilateral institutions. The market incentive also works asymmetrically in the case of
industrialised and emerging-market economies. Although industrialised
countries do borrow from private capital markets, these markets do not
necessarily take the degree of their adherence to international standards
into account. For example, Germany at the time of writing does not comply with fiscal transparency, but this does not have a serious effect on its
credit rating and ability to borrow, as would be the case in an emerging
market's economy. Furthermore, the incentive for industrialised countries to comply with many standards may not be very strong because,

Box 2.2   Why identified incentive structures may not work in the case of industrialised countries

Positive incentives

- Self-interest is muted because the recent crises have been domestic financial crises combined with external payments only in developing and transition economies
- There is reduced exchange risk compared with developing countries, as it is possible for them to borrow in their own currencies
- They do not need technical assistance as an incentive

Official incentives

- Inapplicable as the industrialised countries no longer borrow from multilateral institutions

Market incentives

- There is asymmetry in the way the market assesses the same information for industrialised, emerging markets and developing countries. For example, one of the G-7 countries currently does not comply with fiscal transparency but this does not affect its credit rating seriously or its ability to borrow from private markets
- Thus the idea that the market can punish for non-compliance through higher costs or the drying-up of funds may not be valid for the industrial countries.

unlike emerging-market economies, it is possible for them to borrow capital in their own currency. Hausmann and Panizza (2002) refer to this as the 'original sin'. Developing countries are faced with the exchange-risk impact on their balance sheets because they almost always borrow in a foreign currency; industrialised countries can avoid this risk, and there is therefore less incentive for them to implement standards. This is presumably because domestic financial crises have been combined with external payments crises only in developing and transition economies.

Another approach, adopted with some success both by the OECD's Financial Action Task Force (FATF) with regard to countries that do not combat money laundering actively enough, and by the OECD in dealing with tax havens (Speyer, 2001), is 'name and shame'. Key sanctions under 'naming and shaming' are advisories that raise transaction costs in dealings between non-co-operating and co-operating countries.

Research on the relationship between the implementation of standards and the development of the macroeconomy, and of financial stability, is scanty. A better case for 'ownership' can be made if countries can be persuaded that implementation of standards and codes is in their national interest in order to maintain domestic financial stability and hedge against external shocks. A crisis is a costly affair, and it is in a country's interest to avoid it. Moreover, a strong, healthy, financial sector is essential for the efficient allocation of resources and improved growth performance. Thus, self-interest is the best incentive.

How voluntary is voluntary?

'Adoption of standards and participation in external assessments should be voluntary' (FSF, 2000: 10). The Executive Board of the International Monetary Fund (29 January 2001) has voiced similar sentiments. The Directors agreed that the adoption and assessment of internationally recognised standards will remain voluntary. They recognised that priorities for implementing standards would differ by country and over time, and that assessments would need to take into account differences in members' economic circumstances and stages of development (IMF, 2001a).

Although initial public statements concentrated on the voluntary principle, a shift in focus is perceptible. For example, Eichengreen (2001: 43) makes a case for conditionality. In his view,

> upgrading practices in such areas as macroeconomic policy and transparency, financial market infrastructure, and financial regulation and supervision is essential in a financially integrated world. And international standards, with pressure to comply to be applied by multilateral surveillance, IMF conditionality, regulation and market discipline, are the only available means to this end in a world of sovereign states.

He sees the Asian model as needing to be reformed to comply with international best practice. The argument contains a certain amount of 'idealism', a 'wish list' of what lenders ideally would like to have without any reciprocal arrangements.[14] Eichengreen does not take into account the practical aspects of applying a universal rule in diverse conditions. The idea of conditionality, as evidenced by the quotation at the beginning of this chapter, has support from high-ranking individuals in the industrialised world.

Developing countries have expressed concern that compliance with standards and codes should not become a part of conditionality; they believe that compliance should be voluntary (see, for example, Reddy, 2001). Many, including Brazil (Gottschalk, 2001: 16) and Russia (Granville, 2001: 7) have also expressed the view that capacity-building is more important than conditionality. While developing countries have been supportive of the need to observe certain minimum standards in areas relevant to the maintenance of the international monetary system, including greater transparency, there is less agreement on the design of some codes as being relevant and applicable in economies with different legal institutional set-ups and at different stages of development.[15]

How is 'ownership' of policies ensured if compliance with standards becomes a part of IMF conditionality? Furthermore, conditionality can take the form of formal or informal conditionality. If the view put forward by the Bretton Woods institutions and statements from high-ranking individuals in the industrialised countries leads to the perception that a universal rule ensures financial stability, the market participants will respond accordingly, and even if adherence to S&C is not a part of formal conditionality, the market mechanism will in practice work to achieve the same end through different means.[16]

Developing countries are already overburdened with conditionality. How will the IMF streamline conditionality if a new raft of conditions is added? Moreover, one cannot discuss conditionality when there is no economic proof that standards and codes are effective in developing countries. Failures of companies such as ENRON, WorldCom and so on have demonstrated the possible problems with effectiveness in the industrialised countries as well.

It is premature to be discussing S&C as a condition for finance.[17] Even informal conditionality through the market incentive is problematic. If credit-rating agencies are assimilating information from ROSCs on the credit ratings of individual developing countries, this confirms their concerns voiced about outreach activities. ROSCs are considered by developing countries to be a useful benchmark – as shown, for example, by the responses of Armenia (IMF, 2000: 7) and Russia (Granville, 2001: 7). But there is concern that the judgements expressed may become a way of giving a simple score to a country facing a complex process (Gottschalk, 2001: 13). The complexity of the S&C process and the problems in global monitoring make it difficult to set up binary yes/no judgements or a scale of the degree of implementation. Market incentives incur the danger of being based on partial and subjective information on compliance, or on a lack of judgement about the usefulness of a particular code in a developing-country setting. The international debate needs to focus greater attention on the possibilities of bad judgements. To reiterate, in order to understand the issues involved fully, research is necessary on the usefulness and effectiveness of codes, and countries' experiences with their implementation. Market incentives have been brought into uncharted territory too early for single rules to be applied globally.

Resources

The resources required for the implementation of standards and codes are expected to be enormous, and many countries face serious practical constraints. Some developing countries have expressed the view that these efforts may be made at the expense of socially vulnerable groups. In a DFID-funded survey on standards and codes, the response of many participants was that implementation would be costly in terms of time and resources, and the need for effective technical assistance was stressed (Gottschalk, 2001: 13; Granville, 2001: 26; Charpentier, 2001: 17). In some cases it is doubtful if implementing S&C ought to be a priority for countries with very limited resources and deep poverty problems (Charpentier, 2001: ii).

It is for this reason that capacity-building efforts are seen as being crucial to strengthening financial systems. The resource constraint has been identified as the major problem in implementing standards and codes, and therefore the Bretton Woods institutions, the Bank for International Settlements and the standard-setting bodies are all supporting implementation through technical assistance. The UK government has taken the lead by setting up the Financial Sector Reform and Strengthening (FIRST) Initiative, a technical assistance programme for implementation, in conjunction with other donors. A global directory of training opportunities has been sponsored by the FSF (see www.fsforum.org/training/home.htm). The initial focus is on banking supervision. It is planned to expand the training to other areas of financial activities including insurance supervision and payment and settlement systems.

The number of countries with zero or incomplete compliance is large, and the demands for resources are likely to be large. There is likely to be a resource constraint at both domestic and international levels. So far, no estimation of the costs of implementation is available. The task of estimating costs is complex, because different countries are at different stages of compliance. Some case-study analysis needs to be carried out to gauge what the resource constraints are likely to be. Technical assistance efforts will need to identify the countries to be targeted, and how much assistance over a considerable period of time is required, as implementation is going to be a long process. Resources are also needed for the assessment exercise to gauge where developed and developing countries are across the spectrum.

Transition period

If one accepts that globalisation is here to stay, then the challenge is to prepare developing countries for a highly integrated world. The risk inherent in opening up capital markets requires a well-thought-out preparatory stage. In referring to transition periods for fulfilling the pre-conditions for opening up the capital account, the principles behind the standards and codes exercise form part of those preconditions. Capital account liberalisation requires that central banks have effective regulatory, supervisory, enforcement and informational structures in place. Liberalisation must not be seen to require authorities to retreat from these essential functions. Priority setting and sequencing of the implementation exercise for standards and codes therefore need to be linked to the timing and sequencing of capital account liberalisation.

As stressed earlier, research on country experiences needs to be collated in order to understand fully the implications of applying internationally defined codes to countries with divergent systems. The risks inherent in introducing codes without an understanding of the outcomes justify a gradual approach to implementation. The experiences of using a 'big-bang' approach to capital account liberalisation are well documented in the literature (see, for example, Schneider, 2001). Gradualism also allows time for the inevitable learning curve in developing countries.

The transition period needs to be considered carefully, to take into account the institutional framework, such as the legal structure, administrative and human capacity, and financial resources. Technical assistance can play a very important role in the transition period. Priorities need to be established for countries at different stages of development, as well as with regard to the degree of openness of their financial systems. For official and financial incentives, an understanding of the transition period is crucial for the initiative to work to ensure financial stability. The IMF and the World Bank can play an important role in helping member countries in this regard. The ROSC exercise may not provide information with respect to compliance in the form desired by the private sector, but it can be useful in identifying constraints in member countries and in working out transition periods.

Some examples of limitations to standards and codes

Despite the progress made in formulating an international set of standards and codes, the goals of financial stability are better served if some of the limitations in defining the codes themselves, and in the process of their implementation, are recognised. Moreover, countries implementing these standards need to recognise that these are not static rules or principles but will need constant improvements and adjustments to keep pace with the dynamic process of change and increasing sophistication in financial markets. Flexibility is important, and governments need to take care not to waste resources on standards that may already be outdated. This section examines some of the limitations of S&Cs. Implementing codes is a very recent exercise, and discussion of their effectiveness and limitations is therefore limited to a few specific codes which have been the subject of recent research.

It is important to acknowledge that financial stability depends on macroeconomic fundamentals, and sometimes on the endogenous consequences of a rapid expansion of lending, and that this poses a limitation on the regulation and supervision of a country's financial system. For example, most bank assets are subject to changes in their quality resulting from broader changes in economic conditions, which are often characterised by cycles of 'boom and bust'. Moreover, cross-border financing and herd behaviour on the part of investors, along with macroeconomic fluctuations, can further intensify problems in the financial system (UNCTAD, 2001). Thus macro stability is a prerequisite for the success of the present exercise in new financial architecture.

Transparency codes

International organisations have put increasing emphasis on transparency in macroeconomic policy and data in order to ensure financial stability.[18] The rationale for greater transparency is based on the argument that (i) it forces public and private institutions to be accountable; (ii) it helps lenders and investors to evaluate risk; and (iii) it prevents herding and contagion. Support for this view was voiced soon after the Mexican crisis and reinforced after the outbreak of the East Asian crisis. The G-7 finance ministers reported to the Cologne Summit that 'the availability of accurate and timely information is an essential ingredient for well-functioning financial markets and market economies' (G-7, 1999).

Although the benefits of transparency have been recognised, views from both the market and governments in developing countries have also indicated that too much of a good thing may not necessarily be good. The G-22 report on transparency points out that 'confidentiality may be warranted in some circumstances: for example, to encourage frank internal policy deliberations. In determining the optimum degree of transparency, the benefits must be balanced against the costs' (Group of 22, 1998). For example, many IMF members have been concerned about releasing data on foreign-exchange reserves as they may reduce the effectiveness of market interventions. These data are therefore now provided follow-ing a one-month lag. Thus, although transparency is necessary, there is a question mark over how transparent developing countries should become. Similar points were made at the Overseas Development Institute conference in June 2000.[19]

The case for transparency rests on the belief that information and transparency are central to successful policy in developing countries. Precise, regular information is essential to attract investors. For example, a case can be made that the marginal product of information in Africa is still very high, given the poor record of disclosure there, and investor ignorance of the region. Many have also argued that the vulnerability of developing countries to self-fulfilling crises is caused by their lack of transparency, which leads to herd-like behaviour in the financial mar-kets. However, the private sector also acknowledges that the provision of information can backfire, since it might highlight faults that are shared by many countries but publicised by only a few. Another view from the market is that of Persaud (2001), which argues that, while transparency is a good thing, too much transparency may be self-defeating. This mar-ket research makes a convincing case for not making available on a daily basis information on reserves and so on.

Persaud's study bases its argument on the following:

- In the short run, there is compelling evidence to indicate that the markets cannot distinguish between the good and the sustainable.
- In a herding environment, tighter market-sensitive risk-management systems and more data transparency in fact make markets more prone to a crisis.
- The growing fashion in risk management is to move away from dis-cretionary judgements about risk to more quantitative and market-sensitive approaches. Analysis is based on the daily earnings at risk. A rise in market volatility hits the daily earnings ratio (DEAR) limits of some banks, causing a hit in the DEAR limits of other banks. Several banks sell the same asset at the same time, leading to an increase in market volatility and higher correlations.
- Banks or investors like to buy what others are buying, and sell what others are selling. Their performance is rated relative to each other. Employees are more likely to be dismissed for being wrong and alone than for being wrong and in company.
- Transparency alone cannot avert a crisis or contagion. Moreover, in a contagion situation there is a distinction between fully informed traders who follow fundamentals, and less-informed 'noise traders'.

In the Keynesian 'beauty contest' world, informed traders anticipate irrational trading by noise traders since it is not a question of what one's own beliefs or knowledge are regarding fundamentals but rather that of the common perception. Information may help to ameliorate this situation but it is unlikely to eliminate it entirely.[20] For example, while the Special Data Dissemination Standard (SDDS) was implemented before the crises in Turkey and Argentina, the new disclosure rules failed to serve as an effective warning system.[21] Availability of information on the differences in macroeconomic scenarios in the countries hit by contagion failed to act as a warning signal and prevent the contagion.

The approach to transparency is also asymmetric. 'Ownership' of regulatory policies will be facilitated greatly if there is symmetrical treatment between borrowers and lenders. One of the FSF working group reports on capital flows, for example, focuses attention on improved risk-management practices and enhanced transparency on the part of the public and private sectors in borrowing countries (Cornford, 2000a). It also identifies the factors that may lead to short-term volatile capital inflows into developing countries. The burden of providing information is asymmetric; transparency rules are adhered to by the developing world, but not necessarily by the lenders. Information on the portfolio share allocated to a particular country, and the time horizon in which this share would be reached, would enable developing countries to plan for their resource gaps in a more effective manner and to finance development from alternative sources. Stability would be enhanced if high-frequency data on the largely short-term position of assets denominated in a country's currency held by foreign firms other than banks were endorsed by international action to enable timely action by the national authorities in their foreign-exchange and other financial markets.

The positive and negative incentives discussed in this chapter are valid mainly in the case of emerging markets and developing countries. Transparency can enhance financial stability only if all countries participating in international financial markets implement transparency procedures.

Example 1:   Some limits in implementing transparency

Achieving transparency through the SDDS is still a problem, although it has been in operation since the Asian crisis of 1997. As of March 2003, only 61 out of the 183 IMF member countries have subscribed to the SDDS. Thus incomplete information remains a problem for world financial markets. A study by Mosley (2002) identifies two constraints with respect to poor implementation: a weak market response, and a weak response from countries.

The study investigates a government's incentives to subscribe to the SDDS. On the basis of surveys, Mosley argues that the benefits of SDDS compliance are quite low, while the potential costs are high. She also points to lack of market awareness and use as the disincentive for governments to subscribe to the SDDS. The results of a survey of mutual fund managers show their reliance on private agents such as brokerage houses and credit-rating agencies for information.[22] Credit-rating agencies apparently make more use of the SDDS than other market participants, which implies that the SDDS is utilised indirectly. This survey result is consistent with the outreach exercise performed by the FSF which also found that few participants in the market took into account an economy's observance of standards in their lending and investment decisions, though observance of the SDDS was found to influence credit ratings (FSF, 2000: sect. III).[23] Nevertheless, the use by credit-rating agencies and the possible indirect use by the market do not appear to be sufficient to induce governments to subscribe to the procedure.

Second, the costs of implementation or transition costs can be a reason for the under-subscription of the SDDS. This is a problem in particular for developing countries that are generally not accustomed to disclosing and providing information in a systematic way. Implementation of the SDDS requires not only changes in national practices but also an increase in resources. Mosley (2002) surveyed the government officials of subscribing countries and found that, though there were some transition costs, most subscribers to the SDDS were not required to overhaul their national systems completely. From a cost–benefit analysis point of view, one can deduce from this, as Mosley does, that a country is less likely to join the system if the cost is prohibitively high.

The third potential reason for under-subscription of the SDDS is concern about 'too much' transparency, as mentioned in the previous section.[24] To sum up Mosley's findings, the perceived costs from signing on to the SDDS outweigh the benefits, which are limited because of lack of use by market participants. The SDDS can be effective in achieving its goals if the private sector embraces it actively; this, in turn, would induce governments to accept the standard.

Under-subscription to the SDDS limits the information available in markets. Although transparency is a desirable quality, unless the codes on transparency are implemented globally, its usefulness is limited. Research similar to Mosley's work or the outreach activities by the FSF is not available with regard to the other transparency procedures.

Example 2:   Some limits in implementing transparency in
banking supervision and regulation

Even with the best intentions, transparency in the field of banking supervision and regulation can be blurred. Difficulties arise because of off-balance-sheet items in national accounts and corporate balance sheets. Accounting rules cannot cover these items adequately and thus, in spite of transparency, it may be difficult to assess exposure and its distinction between the short and long term. Cross-border hedging makes it difficult to give advance warnings of financial-system weaknesses and pressures (Basle Committee on Banking Supervision, 2000a: para. 28). Also, financial innovation affects the transparency required for regulation and supervision. The balance sheets of many financial firms have an increasingly chameleon-like quality that reduces the value of their financial returns to regulators. The tensions between financial innovation and effective regulation in modern financial markets are unlikely to disappear, and pose a challenge for financial regulators. The limits of financial regulation have been exemplified in recent times by the fall of ENRON, WorldCom and Global Crossing, for example. These failures also highlight the need for better and more innovative supervision and regulation in the industrialised economies.

Codes on banking supervision

Example 1:   Licensing

Another illustration of the limitations of standards can be demonstrated from the vital field of banking supervision. Take the licensing of banks, for example. In some countries, the criteria were designed primarily to ensure the distinction between the owners and those controlling a bank. But licensing is often also used to serve objectives such as the avoidance of 'overbanking', limitation of financial conglomeration, and (in the case of foreign entities) restricting foreign ownership of the banking sector or ensuring that the parent institution is supervised adequately in its home country. The objectives of licensing may have (usually proximate) relations to banking stability but cannot prevent serious banking instability or banking crises (UNCTAD, 2001).

Example 2:   Banking capital adequacy standard

The capital adequacy standard has been implemented widely and serves as a useful illustration of the limited applicability of a rule-based system. This standard has gained importance in a world of open capital accounts in the industrialised countries as well as in many emerging and developing economies. It was first applied to the initial twelve members of the Basle Committee on Banking Supervision but has now grown to more than a hundred countries, encompassing banks that operate in domestic markets. The information arising from the implementation of these principles is intended to reduce the occurrence of the contagion effect by providing improved information on the level of risk in the banking system, and thus an early warning of an impending crisis. In fact, Argentina had complied with this standard above the required minimum of 8 per cent.

Rojas-Suarez (2002) discusses the appropriateness and effectiveness of the banking capital adequacy standard. Sufficient banking capital is considered to be a good indicator of bank soundness, as it acts as a buffer to absorb unexpected adverse shocks. However, there is evidence that banks' capital requirements had very little usefulness as a supervisory tool in recent experiences of banking crises in developing countries, compared with industrialised countries. Rojas-Suarez shows that, for the developing countries that faced banking crises during the 1990s, growth in net equity capital was high and positive, while for industrialised countries the growth rate was negative.[25] The capital standard did not prove to be an appropriate indicator of bank soundness in developing countries and in fact could have been misleading. The reason why the capital standard has not been an effective tool for developing countries is because there are some preconditions that first need to be met, Rojas-Suarez argues: 'Effective banking supervision may, therefore, need to take into account particular features of developing countries that are different from those of industrialised countries' (Rojas-Suarez, 2002: 14). The first condition for the appropriate performance of the capital requirement is compliance with adequate infrastructure; an appropriate legal, judicial and accounting framework must first be in place. The second condition relates to the depth and efficiency of capital markets. Liquid markets for bank shares, subordinated debt, and other bank liabilities and assets are needed to validate the 'real' value of bank capital as distinct from its accounting value. However, when a capital market lacks liquidity and depth, as is the case for many developing countries, changes in the market value of bank capital do not provide much useful information regarding the quality of reported capital. In addition, the market for capital tends to be small and uncompetitive because of highly concentrated asset ownership. This concentration of wealth provides incentives for bank owners to undertake higher risks than in industrialised countries, as it becomes easy to raise low-quality bank capital relative to the bank's capital base. This feature can explain why emerging-market countries have had high and positive net capital growth when on the brink of banking crises. In sum, the degree of financial development is an important factor for the effectiveness of capital adequacy standards.

The conditions point to the importance of sequencing and capacity for implementing the capital standard. The nature of sequencing differs according to the level of overall economic and financial development. Moreover, Rojas-Suarez argues that a strict application of the capital standard can have unintended consequences in emerging markets, such as weakening the bank systems. For example, the regulatory treatment of banks' claims on government tends to reduce the soundness of banking systems in emerging markets (see Rojas-Suarez, 2002: 18–20 for expansion of this point).

The new Basle Accord (Basle II) presents some new characteristics that have the potential to worsen the condition of emerging markets and developing countries (Griffith-Jones and Spratt, 2001). The proposed reform to the Basle code sets out two different systems for measuring credit risk: the standardised approach based on the ratings of external independent agencies, and the internal risk based approach (IRB), a complex mechanism based on the bank's own internal rating system. Both have been criticised in the literature because they may increase the volatility of private debt flows to developing countries, intensify pro-cyclical lending and enforce short-term rather than long-term inter-bank lending; they can thus cause a further weakening of the financial markets in developing countries (Griffith-Jones and Spratt, 2001; Cornford, 2001; Reisen, 2001). Moreover, the IRB approach is unlikely to be adopted by newer banks, which may suffer a competitive disadvantage in international markets.

A disadvantage of these model-based approaches to risk assessment is that there is very little room left for discretionary judgements. All the information has to be in a simple format to feed into mathematical models. It is likely that they generate similar assessments about countries, so that there will be only one-way expectations in markets. One of the challenges for the international financial architecture is how to generate two-way expectations in the market, to avoid herding.

Reisen (2001) simulated the effects of applying the standardised approach and the IRB to the financial markets and found that 'the potential impact of changing risk weights in Basle II can be dramatic'. The countries with a rating of BB (the majority of non-OECD sovereign states) or inferior would face an exponential increase in their weights of risk, the possible result being an increase in the capital cost for speculative grade developing countries and an increase in volatility. Other aspects, such as the incentives for short-term lending and the rigidity of the 8 per cent capital ratio, may further increase the volatility of the system.[26] Under these terms, Basle II is unlikely to protect the international financial system from instability and, moreover, 'will not be of help to widen the range of countries likely to benefit from private capital inflows' (Reisen, 2001).

Some limits of codes on securities regulation: securities listing standards

Market incentives are explored in Saar (2001) by examining the benefits of compliance with securities listing standards, with special reference to the depository receipt market.[27] The study analyses the importance of reporting and disclosing standards for the amounts of equity capital raised in international markets. The analysis used the American Depository Receipt (ADR) market because the differences in types of ADRs are based on the differences in compliance procedures. Since developing and industrialised countries issue different types of ADRs, the analysis also uncovered differences explainable by the stage of development. Saar finds that the costs of implementing stringent securities listing standards may exceed the benefits. For lower levels of compliance, the results show that factors associated with the stage of development of the issuing firm's country explain the lower levels of capital raised. Thus investing resources in complying with higher standards may not be efficient. The main policy conclusion is that compliance with securities listing standards is not cost-efficient and should remain voluntary. The results indicate that a cost-effective strategy would be to let developing countries decide when implementation is needed, and that official incentives to foster implementation would also not be cost-effective.

Monitoring and administrative capacity: a limiting factor in ensuring implementation

The task of assessing standards implementation began with the IMF and World Bank co-operating in the job of monitoring. The work is carried out by the Financial Sector Assessment Programme (FSAP) and IMF Article IV surveillance, which includes progress in standards implementation among the subjects of surveillance under the heading of the strength of the financial sector more generally.

The administrative capacity of the IMF is likely to be stretched by the Reports on Observance of Standards and Codes (ROSCs) that have been conducted for a limited number of codes for some countries. If the administrative capacity were to be supported by other organisations, the issue of their judgement would arise. And, in the case of the IMF, it would be fair to make the evaluation of monitoring ROSCs independently of its other functions, such as lending.

At the country level, the assessment exercises will often place an additional burden on a limited supply of supervisory capacity. Expanding this capacity takes a considerable time. And countries are then faced with the prospect of the flight of human capital. A well-trained supervisor may be tempted by attractive alternative employment opportunities in the private sector, or even in the IMF or the World Bank themselves (they have recently been increasing the number of their staff with expertise in this area). These organisations are, of course, aware of the problem of human resources, as are the Basle Committee for Banking Supervision (BCBS) and the Core Principles Liaison Group (CPLG), and efforts are being made to co-ordinate initiatives and to ensure that scarce expert resources are used in the most efficient way. However, there remains a real danger that international assessment of countries' supervision will be at the expense of actual supervision on the ground.

A serious limitation of the monitoring process is that there is no public schedule with regard to the timing of future publications, and no information on the criteria followed in prioritising one country or one code over another. It is therefore impossible to discover whether a ROSC has not been updated because no substantial changes took place in the country, or because there were no resources or time for further analysis. At this stage it is uncertain how this exercise will prove to be a reliable source of information for investors and credit-rating agencies in order that market incentives will be able to work. Currently ROSCs are available for only 75 out of the 183 members of the IMF. Although improvement in information is likely to contribute to financial stability, at an operational level information is scanty.

The IMF has indicated that work is in progress on standardising ROSCs. Thus both human and financial resources and capacity constraints are identifiable in the Bretton Woods institutions (BWIs) serving as global monitors. One alternative would be greater use of self-assessment combined with a peer review process. The FATF model is a useful example. The BWIs could then be assigned an important role in co-ordinating the process and providing technical assistance to assist some countries in self-assessments and implementation. The BWIs could also play a useful role as providers of links to sources of information at country level on self-assessment, thus facilitating the use of this information by market participants. The first step forward may be country self-assessment available on the treasury website. The USA has set an example with self-assessment; the format is simple and may serve as one example for the simplifying of information. Among emerging markets, India has undertaken an exercise with the technical details of ten standards and posted their assessment on the Reserve Bank of India website. Technical assistance for self-assessment of the kind India has undertaken may be a better way forward than the use of negative incentives for compliance. Moreover, identification of where different countries are with respect to their institutional, legal and regulatory framework *vis-à-vis* the codes will also help to identify the real problems in applying a uniform rule across countries. The exercise will also be useful in defining the transition period needed for implementation. Another result of such an exercise will be in defining the areas in which a rule can be applied, and in which voluntary principles can best be utilised.

Open questions

The issues that have been raised and discussed in this chapter lead us to sum up as follows:

- Compliance with standards and codes is a global issue, although the incentive structure, monitoring mechanism and resources needed for assessment and implementation do not guarantee this.
- The arguments for making it a voluntary process and not a part of conditionality for developing countries lie in the advantages to be found in embedding the whole process in countries' self-interest in order to ensure 'ownership'. 'Conditionality' and 'ownership' do not go together.
- Research on the effectiveness and appropriateness of the codes in a diverse set of country situations produces arguments in favour of operating with principles rather than rules, and working out transition periods for implementing them.

The following questions reiterate some of the issues raised and further open up the discussion.

Can we ensure global participation in the implementation of standards and codes? Are standards and codes meaningful for all countries?

Financial stability is a global concern. Crises emerging in any part of the world can have a contagion effect and can threaten the financial stability of other countries around the globe. The incentive structures prioritised in the present discussion make the implementation of standards and codes of interest to a country only if it proposes to borrow from the commercial financial markets or from bilateral or multilateral official sources. Since the G-7/G-10 countries no longer borrow from multilateral institutions, only the market incentives would be operative. But markets do not necessarily take the standards into account in the context of the industrial countries, and the latter's ability to borrow in their own currency is another factor operating to reduce the incentives. These asymmetries are not dealt with in the FSF reports on the subject, presumably because domestic financial crises have been combined with external payments crises only in developing and transition economies. But the past is not necessarily a good guide to the future. Imagine for a moment the problems that might be spawned by the failure of one of the few global banks, or by a meltdown in the US financial market contained less successfully than that of 1987.[28] How far is the emphasis on emerging markets and developing countries in the discussion of S&C implementation justified? Can a future crisis only arise in this part of the world? Is implementation the first priority for countries that are not financially integrated into global markets?

How do we ensure global monitoring of compliance with standards and codes?

The preceding paragraph raises the issue of monitoring. Are all countries covered by the monitoring activity of ROSCs and the FSAP? The answer is probably no. Is it possible to cover at least all the countries participating in international financial markets? The answer lies in the fact that only some of the codes are covered for all countries under the current arrangement, but for others, surveillance is an issue. Aziz Ali Mohammed will discuss this issue further in Chapter 3. The results of ROSCs and FSAP exercises may prove to be of limited use as an early warning indicator of crisis because of the lack of universal coverage. How far does the progress made in the international financial architecture ensure that the goals of financial stability will be met by compliance on the part of countries not borrowing from multilateral institutions?

Is there a case for separating the monitoring of standards and codes from lending operations in order to ensure global stability?

If there is such a case, how do we ensure that monitoring remains distinct from lending operations, so that each exercise can be carried out more effectively? Currently, monitoring is carried out mainly under IMF Article IV consultations, and there is a tension between the two operations. Will financial stability be better served if monitoring of standards is global and not linked to the lending function?

Who is responsible for providing information? Is the private sector the answer?

Information on compliance is vital for surveillance activity and assessment of risk by the private sector. The information generated by ROSCs and the FSAP is limited in its country coverage and is not a continuous data stream across the globe. The IMF has announced its intention to provide updates but will still not produce a continuous data stream.

Oxford Analytica and the Global Financial Services Forum have started a service to provide information on compliance with the core standards and codes for subscribers on the Internet. What are the advantages of the private sector supplying such information? What kind of peer review process would ensure that it functions better than credit-rating agencies in assessing information on standards and codes? Is self-assessment with a peer review process another alternative to global monitoring, since global monitoring faces a resource constraint? Should information not be a global public good?

What measures can the international community take to ensure that there is reciprocity in transparency?

At present the degree of transparency varies across countries, and this incongruity can undermine its effectiveness. Transparency can enhance financial stability effectively only when it takes place across countries and markets.

Do principles work better than rules?

The research available on some of the codes indicates that there are limits to their effectiveness in predicting or preventing a crisis. The example of ENRON illustrates that even in a rule-based system crises are possible.

Too much time may be spent in adhering to its letter of the law rather than its spirit. It is not easy to monitor compliance by the letter of the law; judging by the ENRON experience, it is a good idea to move away from legislative (rule-based) operations. The UK provides an example of financial reporting procedures being based on broad principles.

Do we need the same model of corporate structure globally?

Financial stability is an objective of interest to all countries. Some codes, such as the corporate governance code, require structural changes in the way economies function. Such changes are a political process and carry the exercise on standards and codes far beyond its initial objective. Changes in structures that are not supported by participants in the market can lead to more instability than stability. Can the objective of financial stability be secured by accepting the codes in principle – that is, by ensuring that the balance sheets of the corporate sector are healthy and do not subject the economy to risk? Is it necessary to impose the Anglo-Saxon model on countries with different structures and institutions? One argument may be that information coming out of similar structures is easily standardised and usable by the markets in risk assessments. Is it justifiable to expect countries to change their structures and adopt imposed models of corporate structure, for which there is no evidence that they can work efficiently, simply in order to attract international finance that is a small fraction of their GDP?

Is it not a good idea to encourage self-assessments on compliance?

This brings up the issue of whether national rather than international assessments of S&C compliance might be preferable. The process will need to be a voluntary one, with technical assistance in areas where there are gaps in skills. It is more practical to have national assessments of the risks to balance sheets. Common principles providing best practice would be very useful for benchmarking, and would also provide the opportunity to take country-specific factors into account. It is also conceivable that the market has resident consultants who can provide information in countries where it is investing, and in many spheres of market information this is already the case. Moreover, the argument that there is too little information is not a convincing one. The market has also failed to use existing information in past crises.

Are suggestions that S&C become a part of conditionality a good idea, given that it is difficult to standardise different structures and systems across the world under a single rule?

Attempts to do so may lead to more instability as the implementation process is a political one, and opposition to changing structures is to be expected. Is it possible that the debate is moving beyond the remit of international financial architecture into intrusion into the politics of sovereign countries? And is access to finance from multilateral institutions not burdened already with over-conditionality? How will the IMF streamline conditionality if at the same time a whole raft of new conditions is added?

In view of these difficulties, what is the way forward?

Self-assessment and voluntary principles can be supported by a background process, which would provide the necessary support for such an initiative. This could probably take the form of a major research programme, possibly co-ordinated by the IMF and World Bank, in a sample of countries representative of the different structures and systems across the globe, on the appropriateness of different standards and their effectiveness, along with issues of defining transition periods, priorities and sequencing. How are 'ownership' and 'appropriateness' to be ensured? It is noteworthy that the few existing research studies do point to the limited usefulness of some codes in the developing country context.

How do we resolve the resource constraints for implementation?

Issues of administration are immense, at both surveillance and country levels. There are issues of capacity and resources. While technical assistance will undoubtedly play a very important role in helping countries to strengthen their financial sectors, is the scale of the required resources sufficient to support implementation in all countries participating in international financial markets? Have the agencies offering technical assistance any estimate of the scale of resources required?

How do we improve ownership and self-interest?

Standards and codes have been found to be more effective in terms of intrinsic use and implementation when countries have the right incentives and when it is in their interest to adopt them. This can occur when countries feel that they 'own' the policies. A conscious effort to increase the involvement of under-represented countries in the design and development of standards is necessary to break the cycle of lack of incentives leading to limited effectiveness of the S&C. The appropriateness of standards is also essential.

Should the emphasis not be on sound balance-sheet management?

Healthy balance sheets in both the macro and corporate financial sectors are crucial in averting disaster. The World Bank is already working on indicators of financial soundness. Technical assistance can play a role in ensuring the quality of financial sector balance sheets. Wide encompassing rules, whether formal or informal, take the form of conditionality and can distract attention from this vital area. In terms of prioritisation, is this not the first priority?

What are the other priorities?

In terms of the twelve codes, is there any basis for demarcating some codes as being of higher priority? Which codes do fund managers and credit-ratings agencies take into account? Is it right to have a market-driven process in deciding codes?

Is the initiative enough to ensure global financial stability? How do we ensure stability in the transition period?

The prioritised twelve standards will take years to implement. How is financial stability to be ensured in the transition period? Moreover, we do not know enough to be sure that, even at the end of the transition period, the twelve codes will encourage financial stability. Financial crises have many causes, and the danger is that too much emphasis on standards can detract attention from other policy measures.

Appendix

Table 2.1   ROSC modules published by 13 June 2002

Data dissemination	Fiscal transparency	Monetary and financial policy transparency	Banking supervision	Insurance supervision	Securities market regulation	Payments system	Corporate governance	Insolvency and creditor rights	Accounting and auditing
OECD countries									
Australia, 1999	Australia, 1999	Australia, 1999	Australia, 1999	Canada, 2000*	Canada, 2000*	Canada, 2000*	Czech Republic, 2002**, 2001*	Slovak Republic, 2002*	Slovak Republic, 2001**
Czech Republic, 2001, 2000	Czech Republic, 2002, 2001, 2000	Canada, 2000*	Canada, 2000*	Czech Republic, 2002, 2001*	Czech Republic, 2002, 2001* 2000	Czech Republic, 2002, 2001*	Slovak Republic, 2002*	Czech Republic, 2001**	Poland, 2002**
France, 2001, 2000	Finland, 2001*	Czech Republic, 2002, 2001*	Czech Republic, 2002, 2001*, 2000	Finland, 2001*	Finland, 2001*	Euro Area, 2001*	Poland, 2001**		
Hungary, 2002	France, 2002, 2001	Euro Area, 2001	Hungary, 2002*, 2001	Hungary, 2002*	Hungary, 2002*, 2001	Finland, 2001*	Turkey, 2000**		
Italy, 2002	Greece, 2002, 2001, 1999	Finland, 2001*	Iceland, 2001*	Ireland, 2001*	Iceland, 2001*	Hungary, 2002*, 2001			

Sweden, 2002, 2001	Hungary, 2002, 2001	France, 2002	Ireland, 2001*	Luxembourg, 2002*	Ireland, 2001*	Luxembourg, 2002*
Turkey, 2002	Italy, 2002	Hungary, 2002*	Luxembourg, 2002*	Mexico, 2001*	Luxem-bourg, 2002*	Mexico, 2001*
United Kingdom, 1999	Japan, 2001	Iceland, 2001*	Mexico, 2001*	Poland, 2001*	Mexico, 2001*	Poland, 2001*
	Korea, Republic of, 2001	Ireland, 2001*	Poland, 2001*	Slovak Republic, 2002*	Poland, 2001*	Slovak Republic, 2002*
	Mexico, 2002	Luxembourg, 2002*	Slovak Republic, 2002*	Sweden, 2002*	Slovak Republic, 2002*	Sweden, 2002*
	Poland, 2001	Mexico, 2001*	Sweden, 2002*	Switzerland, 2002*	Sweden, 2002* 2002*	Switzerland, 2002*
	Sweden, 2002, 2000	Poland, 2001*	Switzerland, 2002*		Switzerland, 2002*	
	Turkey, 2000	Slovak Republic, 2002*	United Kingdom, 1999			
	United Kingdom, 1999	Sweden, 2002*				
		United Kingdom, 1999				

Table 2.1 (Contd.)

Data dissemination	Fiscal transparency	Monetary and financial policy transparency	Banking supervision	Insurance supervision	Securities market regulation	Payments system	Corporate governance	Insolvency and creditor rights	Accounting and auditing
Albania, 2000	Argentina, 1999	Argentina, 1999	Algeria, 2000	Barbados, 2003*	Barbados, 2003*	Barbados, 2003*	Barbados, 2003*	Argentina, 2002**	Croatia, 2002**
Argentina, 1999	Armenia, 2002	Barbados, 2003*	Argentina, 1999	Bulgaria, 2002*, 2001, 2000	Bulgaria, 2002*, 2001, 2000	Bulgaria, 2002*	Bulgaria, 2002**	Bulgaria, 2001, 2000	Kenya, 2001**
Armenia, 2002	Azerbaijan, 2000	Bulgaria, 2001, 2000	Barbados, 2003*	Cameroon, 2000*	Croatia, 2002*	Cameroon, 2000*	Croatia, 2001**	Lithuania, 2002**	Lithuania, 2002**
Botwana, 2002	Benin, 2002	Bulgaria, 2002*	Bulgaria, 2002, 2001	Croatia, 2002*	Estonia, 2002, 2000	Croatia, 2002*	Egypt, 2001**		Morocco, 2002**
Bulgaria, 2001, 2000	Brazil, 2001	Cameroon, 2000*	Cameroon, 2000*	Estonia, 2002, 2000	Senegal, 2001*	Estonia, 2002, 2000	Georgia, 2002**, 2001*		Philippines, 2001**
Cameroon, 2001	Bulgaria, 2001, 2000	Croatia, 2002*	Croatia, 2002*	Gabon, 2002	Slovenia, 2001*	Georgia, 2001*	India, 2000**		Ukraine, 2002**
Chile, 2001	Burkina Faso, 2002	Estonia, 2002, 2000*	Estonia, 2002, 2000	Georgia, 2001*	Tunisia, 2002*	Israel, 2001*	Latvia, 2002**		
Costa Rica, 2002	Cameroon, 2000	Gabon, 2002	Georgia, 2001*	Israel, 2001*		Slovenia, 2001*	Lithuania, 2002**		

Estonia, 2002, 2001	Estonia, 2002	Georgia, 2001*	Hong Kong SAR of China, 1999	Israel, 2001*	Tunisia, 2002*	Malaysia, 2000**
Hong Kong SAR of China, 1999	Honduras, 2002	Hong Kong SAR of China, 1999	Israel, 2001*	Latvia, Republic of, 2002*	United Arab Emirates, 2003*	Mauritius, 2002**
Hungary, 2001	Hong Kong SAR of China, 1999	Hungary, 2001*	Latvia, 2002	Lithuania, 2002		Philippines, 2001**
Jordan, 2002	India, 2001	Israel*, 2001*	Lithuania, 2002	Senegal, 2001*		Zimbabwe, 2000**
Lithuania, 2002	Iran, 2002	Senegal, 2001*	Senegal, 2001*	Slovenia, 2001*		
Mauritius, 2002	Kyrgyz Republic, 2002	Tunisia, 2002*, 2001, 1999	Slovenia, 2001*	Tunisia, 2002*		
Mongolia, 2001	Latvia, 2001	Uganda, 1999	Tunisia, 2002*, 2001, 1999			
Namibia, 2002	Lithuania, 2002	United Arab Emirates, 2003*	Uganda, 1999			

Table 2.1   (*Contd.*)

Data dissemination	Fiscal transparency	Monetary and financial policy transparency	Banking supervision	Insurance supervision	Securities market regulation	Payments system	Corporate governance	Insolvency and creditor rights	Accounting and auditing
Romania, 2001	Malawi, 2002		United Arab Emirates, 2003*						
Senegal, 2002	Mali, 2002								
South Africa, 2001	Mauritania, 2002								
Sri Lanka, 2002	Mongolia, 2001								
Tunisia, 2001, 1999	Mozambique, 2002, 2001								
Uganda, 1999	Nicaragua, 2002								
Uruguay, 2001	Pakistan, 2002, 2000								
	Papua New Guinea, 2000								
	Philippines, 2002								
	Romania, 2002								

Slovenia,
2002
Sri Lanka,
2002
Tunisia,
2001
Uganda,
1999
Ukraine,
1999
Uruguay,
1999

Notes
* Indicates the module was derived from an FSAP;
** World Bank ROSCs.

Table 2.2   Countries' participation in standard-setting bodies

	Monetary policy and financial policies	Fiscal transparency	Data dissemination	Insolvency and creditor rights systems	Corporate governance	International accounting standards	International auditing standards	Systematically important payment systems	Banking supervision	Securities regulation	Insurance core principles
Organisation	*IMF*	*IMF*	*IMF*	*WB*	*OECD*	*IASB*	*IFAC*	*CPSS*	*BCBS*	*IOSCO*	*IAIS*
	International Monetary Fund 183	International Monetary Fund 183	International Monetary Fund 183	World Bank 183	Organization for Economic Co-operation 30	International Accounting Standards Board 106	International Federation of Accountants 122	Committee on Payment and Settlement Systems G-10	Basle Committee 13	International Organisation of Securities Commissions 99	International Association of Insurance Supervisors 66
					Austria				Belgium		
					Austria				Canada		
					Belgium				France		
					Canada				Germany		
					Czech Republic				Italy		
					Denmark						
					Finland				Japan		
					France				Luxembourg		
					Germany				Netherlands		
					Greece				Spain		
					Hungary				Sweden		
					Iceland				Switzerland		
					Ireland				United Kingdom		
					Italy				United States		
					Japan						
					Korea						
					Luxembourg						

Mexico
Netherlands
New Zealand
Norway
Poland
Slovak
 Republic
Spain
Sweden
Switzerland
Turkey
United
 Kingdom
United States

Source: Organisations' websites – hyperlinked at: http://www.fsforum.org/Standards/keystds.html.

Table 2.3 Membership in FSF working groups

	Task Force on Implementation of Standards	*Incentives to Foster Implementation of Standards*	*Working Group on Capital Flows*	*Working Group on Offshore Centres*	*Working Group on Enhanced Disclosure*	*Working Group on Highly Leveraged Institutions*	*Working Group on Deposit Insurance*
Established	Sept 1999	April 2000	April 1999	April 1999	June 1999	April 1999	April 2000
Ended	March 2000	Sept 2001	April 2000	April 2000	April 2001	April 2000	April 2001
ToR	To explore issues related to and consider a strategy for fostering the implementation of international standards for strengthening financial systems	To monitor progress in implementing core standards and further raise market awareness of standards	To evaluate measures in borrower and creditor countries that could reduce the volatility of capital flows and the risks financial systems of excessive short-term external indebtedness	To consider the significance of offshore financial centres for global financial stability	To assess the feasibility and utility of enhanced public disclosure by financial inter-mediaries	To recommend actions to reduce the destabilising potential of institutions employing a high degree of leverage (HLIs) in the financial markets of developed and developing countries	To review recent experience with deposit insurance scheme and consider the desirability and feasibility of setting out international guidance for such arrangements
Final report	Issues of the task force on implementation of standards	Final Report of the Follow-up Group on Incentives to Foster Implementation of Standards	Report of the Working Group on Capital Flows	Report of the Working Groups on Offshore Centres	Multi-disciplinary Working Group on Enhanced Disclosure Final Report	Report of the Working Group on Highly Leveraged Institutions	Guidance for Developing Effective Deposit Insurance Systems

Member countries						
Australia	Argentina	Brazil	Canada	Australia	Australia	Argentina
Canada	Australia	Canada	France (Chair)	Canada	Canada	Canada (Chair)
China	Canada	Chile	Germany	France	France	Chile
France	France	France	Italy	Germany	Germany	France
Germany	Germany (Chair)	Germany	Japan	Japan	Hong Kong	Germany
Hong Kong (Chair)	Hong Kong	Italy (Chair)	Singapore	Mexico	Italy	Hungary
India	India	Japan	Switzerland	Sweden	Japan	Italy
Italy	Japan	Malaysia	Thailand	UK	Netherlands	Jamaica
Japan	Sweden	South Africa	UK	USA	UK (Chair)	Japan
Mexico	UK	UK	USA		USA	Mexico
Netherlands	USA	USA				Philippines
South Africa						USA
Sweden						
UK						
USA						

Source: Financial Stability Forum: www.fsforum.org.

54

Table 2.4 A summary of Reports on the Observance of Standards and Codes for selected countries

---

Argentina
Report dated 15 April 1999

General comments	Argentina made important improvements in its transparency practices. Although some aspects could be further improved, the compliance with the standards is very high. The report also includes a self-assessment of the country in Securities and Market Regulation, Accounting Practices and Auditing Practices.
Data dissemination	Argentina has subscribed to SDDS since 1996 and compliance with the standard is in progress.
Fiscal transparency	Argentina achieved a high degree of fiscal transparency but in some areas it was required to: • simplify the rules relating to intergovernmental fiscal relations; • strengthen tax regulation and administration; improve information on general government; and • finalise the draft legislation on fiscal responsibility.
Monetary and financial transparency	The central bank's policies are transparent and the financial framework is clear. Argentina has a very high compliance with this standard. The report stresses the importance of continuing the policy of independence by the Bank Supervising Agency.
Banking supervision	Argentina's practices appear to be consistent with the disclosure aspects of the Basle core principles. 'Increasing public awareness of riskier institutions can be expected to impose market discipline on their management and promote (healthier forms of) competition among banks.'

Greece
Report dated December 1999, updated in February 2001 and March 2002

General comments	The code was already implemented before the ROSC review in 1999, and the report of 1999 suggested several areas where improvements were necessary: • clarity of roles and responsibilities; • public availability of information; • open budget preparation; • execution and reporting; and • independent assurances of integrity.

Japan
Report dated August 2001

Fiscal transparency	Japan meets high standards of fiscal transparency and recent initiatives have improved the adoption of the standard.

Table 2.4   (Contd.)

Nevertheless there is still room for major progress in key areas: more attention in providing timely information on the overall stance of fiscal policy; preparation of medium-term budget plans; and the role and consequence of public financial intermediation through the FILP (Fiscal Investment and Loan Programme) should be clarified.

United Kingdom
Report dated 15 March, 1999

General comments	'The United Kingdom has achieved high levels of transparency in the four areas assessed here.' The report also contains UK self-assessments of Securities Market Regulation, Insurance Industry Regulation, Accounting Practices and Auditing Practices.
Data dissemination	At the time of the report, the UK was implementing SDDS and was still not disseminating the data on central and general government operations. The ROSC also stressed the importance of revising metadata.
Fiscal transparency	'The United Kingdom has achieved a very high level of fiscal transparency.'
Monetary and financial transparency	'The new monetary policy framework is highly transparent with respect to all four principles underlying the draft Code.' With respect to financial policy the report asks for more transparency in the mechanism that may lead to the dismissal of the FSA (Financial Services Authority) board.
Banking supervision	'While existing supervisory practices in the areas outlined above already appear consistent with the disclosure aspects of the Basle Core Principles, the picture can be expected to become somewhat sharper once the current period of regulatory transition is resolved, in particular with the passage of legislation underpinning the FSA.'

India
Report dated February 2001

General comments	The ROSC on fiscal transparency has been prepared by the IMF and the ROSC on corporate governance by the World Bank.
Fiscal transparency	'India has achieved a reasonably high standard of fiscal transparency.' Nevertheless, lists issues that need to be improved:

- enact the Fiscal Responsibility and Budget Management Bill (the report also stresses the opportunity to revise some of its aspects);
- further simplification and clarification in the area of intergovernmental fiscal relations;

Table 2.4   (*Contd.*)

	• the role of the central government in enforcing fiscal discipline on the states should be established more clearly; • the current nine-month lag in producing reliable and detailed general government accounts is too long; • the budget documents should provide more background information and analysis (for example, there is a lack of long-term projections and assessment of fiscal risks); • the expenditure framework needs to be strengthened; • Clarify the principles governing RBI (Reserve Bank of India) financing of the central government (the report suggests granting legal autonomy to the RBI); • continued efforts also are needed to stem the scope for corruption among tax officials and others; and • the recently established National Statistical Commission ought to address the issue of the technical independence of the Central Statistical Organisation.
Corporate governance	India adheres only in part to the OECD principles of corporate governance. Compliance is not complete in all the areas taken into account: • basic shareholders' rights; • equitable treatment of shareholders; • role of stakeholders in corporate governance; • disclosure and transparency; and • responsibilities of the Board.

Cameroon
Report dated May 2000

General comments	Report prepared in the context of a FSAP.
Banking supervision	'The assessment of observance of each of the 25 Core Principles (30 after subdividing the first Core Principle into six sub-principles) has revealed a number of weaknesses … the legal and regulatory framework appear to be compliant or largely compliant with 18 of the 26 Core Principles that are relevant.' Principles with which Cameroon is non-compliant (or broadly non-compliant are: • human resources (that are insufficient); • capital requirements (the current minimum solvency ratio is too low and should be raised to 8 per cent); • loan policies; • connected lending (legal provisions are insufficient); • other material risks (many important risks have not been considered in the regulations); • money laundering; and • accounting and disclosure.

Table 2.4 (Contd.)

| | The report stresses the importance of the lack of human resources within the regional banking commission (COBAC) and 'recommends that COBAC be given a specific budget consistent with its need and that the latter be ranked top priority'. |

Korea
Report dated January 2001

Fiscal transparency — 'Korea meets international best practices in fiscal transparency in many areas.' For further improvements, IMF staff suggested that the government should:

- take the opportunity, now that the effects of the financial crisis are waning, to reassess and define its fiscal role more clearly;
- affirm the universality of the budget as the principal instrument of fiscal control;
- improve the annual budget documents;
- improve the quality of information on local government, on its financial assets and on the working methods and assumptions underlying the fiscal forecasts;
- simplify the tax system significantly; and
- continue to expand on its initiatives to improve taxpayer services.

Notes

1 The views expressed in this chapter are those of the author and do not necessarily express the views of UNCTAD.
2 Its membership consists of representatives of the national authorities responsible for financial stability in selected OECD countries, Hong Kong and Singapore, and of major international financial institutions, international supervisory and regulatory bodies and central bank expert groupings.
3 Some examples are the Principles for the Supervision of Banks' Foreign Establishments agreed by the Basle Committee on Banking Supervision in 1983, and a Framework for International Convergence of Capital Measurement and Capital Standards, published in 1988. Work on some standards, such as those for data dissemination and fiscal transparency, existed prior to the outbreak of the East Asian crisis. The Special Data Dissemination Standard (SDDS), for example, was developed by the IMF in response to the deficiencies in major categories of economic data following the Mexican crisis in December 1994.
4 See Table 2.1 in the Appendix to this chapter for a summary coverage of countries and codes by ROSCs.
5 The US Treasury website provides a self-assessment of the US position on the twelve core standards as at 25 June 2001.
6 For example, Acharya (2001: 38) writes, 'As a rule of thumb, most OECD countries are in compliance (or are close to compliance) with most standards, while many developing countries are at varying distances from compliance with regard to most standards.'

7   At the time of writing, the FSF has a total of forty members, comprising three representatives from each G-7 country (one each from the treasury, central bank and supervisory agency); one each from Australia, Hong Kong, Singapore and the Netherlands; six from international organisations (International Monetary Fund (two), World Bank (two), Bank for International Settlements (one) and OECD (one); six from international regulatory and supervisory groupings (Basle Committee on Banking Supervision (two), International Organisation of Securities Commissions (two) and International Association of Insurance Supervisors (two)), and two from Committees of Central Bank experts (Committee on the Global Financial System (one) and Committee on Payment and Settlement Systems (one), plus the chairman, Mr Crockett).

8   See Table 2.2 for a list of countries represented in the various standard-setting bodies and Table 2.3 for the countries represented in the various working groups; both are in the Appendix to this chapter.

9   The reports of the various committees are available on the RBI website.

10   Nor have studies carried out so far given sufficient economic proof.

11   The key requirements for this to be effective would be (i) market familiarity with international standards; (ii) their assessment of its relevance for assessments of market risk; (iii) market access to information on compliance and the degree of compliance; and (iv) use of information by the market in risk assessments.

12   The period for assessing the effectiveness of market incentives is, admittedly, very short. Nevertheless, assessment of some codes in the literature points to the limited use of the market incentive. See, for example, Mosley (2001).

13   For a further discussion on this issue see UNCTAD (2001).

14   The wish-list is an intrusion in the affairs of emerging markets and developing countries. The destabilising activities of Highly Leveraged Institutions have been ignored in the discussion. The Report of the Working Group on HLIs (April 2000) identified the capacity of HLIs to establish large and concentrated positions in small and medium-sized markets, and with this capacity the potential to exert a destabilising influence. Some aggressive practices by HLIs include heavy selling of currencies in illiquid markets, selective disclosures, rumours about future developments, and correlated position-taking in the markets for different assets within a country and across countries, with the objective of achieving profitable movements in relative prices.

15   Mr Jin Liqun, Deputy Finance Minister of China, for example, voiced this at a conference organised by the IMF: 'Developing countries are given to understand that they can pre-empt a financial crisis and achieve economic stability, providing they follow rigorously the international standards and codes. But there are two questions to answer: first, are the standards and codes suitable to developing countries at their stage of development; and second, do they have a minimum institutional capacity to apply these standards and codes at the same level as developed countries?', *IMF Survey*, vol. 30, no. 7, 2 April 2001, p.103.

16   See Axel Nawrath (Chairman of the Follow-Up Group on Incentives to Foster Implementation of Standards) to William McDonough (chairman of the BCBS) (4 April 2001): 'I am of the view that the new [Basle] Accord can provide incentives, albeit indirectly, to banks and other market practitioners to pay attention to Standards. This should in turn raise awareness among

economies to the need to upgrade the implementation of Standards in their jurisdictions.'

17 Conditionality is a highly contentious issue. We do not go into this discussion here. For a discussion on effectiveness see, for example, Kapur and Webb (2000); Killick (1995).

18 See the Code of Good Practices on Transparency in Monetary and Financial Policies at http://www.imf.org/external/np/mae/mft, and fiscal transparency at http://www.imf.org/external/np/fad/trans.

19 See *Development Policy Review*, vol. 19, no. 1, March 2001; and *Conference Report* (2000) on www.odi.org.uk.

20 Ibid.

21 The SDDS was launched in April 1996 and became operational in September 1998.

22 The subjects of the survey were specifically managers of internationally-orientated US mutual funds and managers of UK funds which invest at least 5 per cent of assets in emerging-markets regions. For more details, see Mosley, 2002: 13.

23 The report was based on an informal dialogue with participants from 100 financial firms in eleven jurisdictions, mainly developed countries. Overall, the FSF found limited awareness of the twelve key standards. Observance of the standards was considered to be less important than the adequacy of a country's legal and judicial framework; political risk and economic and financial fundamentals were more important factors.

24 'For a variety of reasons, ranging from legitimate economic policy-making concerns to pure political opportunism, governments may prefer not to be completely transparent in their dissemination of economic information' (Mosley, 2002: 26).

25 Furthermore, in a related study, where Rojas-Suarez (2001) compares various early-warning indicators of banking problems in developing countries, capital ratio performed the worst. The same indicator is found to be much more efficient in analysing the soundness of the banking system of developed countries.

26 Under the new Accord, the short term is considered to be a maximum of three months instead of one year. See also Cornford (2000b).

27 Depository Receipts are negotiable certificates that certify ownership of a company's publicly traded equity or debt; they differ exclusively by the degree of compliance with transparency codes. There are different types of DRs. The American Depository Receipt (ADR) of Level I, II, III and the rule 144A ADR issued and traded in the US Global Depository Receipts (GDRs) issued to US and non-US are traded outside the USA. Level III ADRs can be traded at NASDAQ and the New York Stock Exchange, and require full compliance with the SEC disclosure standards. Level II can also be traded at NYSE and NASDAQ, but has less stringent requirements. Level I ADRs need the least compliance with the standard.

28 Another example of threats of a global meltdown is the crisis in Long-Term Capital Management. In September 1998, Russia's default on its sovereign debt created losses for many large financial institutions, a widening of credit spreads, and pressure on highly leveraged institutions such as the LTCM. The consequences of a bankruptcy of the LTCM would have been enormous for the entire world economy. The LTCM was saved by the intervention of

the US Federal Reserve and the principal international banks which, after 23 September 1998, owned 90 per cent of the fund and established a board to supervise its activities.

References

Acharya, S. (2001) 'New International Standards for Financial Stability: Desirable Regulatory Reform or Runaway Juggernaut?', in S. Griffith-Jones and A. Bhattacharya (eds), *Developing Countries and the Global Financial System*, London: Commonwealth Secretariat.

Basle Committee on Banking Supervision (1983) *The Principles for the Supervision of Banks' Foreign Establishments*, Basle: Bank for International Settlements.

Basle Committee on Banking Supervision (1988) *Framework for International Convergence of Capital Measurement and Capital Standards*, Basle: Bank for International Settlements.

Basle Committee on Banking Supervision (2000a) *Report of the Working Group on Capital Flows*, Basle: Bank for International Settlements.

Basle Committee on Banking Supervision (2000b) *Report of the Working Group on Highly Leveraged Institutions*, Basle: Bank for International Settlements.

Charpentier, S. (2001) 'Nicaragua: Case Study on the Application of Priority Standards and Codes for International Financial Stability', unpublished.

Clark, A. (2000) 'International Standards and Codes', Remarks at a conference on the Role of Regulation in a Global Context, City University Business School and University of London.

Cornford, A. (2000a) *Commentary on the Financial Stability Forum's Report on the Working Group on Capital Flows*, G-24 Discussion Paper Series No. 7, Geneva: UNCTAD, December.

Cornford, A. (2000b) *The Basle Committee Proposal for Revised Capital Standards: Rationale, Design and Possible Incidence*, Geneva: UNCTAD.

Cornford, A. (2001) *The Basle Committee Proposal for Revised Capital Standards: Mark 2 and the State of Play*, UNCTAD Discussion Paper No. 156, Geneva: UNCTAD.

Eichengreen, B. (1999) *Toward a New International Financial Architecture*, Washington, DC: Institute for International Economics.

Eichengreen, B. (2001) 'Strengthening the International Financial Architecture: Open Issues, Asian Concerns', Paper prepared for the IMF/KIEP Conference on Recovery from the Asian Crisis, Seoul, May.

FSF (Financial Stability Forum) (2000) 'Report of the Follow-up Group on Incentives to Foster the Implementation of Standards', prepared for the meeting of the FSF, 7–8 September.

Gottschalk, R. (2001) 'A Brazilian Perspective on Reform of the International Financial Architecture', Report commissioned by DFID, unpublished.

Granville, B. (2001) 'International Financial Architecture: Russia Case Study', Report commissioned by DFID, London: Royal Institute of International Affairs, unpublished.

Griffith-Jones, S. and S. Spratt (2001) 'Will the Proposed New Basle Capital Accord Have a Net Negative Effect on Developing Countries?', Brighton: Institute of Development Studies, University of Sussex (mimeo).

G-7 (1999) 'Strengthening the International Financial Architecture', Report of G-7 Finance Ministers to the Cologne Economic Summit, June.

Group of 22 (1998) 'Report of the Working Group on Transparency and Accountability', Washington, DC: Group of 22.

Hausmann, Ricardo and Ugo Panizza (2002) 'The Mystery of the Original Sin: The Case of the Missing Apple', prepared for the conference 'Currency and Maturity Mismatching: Redeeming Debt from Original Sin', The Inter-American Development Bank, 21–22 November 2002.

IMF (International Monetary Fund) (2000) *Reform of International Financial Architecture: Armenia Case Study*, Washington, DC: IMF.

IMF (International Monetary Fund) (2001a) *Public Information Notice* (PIN) No. 01/17/ 5, March, http:www.imf.org.

IMF (International Monetary Fund) (2001b) *IMF Survey*, vol. 30, no. 7, 2 April.

Kapur, D. and R. Webb (2000) *Governance-Related Conditionalities of the International Financial Institutions*, G-24 Discussion Paper No. 6, Geneva: UNCTAD, August.

Killick, T. (1995) *IMF Programmes in Developing Countries*, London: Routledge.

Mosley, L. (2001) 'Attempting Global Standards: National Governments, International Finance, and the IMF's Data Regime', unpublished.

Mosley, L. (2002) *Financial Globalisation and Government Policymaking*, Cambridge and New York: Cambridge University Press.

Persaud, A. (2001) 'The Disturbing Interactions between the Madness of Crowds and the Risk Management of Banks in Developing Countries and the Global Financial System', in S. Griffith-Jones and A. Bhattacharya (eds), *Developing Countries and the Global Financial System*, London: Commonwealth Secretariat.

Pistor, K. (2000) *'The Standardization of Law and its Effect on Developing Economies'*, G-24 Working Paper No. 4, Geneva: UNCTAD.

Reddy, Y. V. (2001a) 'Implementation of Financial Standards and Codes: Indian Perspective and Approach', Speech at Conference on International Standards and Codes organised by the IMF and World Bank, Washington, DC, 7–8 March.

Reddy, Y. V. (2001b) 'Issues in Implementing International Financial Standards and Codes', Speech at Centre for Banking Studies of the Central Bank of Sri Lanka, Colombo, 28 June.

Reisen, H. (2001) 'Will Basle II Contribute to Convergence in International Capital Flows?', Paris: OECD Development Centre, unpublished.

Rodrik, D. (2000) *Exchange Rate Regimes and Institutional Arrangements in the Shadow of Capital Flows*, Cambridge, Mass.: Harvard University Press, September.

Rojas-Suarez, L. (2001) *Can International Capital Standards Strengthen Banks in Emerging Markets?*, IIE Working Paper No. WP01–10, Washington, DC: Institute for International Economics.

Rojas-Suarez, L. (2002) 'International Standard for Strengthening Financial Systems: Can Regional Development Banks Address Developing Countries' Concerns?', Paper prepared for Conference on Financing for Developing: Regional Challenges and the Regional Development Banks, Institute for International Economics, Washington, DC, February.

Saar, A. (2001) *Benefits of Compliance with Securities Listing Standards: Evidence from the Depository Receipt Markets*, IMF Working Paper, WP/01/79, Washington, DC: International Monetary Fund, June.

Schneider, B. (2001) 'Issues in Capital Account Liberalisation', *Development Policy Review*, Vol. 19, No. 1, March.

Speyer, B. (2001) 'Standards and Codes – Essential Tools for Crisis Prevention', *Deutsche Bank Research Bulletin*, March.

UNCTAD (2001) *Trade and Development Report*, Geneva: UNCTAD.

3
Implementing Standards and Codes through the BWIs: An Overview of the Developing-country Perspective

Aziz Ali Mohammed

Introduction

The subject of standards and codes (S&C) entered into the debates on the reform of the international financial architecture in the aftermath of the financial crises that engulfed the East Asian countries and Korea in 1997–8. In the subsequent discussions, the significance attributed to the implementation and observance of standards and codes has ranged widely. At one end of the spectrum is the position articulated by the UK Chancellor of the Exchequer,[1] who characterised standards and codes as the 'new rules of the game' that are 'not incidental to the financial architecture for the new global economy: they *are* the financial architecture for the new global economy'. At the other end is the view that 'rich countries are long on norms when they are short on resources' and are advancing them to 'deflect attention from broader issues of the nature and quality of international financial regulation' (Kapur, 2002).

This chapter proceeds from a recognition of the usefulness of standards and codes as one component of a set of crisis prevention tools that the international community is deploying through the Bretton Woods institutions (BWIs) to strengthen the stability of the international financial system and to help developing countries integrate better into the global capital market. Standards and codes are also seen as a means for these countries 'to evaluate their own systems against international benchmarks, to identify vulnerabilities and gaps in regulatory structures and practices, and to indicate medium-term development needs and priorities' (Mohammed, 2001).

The next section describes the work being done in the BWIs to monitor and report on the implementation and observance of S&C in relation to their developing member countries. For this purpose, the term 'developing countries' excludes the transition economies as defined by the IMF's *World Economic Outlook*. The Standards and Codes initiative of the BWIs covers eleven areas out of a much larger universe, on the basis that these areas are especially useful for the operational work of the IMF and World Bank, and areas for which assessments would be undertaken and issued as Reports on the Observance of Standards and Codes (ROSCs).[2] Subsequently, a twelfth area has been added, namely, anti-money laundering (AML) measures proposed by the Financial Action Task Force (FATF) and designated as FATF 40, to which have been added eight measures for combating the financing of terrorism (CFT). Following the description of BWI activity, the next section summarises the evolution of developing-country thinking on the subject of standards, as indicated by ministerial statements made in the context of the Group of 24 (G-24) communiqués. The fourth section discusses some issues arising out of the implementation of the ROSC initiative by the BWIs and the appropriateness of their role in monitoring compliance on the part of their developing-country members. The final section provides a summary and conclusions.

BWI activities with standards and codes in developing countries

In the aftermath of the financial crises of the mid- and late-1990s, the IMF began, in January 1999, to experiment with the preparation of 'transparency reports'. These were case studies designed to assess the extent to which countries were observing international standards in areas of direct operational relevance to the IMF, and where it had relevant technical expertise – that is, in data dissemination, fiscal policy transparency, monetary and financial policy transparency, and banking supervision. In the last-mentioned case, the studies mainly covered the transparency aspects of the Basle core principles, although in some cases they assessed observance of the core principles in total. These studies (merged into ROSCs) were prepared initially by IMF staff with the co-operation of the respective country authorities, and in a few cases with the assistance of the World Bank. In September 1999, the Fund agreed to an approach to the preparation of ROSCs whereby different institutions could be invited to take primary responsibility for the undertaking of assessments in the areas related to their competencies.[3]

Meanwhile, collaboration with the World Bank was also proceeding through another channel. The Financial Sector Assessment

Programme (FSAP) was launched jointly in May 1999 'to strengthen the monitoring of financial systems in the context of the IMF's bilateral surveillance and the Bank's financial sector development work'. The objective of the pilot programme covering twelve countries was primarily that of crisis prevention, and hence the focus was on selecting cases of 'systemic importance' and covering a wide range of issues, including 'external sector weaknesses or financial vulnerability; the nature of the exchange rate and monetary regime'.

At the first Board review of the pilot programme in the spring of 2000, it was agreed to expand the pace of the programme to around twenty-four countries per year. While priority would still apply to 'systemically important countries', a preference was expressed for maintaining a broad country coverage, to afford a variety of members 'the opportunity to participate in the FSAP to help them strengthen and develop their financial sectors, to prevent costly financial crisis and, where relevant, to prepare the ground for financial sector liberalization and greater access to the international capital markets'. Given this broadening of objectives, a wide range of analytical tools and techniques was deployed, including macro-prudential analysis, stress testing and scenario analysis, and assessments of observance and implementation of relevant international financial sector standards, codes and good practices. The 'detailed assessments' being undertaken in the context of the FSAP exercise became part of the 'summary standards assessments' that, in turn, were incorporated as the financial sector modules of the ROSC initiative.[4]

This initiative clearly goes beyond financial sector assessments to cover a broad range of standards in other sectors, and it has additional objectives – notably to provide domestic policy-makers with benchmarks of good practice in key areas of policy and, by promoting the use of consistent definitions and the release of accurate information to private markets, to allow 'potential investors and international capital markets to make informed cross-country comparisons'.[5] Moreover, these objectives are no longer restricted to helping emerging market and other developing countries: the international standards have to be implemented by developed countries as well. This ambitious effort required close BWI co-operation with standard-setters in several areas, and with the Financial Stability Forum (FSF).[6] Meanwhile, in addition to its contribution to the modules for ROSC that were derived from FSAP, the World Bank identified areas in which it would undertake the preparation of ROSC assessments consistent with its mandate for capacity-building and poverty reduction, including corporate governance, accounting and auditing, and, when standards became available, in the area of insolvency and creditor rights.

Table 3.1 sets out the progress made by the BWI under the FSAP/ROSC initiatives, it being estimated that each FSAP exercise, on completion, has yielded on average an assessment of five financial sector standards. (There is a trend, however, to become more selective, by tailoring the coverage of topics more closely to country circumstances, and to aim in a typical FSAP for detailed assessments of three standards in the future.) Of the 44 FSAP exercises completed by the end of December 2002, as many as 23 were for emerging-market and other developing countries, as were 12 out of another 21 exercises currently under way. For FSAPs in the planning stage, 21 participants out of a confirmed list of 31 countries belong to the same grouping. This suggests that a fairly broad mix of developing countries has an expectation of acquiring, or improving, access to international capital markets with the help of the FSAP programme. The picture is somewhat less promising in the case of ROSC modules, where more than half of the 320 completed modules are outside the developing country category. Moreover, the share of modules that have been published is much smaller for developing countries compared with the transition economies or the advanced countries, where practically all completed ROSCS have been published, as shown in Table 3.2.

It is evident from the distribution of published ROSCS, classified by category, that work on Group 1 (transparency) that started earlier in the IMF than the joint FSAP exercise (Group 2) produced a much greater number of modules, whereas the World Bank, which started work on Group 3 (financial integrity) modules even later, has published fewer of

Table 3.1 FSAP/ROSC indicators for member countries (as at 31 December 2002)

	Africa	Developing Asia	Western Hemisphere	Middle East, Turkey & Malta	Transition economies	Advanced economies	Total
No. of member countries	51	29	32	16	28	28	184
FSAPs completed	8	4	7	4	13	8	44
FSAPs under way	4	1	6	1	3	6	21
FSAPs confirmed for future	4	1	11	5	3	6	30
ROSCs modules completed no. of members	63	24	42	25	107	59	320
ROSCs committed	45	22	58	23	42	51	241
SDDS subscribers	2	5	9	1	9	23	49
GDDS participants	22	6	11	5	8	0	52

Note: Country classification based on *World Economic Outlook* (April 2002).

Source: International Monetary Fund.

Table 3.2   Distribution of published ROSCs by region and category (as at 31 December 2002)

	Africa	Developing Asia	Western Hemisphere	Middle East, Turkey & Malta	Transition economies	Advanced economies[b]	Total
No. of modules completed[a]	63 (20)	24 (8)	42 (13)	25 (8)	107 (33)	59 (18)	320 (100)
ROSC modules published	43	11	18	5	102	64	243
1 Data dissemination	8	1	4	2	9	5	29
2 Fiscal transparency	10	6	6	1	15	10	48
3 Monetary and financial transparency	6	0	2	0	13	13	34
4 Banking supervision	7	0	2	0	14	11	34
5 Securities markets regulation	2	0	1	0	11	8	22
6 Insurance regulation	4	0	1	0	13	8	26
7 Payments systems	2	0	1	0	12	9	24
8 Corporate governance	2	3	0	2	8	0	15
9–10 Accounting and auditing	2	1	0	0	4	0	7
11 Insolvency regimes/creditor rights	0	0	1	0	3	0	4

Notes: Country classification based on *World Economic Outlook*.
[a] Figures in brackets show percentage of total modules completed;
[b] Includes Euro Area (2 modules) and Hong Kong SAR (4 modules).

Source: International Monetary Fund.

them to date. The Fund has been the standard-setter in the transparency group, followed by banking supervision, which was the one standard in Group 2 where the IMF was already at work in collaboration with the Basle Committees before the start of the FSAP exercises. Developing countries with the largest number of completed modules by the end of 2002 are Brazil and South Africa (10 modules each); Tunisia (9); Egypt and the Philippines (8 each); followed by Cameroon, India and Mexico (6 each); Argentina, Guyana and Senegal (5 each); and Nigeria, Dominican Republic, Turkey, Uganda and Zambia (4 each). Gabon, Iran, Guatemala, El Salvador, Peru, Lebanon, UAE and the Yemen have completed three each, with the rest of the developing world having not more than one or two each. There is evidently a concentration of interest, especially in the emerging-market category, where their desire to improve access to capital markets and the BWIs' interest in preventing financial crises have favoured their priority inclusion in FSAP exercises.

There remain, nevertheless, a large number of developing countries that have not yet participated in the FSAP/ROSC exercises, reflecting a degree of concern that has been voiced by a number of them with the outcome of the exercises, as shown by the G-24 communiqués summarised in the next section.

Developing-country views on S&C

The G-24 members[7] hold plenary sessions semi-annually (usually in April and September) to expound their thinking on various international monetary and development issues of the day that feature on the agendas of the international community.[8] Being represented by member states at the level of ministers of finance and/or governors of central banks, the consensus positions reflected in their press communiqués provide an authoritative indication of their evolving thinking on S&C issues (the relevant paragraphs are reproduced in Appendix 3.1).

Prior to the outbreak of the East Asian financial crisis, there were two specific references, later covered under the rubric of S&C – namely, the efforts of the Basle Committee on Banking Supervision to develop regulatory guidelines and supervision standards, and the efforts being made in the IMF to reach agreement on the General Data Dissemination System. Also at this early stage, there was a mention of two issues that became something of a refrain in subsequent communiqués, namely, the need for 'adequate and timely technical assistance', and for the participation of developing countries 'fully in the deliberations and decisions on international supervisory issues'.

The first communiqué (September 1997) following the outbreak of the financial crisis in Thailand noted recent efforts by the BWIs 'to clarify their potential roles within their respective mandates in the strengthening of governance and reduction of corruption at the national and international levels'. It then added a caution on 'the need to avoid the application of conditionalities based upon subjective judgments in these areas and to ensure uniformity of treatment of members based on objective criteria'. The communiqué introduced a new subject, offering 'full support for co-operative international efforts to combat transnational bribery, money laundering and other forms of economic crime'.

The G-24 ministers met in an Extraordinary Session in February 1998 as the Asian crisis was reaching its peak. While the Caracas Declaration II addressed a broad range of issues of concern to them, it is curiously silent on the subject of standards on codes, suggesting that efforts in this area had not yet reached a salience that would attract a ministerial pronouncement.

The next regular plenary (April 1998) noted ministerial interest in reaching agreement on 'key principles of fiscal transparency', and emphasised the need for their 'symmetrical application with due regard to countries' institutional arrangements and capacities and resource constraints'. The communiqué called on 'the international community, in particular the IMF, to provide the necessary technical assistance to help countries meet the requirements of these principles'.

The October 1998 meeting began to raise a number of S&C issues under the rubric of the architecture of the international monetary and financial system. Ministers welcomed the intensified involvement of the BWIs in financial sector issues, and encourage them 'to disseminate best practices in the financial supervision and regulatory areas' and to promote their own (that is, BWIs') capacity to provide technical assistance in these areas. Their only caution was that any expansion of surveillance activity be 'symmetric as between capital receiving and capital source countries', and they asked for stronger supervision of financial institutions in the major financial markets. Ministers added that they are 'fully committed to the provision of accurate and timely information on economic developments and prospects in their countries', only cautioning against 'premature disclosure' of sensitive information that might interfere with policy implementation. They were also 'fully supportive of transparency in BWI operations' and recognised 'the importance of a dialogue between the BWI and market participants'. Their caveats were that transparency must take into account the need to 'protect the confidentiality and candor of the exchanges between member countries and the BWI'; they wanted to be sure that information was not shared with selectively chosen participants, and that the BWIs were not 'put in the position of serving as rating agencies for market participants'. Finally, they noted the importance of 'strengthening prudential regulation and supervision of their financial systems' and in the case of 'non-financial entities, they underscore the need for improved transparency and corporate governance'.

While the following plenary meeting (April 1999) retained the international financial architecture rubric, the communiqué for the first time began to address explicitly 'the development and implementation of internationally recognized standards' but, curiously, considered these to be 'critical to the proper accountability of international financial institutions' rather than as applying to themselves. In the same breath, however, Ministers sought the symmetrical application of transparency criteria between public institutions and the private sector, and they 'also note[d] that countries at different stages of development will necessarily proceed at different speeds and will require extensive technical assistance in the process of applying these norms, the implementation of which should be voluntary and should not undermine the development of their financial sectors'.

The next three plenary communiqués spanning the year ending September 2000 indicated a sharpening of G-24 concerns, as shown by the inclusion of separate paragraphs under the heading of standards. The September 1999 communiqué accepted the increased attention being given to standards of 'transparency and disclosure' in IMF surveillance 'as long as it remains within the core competencies of the IMF'. The April 2000 communiqué added another qualification, namely, that 'the scope of surveillance should not be extended to cover the observance of such standards and codes'. The last of the three communiqués used rather peremptory language in stating that 'compliance with such standards and codes should not be prematurely integrated into the Article IV consultation process and must not become a condition for the use of IMF resources'. This latter case echoed an earlier statement in the September 1999 communiqué, wherein ministers 'stress that adherence to international standards should not be used in determining IMF conditionality'. All three communiqués underline the voluntary nature of implementing standards and codes, 'taking into account the particular institutional capacities and stage of development of each country'. There was a similarly uniform insistence in all three communiqués on the need for additional technical assistance. The September 2000 communiqué reverted to the issue of symmetry brought up earlier in April 1999, by stating that 'Ministers find the application of codes and standards to be highly asymmetric.' They added that 'standards in the area of transparency are being pressed upon developing countries without commensurate application of corresponding obligations for disclosure by financial institutions,[9] including currently unregulated highly leveraged institutions'. In addition to the ongoing concerns about the voluntary character of compliance with S&C and the apprehension about incorporating them into programme conditionality, the April 2001 communiqué introduced the need for 'additional resources and adequate time … to strengthen developing countries' implementation capacities'. It also mentioned for the first time (since the fleeting reference in April 1998) the subject of money laundering. Ministers agreed that 'money laundering is a matter of global concern', that efforts to combat it 'should be based on a cooperative strategy, involving both developed and developing countries', and that 'monitoring the implementation of any money laundering standards should take full account of members' capabilities and stage of financial sector development and *should not be used as a means of diverting legitimate financial resources away from developing countries'*(italics added).

The subject gained in salience in the most recent communiqués (November 2001 through to September 2002) which incorporated separate paragraphs under the rubric of 'Combating Money Laundering and the Financing of Terrorism'. Ministers are clearly concerned that the work of the IMF and the World Bank in this area be 'consistent with their mandates and core areas of expertise and that they should not become involved in law enforcement matters'. They are apprehensive about the 'non-voluntary and non-cooperative manner in which the FATF 40 Recommendations are applied to non-FATF members', and they caution against 'relying on the FATF for ROSC assessments which should remain the responsibility' of the BWIs.

Developing-country concerns and their resolution

How the concerns expressed by developing countries have been addressed by the BWIs is considered in this section, together with the broader issue of the appropriateness of the BWIs playing such an activist role in the area of standards and codes.

Voluntary character of implementation and observance?

The BWIs have been scrupulous in maintaining that participation by their members has not involved any coercive element. It is clear from Table 3.1 that, in the case of FSAPs, as against completed exercises in fourteen developing countries, as many as twenty-six others were in process at the end of March 2002, and that this would appear to reflect as much a capacity constraint on the part of the BWIs as any marked reluctance on the part of members.[10] With each FSAP yielding four and a half ROSC modules, it is not out of line to find that, as against 95 modules completed in fourteen countries, as many as 120 were in process in an additional eleven developing countries. Another voluntary aspect relates to the publication decision which remains with the member. As against the 95 completions, only 55 of the modules were allowed by members to be published by the same date. There is evidence of more developing countries volunteering for ROSC exercises, although this appears to be associated with preference for the comprehensive, wide-ranging FSAP exercise rather than for individual ROSCs as such. Moreover, as noted earlier, a completed FSAP yields four or more ROSCs, but strictly as a by-product.

However, a dilemma remains. If progress on standards is to 'inform' IMF surveillance discussions under Article IV as well as being deemed essential for the World Bank's policy dialogue and capacity-building efforts, how is this to be reconciled with the voluntary character of participation? While related information might be extracted from other sources, such as technical assistance reports in a particular country, together with any self-assessments made by the country, or by attaching specialist staff with regular Article IV staff missions to look at some aspects of the implementation process with regard to specific standards, there cannot be sufficient assurance that the required information would be extracted from disparate sources for the IMF to carry out its surveillance responsibilities fully. Moreover, reliance on such *ad hoc* sources could undermine the integrity of the ROSC process itself, if it generated a perception that members volunteering for ROSCs were being treated unequally, and were being assessed more rigorously than others. Whether a genuinely voluntary stance can be sustained becomes even more problematic against the growing pressure from major industrial country authorities to incorporate compliance with one or more standards into conditionality for the use of BWI resources,[11] and with the desire of market participants to have comparable information on a cross-country basis in order to inform their own lending and investing decisions (see further discussion below).

Ownership issues

In this area, the concerns of developing countries have been expressed in terms of their lack of appropriate representation in standard-setting bodies and institutions such as the FSF, as well as their exclusion from the deliberations of industrial country groupings where decisions on these matters are made. The BWIs have been careful to point out that all decisions on their involvement with S&C have been taken in the Executive Boards, where developing countries are fully represented.[12] The selected areas were endorsed explicitly by the two Boards as being useful to the operational work of the BWIs, and both the standards and the assessment processes remain subject to periodic review. Priorities in implementing standards are recognised as differing from country to country, and from period to period. There is selectivity in the choice of standards – or parts of standards – against which members are being assessed, and this is ensured by the modular approach to undertaking standards assessments, which allows countries to focus on their own agendas for reform.

Moreover, the BWIs have provided their good offices to enable developing-country representatives to put their views directly to standard-setters in areas where they themselves are not responsible for developing standards. However, this is hardly satisfying for developing country governments, which find themselves excluded from decision-making levels, especially in cases where non-official mechanisms of regulation are involved in standard-setting. It is not clear whether BWI efforts can create a convergence between developing country interests and systemic imperatives sufficient to endow what is essentially a 'third-party' assessment process with a sense of genuine ownership on the part of those being assessed, especially when incentives and sanctions linked to standard-setting become part and parcel of surveillance and conditionality.

Are international standards 'one size fits all' standards?

Developing countries have been concerned that universal standards cannot take into account the diversity of legal and institutional environments in their economies, and the varying stages of development of their markets. Many standards, especially those related to corporate and other elements of governance, have emerged from business practices and norms which have evolved over long periods of time and which reflect compromises among social groups and institutions in advanced countries. Given this historical background for the evolution of several standards, 'the main fear is that, faced with different constraints, at least in the short run, standards designed for industrial countries may not be appropriate for developing countries'.[13] Here again, the BWIs have recognised that it would be unrealistic to expect low-income countries to observe all standards and all elements of standards in the near future, and their focus remains on the gradual improvement of institutions and adherence to standards to encourage a better investment climate.

Moreover, standards, for the most part, establish *good* rather than *best* practice, in the hope that these might be attainable over time by all countries. In a few cases, such as the SDDS, the standard is set at a higher level than the general standard established under the GDDS, the intention being to apply the higher standard only to countries with access to international capital markets. Another example would be the securities standard, which only requires that there be adequate means for enforcing regulations, while recognising that different means of enforcement may be appropriate in different environments. A 'multi-track' approach can be applied in other standard areas as well, taking into account timing and sequencing issues in evaluating them. The BWIs remain convinced, however, that if international standards are to work effectively as benchmarks for monitoring progress, there must be consistency of definitions. Without this, the information and data relied on by policy-makers and market participants will not be comparable across countries, thus undermining the usefulness of standards as a crisis prevention tool. Yet a major challenge remains: how to combine appropriate differentiation with adoption of internationally agreed standards?

Symmetry

Developing countries have shown great concern that the application of certain standards places their financial sectors at a disadvantage *vis-à-vis* financial institutions operating in the more mature capital markets, for reasons additional to those noted in the preceding paragraph. This is illustrated by the application of transparency standards to most of the financial institutions operating in capital-receiving countries (mainly banks), whereas a larger diversity of institutions operating in capital-source countries are not covered. This is particularly true of highly leveraged institutions (notably hedge funds) that do not have reporting obligations to official supervisory authorities in their home countries, let alone to those in developing countries where their operations can produce large disturbances in shallow credit and foreign-exchange markets, and the same applies to over-the-counter transactors in many derivatives markets. These issues of 'market dynamics' – including the 'herding' behaviour of short-term investors, international banks and correlation ploys – have been played down in the analysis of past contagion situations, and this tendency is likely to persist, since S&C disciplines are liable to divert attention from the capital-supply side of the problem. Pressures for the rapid opening of capital accounts have abated in the light of experience, especially following the Asian crises of 1997–8; it is important to keep this experience in mind when seeking to push countries to adhere to standards. The same issues of sequencing and prioritisation, the neglect of which led to past problems in the capital account area, can arise in the standards and codes area as well. Moreover, the pressures operate asymmetrically: developing countries, dependent on the 'good housekeeping' seal of the BWIs in order to access capital markets, are far more subject to them than advanced countries, some of which have failed, for example, to meet basic transparency standards in their fiscal sectors.[14] The asymmetries become egregious if compliance with some standards is made subject to conditionality for the use of BWI resources.

Resource costs relative to benefits

Good studies are not available on the likely costs being incurred by national authorities in meeting standards in the eleven policy areas established by the BWIs (plus the AML/CFT recommendations being negotiated with the FTAF, with the objective of converging on a global standard). Perhaps a general comment that might be ventured is that standards focusing on *process* might be less costly than those dealing with *substance*. The international community has recognised that these costs could be heavy, and has been forthcoming with technical assistance (TA), largely on a grant basis, from bilateral as well as multilateral sources.[15] While this helps to pay for foreign expertise made available on a short-term basis, it cannot compensate for the necessary domestic costs that are incurred in providing counterpart staff and logistical support to the external technicians. Nor can such TA compensate for the energy expended by high-level officials in the recipient countries, who must deal with the phalanx of foreign experts descending in a succession of TA 'missions' and expecting to be received by top policy-makers – whose time is perhaps the scarcest resource in most developing countries.

It can be argued that, against these unavoidable costs must be set the opportunity costs incurred if uncorrected policy deficiencies result in restricting or denying access to international capital markets, and the costs can only mount if and when the country then encounters a financial crisis. There are also certain benefits by way of improved credit ratings and a lower cost of borrowing derived by countries that improve their observance of internationally agreed standards, even if these benefits are sometimes difficult to quantify. The BWIs are aware of this lacuna and are undertaking more intensified research on the relationship between implementation of standards, and macroeconomic and financial stability development.

Serving conflicting audiences

As intergovernmental organisations, the primary objective of the BWIs in launching a major activity such as the FSAP/ROSC initiative must be to serve their members. Interesting private market participants and rating agencies in using the ROSC information to sharpen their risk assessments and to help foreign investors make better investment decisions can be only a secondary objective. To an extent this usage is constructive, as when investors differentiate among borrowing countries more clearly than before, and this becomes reflected in a greater dispersion of spreads on emerging-market debt and in decreasing correlations between spreads across countries. The fact that the Argentine crisis around the turn of the year 2001–2 did not result in widespread contagion might support this view, although the fact that this disaster was so long predicted, and yet so slow in arriving, should dampen much enthusiasm on this score.[16]

Developing countries, as noted in the preceding section, have expressed reservations on how far their own international institutions should go to help private parties make judgements, and the BWIs have been careful in their ROSC assessments to give credit for progress made by members against a given standard or a set of standards rather than providing a snapshot. They have sought to place their assessments in proper context, thereby frustrating the private sector's desire for quantified ratings. The private sector is certainly making its own assessments, and refining its own assessment methodologies – with or without recourse to BWI materials – and it would be unfortunate if undue emphasis on outreach efforts by the BWIs were to result in raising apprehensions in the minds of developing country officials that the BWIs are seeking to impose a market discipline to supplement their own.

Appropriateness of BWI as monitoring agents

The concern that implementation of standards and compliance with them will become an element of conditionality – it has already become an element 'informing' surveillance – remains the principal objection to an activist BWI role in this field of activity, but it is not the only one. The issue of asymmetric pressures exerted by the BWIs has been noted above, as well as the apprehension that the BWIs have accepted codes for monitoring purposes that have been set by non-state standard-setting bodies, and which seek to affect the behaviour of private agents within developing economies.

This raises a more fundamental question. Can intergovernmental organisations be made responsible for applying standards in respect of activities that lie outside the remit of their member governments, and where private interests actively resist the intervention of their own governments?[17] A particularly troublesome issue arises in the case of the

World Bank – namely, the 'jurisdictional gap' it confronts in assessing the observance of standards by its Part I members. The issue has been finessed by organising joint missions with the IMF for FSAPs and OFC assessments, and there is some thought of attaching World Bank staff or consultants with Article IV missions to industrial countries. The legal basis for such efforts remains unclear, especially given the inability of Part II members, in the case of the World Bank Group, to appeal to the principle of the 'uniformity of treatment' of members that applies in the case of the IMF.[18]

Finally, there is the contentious question of BWI involvement in the AML/CFT area, given the very substantial law enforcement and police work component in this activity that clearly falls outside BWI mandates and competencies. There is also the issue of how the *modus operandi* of the standard-setting body in this area – the FATF – can be reconciled with the uniform, voluntary and co-operative nature of the ROSC exercise.

Summary and conclusions

This chapter reviews the work on standards and codes being done by the BWIs with their developing country members, the concerns expressed by the latter through their G-24 communiqués, and the serious efforts of the BWIs to address them. It is concluded that, while developing countries have generally welcomed the BWI role, the multiplicity of objectives involved in the FSAP/ROSC initiatives has made it intrinsically difficult for the BWIs fully to respond to several of the concerns expressed. The BWIs have endeavoured to avoid any coercive element in their assessment work; yet the need to achieve coverage of countries that have the potential to generate instability makes it necessary to exert a degree of pressure on some members to participate even when they are not always persuaded of the benefits to be derived relative to the costs involved. Similarly, the desire of the BWIs to interest private market participants in their S&C work has generated apprehensions that they are seeking to impose a market discipline to supplement their own. Indeed, a final judgement on the effectiveness of the FSAP/ROSC exercises conducted by the BWI will turn, as far as developing countries are concerned, on the benefits they obtain in terms of improved access to private capital markets, relative to the costs they incur in implementing the international standards initiative.

The reality is that many international standards derive from practices evolved from the experience of industrial countries; using them as benchmarks for assessing the performance of countries with less organised financial structures creates competitive disadvantages, despite multi-track approaches or transition allowances. This feeds, in turn, into problems of asymmetry that are grounded in the greater dependence of developing countries on the 'good house-keeping' seal from the BWIs for access to private capital markets. The asymmetry intensifies as BWI assessments move from 'informing' surveillance into becoming considerations that influence lending decisions. Indeed, a final judgement on the appropriateness of the BWIs' role as monitoring agents of the international community could well turn, as far as developing countries are concerned, on the outcome of the current debate as to whether the implementation of standards and compliance with them should be incorporated into conditionalities for the use of BWI resources.

Appendix 3.1   References to standards and codes in G-24 communiqués

27 April 1997

IV   Financial sector issues

7   Ministers noted that, in an environment of globalized financial markets, it is becoming increasingly important to promote and maintain sound banking systems. They urged multilateral institutions to provide adequate technical assistance to help members to strengthen regulatory and supervisory systems and to enhance the transparency of financial markets, as well as to provide financial support to assist in the restructuring of financial sectors. Ministers recognized the efforts being made by the Basle Committee on Banking Supervision and the IMF on the development of appropriate guidelines and standards. They stressed that the developing countries should participate fully in the deliberations and decisions on international supervisory issues.

V   Governance

8   Ministers noted that the principles of good governance of nations include transparency, accountability, and the rule of law. They stressed that the intergovernmental financial institutions, in following these principles in their own operations, should adhere strictly to the mandates embodied in their respective Articles of Agreement. In addition, they called for the fuller participation of developing countries in the decision-making process of the institutions, as well as in their management and staffing patterns.

IX   *General data dissemination system*

13   Ministers recognized the efforts being made to reach agreement on the General Data Dissemination System (GDDS), noting the pragmatic and flexible elements of the system whereby countries can assume the commitment to participate voluntarily. Ministers emphasized the need for developing countries to receive adequate and timely technical assistance to facilitate their early participation in the GDDS.

20 September 1997

III   *Governance*

7   Ministers reiterate their commitment to the principles of good governance, which include transparency, accountability, and the rule of law. While noting the recent efforts of the Fund and the World Bank to clarify their potential roles within their respective mandates in the strengthening of governance and reduction of corruption at the national and international levels, they re-emphasize the need to avoid the application of conditionalities based upon subjective judgments in these areas and to ensure uniformity of treatment of members based on objective criteria. Ministers express full support for cooperative international efforts to combat transnational bribery, money laundering, and other forms of economic crime.

15 April 1998

IV   *Governance*

6   Ministers reaffirm their commitment to the principles of good governance—which include transparency, accountability, and the rule of law—and support the fight against corruption, money laundering, and all other forms of economic crime.

7   Ministers are following with interest the ongoing process toward reaching agreement on key principles of fiscal transparency and emphasize the need for their symmetrical application, with due regard to countries' institutional arrangements and capabilities and resource constraints. They stress the need for the international community, in particular the IMF, to provide the necessary technical assistance to help countries meet the requirements of these principles.

3 October 1998

14 Ministers take note of the intensified involvement of the BWIs in financial sector issues. They encourage the BWIs to help disseminate best practices in the financial supervision and regulatory areas and to strengthen their own capacity to promote technical assistance in these areas. Ministers emphasize that surveillance activities related to financial sector issues must be symmetric as between capital-receiving and capital-source countries. In this context, they stress the importance of strengthening supervision of financial institutions in the major financial markets – including hedge funds, currency traders, and other firms undertaking large cross-border transactions.

15 While fully committed to the provision of accurate and timely information on economic developments and prospects in their countries, Ministers note that premature disclosure of certain types of information remain sensitive and might interfere with policy implementation. While supportive of progress made on transparency in BWI operations, Ministers nevertheless expect that further progress in transparency should take fully into account the need to protect the confidentiality and candor of the exchanges between member countries and the BWIs.

16 While recognizing the importance of a dialogue between the BWIs and market participants, Ministers expect such contacts to be mindful of the confidentiality of their relations with members, avoid sharing information with selectively chosen participants, and not allow themselves to be put in the position of serving as rating agencies for market institutions.

17 Ministers note the importance of strengthening prudential regulation and supervision of their financial systems, in particular to ensure that they are able to intermediate short-term cross border flows efficiently. In the case of non-financial entities, they underscore the need for improved transparency and corporate governance.

26 April 1999

II   Strengthening the architecture of the international financial system

12 Ministers welcome the progress made on issues of transparency, but they emphasize the importance of concentrating on areas related to the core activities of the Fund. They reiterate their concern that publication of Fund staff surveillance reports is likely to compromise the quality and candor of discussions with member countries, thereby

undermining the effectiveness of the Fund's surveillance function. This issue is especially pertinent in the case of a number of countries for which the publication of documents might lead to disproportionately large effects, because, notwithstanding countries' own publications, the Fund staff analysis might be the most visible external assessment of their policies. Ministers emphasize the need for enhancing transparency in the working of private financial entities, especially the highly-leveraged institutions.

13   Ministers recognize that the development and implementation of internationally recognized standards are critical to the proper accountability of international financial institutions. However, they emphasize the need for a symmetrical application of transparency criteria between public institutions and the private sector. Ministers also note that countries at different stages of development will necessarily proceed at different speeds and will require extensive technical assistance in the process of applying these norms, the implementation of which should be voluntary and not undermine the development of their financial sectors.

25 September 1999

II   Surveillance and standards

9   The increased attention given to standards of transparency and disclosure is acceptable, as part of Fund surveillance as long as it remains within the core competencies of the Fund and subscription to international standards remains voluntary. Assessments made on countries' practices in these areas, however, should take fully into account their institutional capacities and stage of development, so as not to place developing countries at a comparative disadvantage in their efforts in developing their financial systems. Appropriate additional technical assistance should be provided to help developing countries prepare for the implementation of international standards. Ministers stress that adherence to international standards should not be used in determining Fund conditionality.

15 April 2000

V   Surveillance, standards, and safeguards

14   While they welcome the development of international codes, standards, and best practices, Ministers consider that the scope of surveillance should not be extended to cover the observance of such standards and codes, which should remain a voluntary choice by each member. Ministers expect the BWIs and other

organizations to be prepared to intensify technical assistance in their respective areas of competence to countries seeking to implement codes and standards.

23 September 2000

International standards and codes

14   Ministers recognize the positive aspects of the development of international codes, standards, and best practices in the spheres of data dissemination, fiscal transparency and transparency in monetary and financial policies, and the management of debt as well as reserves. However, they note that the participation of developing countries in discussions on the development of these standards and codes has been limited, and they call for a more inclusive process. Ministers continue to underline the voluntary nature of implementing such codes and standards, taking into account the particular institutional capacities and stage of development of each country. They also stress the importance of the availability of appropriate technical assistance where needed. Ministers find the application of codes and standards to be highly asymmetric. Standards in the area of transparency are being pressed upon developing countries without a commensurate application of corresponding obligations for disclosure by financial institutions, including currently unregulated highly-leveraged institutions. Ministers would insist that any monitoring of standards and codes within the corresponding competencies of the BWIs should be done on a strictly symmetric basis. Moreover, compliance with such standards and codes should not be prematurely integrated into the Article IV consultation process and must not become a condition for use of IMF resources.

28 April 2001

E   International financial system

9   Ministers note the significant progress made in strengthening the international financial system through the development of international codes, standards, and best practices, to be applied by both developed and developing countries. They continue to underscore the need to ensure that the observance of standards and codes remains voluntary, duly recognizing the country-specific circumstances and stages of development, including administrative and institutional constraints. The work of the Bretton Woods

Institutions (BWIs) on such standards and codes should not extend beyond their core areas, and their observance should not be incorporated in program conditionality. Significantly more technical assistance, additional resources, and adequate time are essential to strengthen developing countries' implementation capacities. Ministers underscore the importance of addressing the existing weaknesses in the regulatory framework of the financial sectors of advanced economies, including in areas such as hedge funds and the supervision of offshore financial centers, to ensure uniform application of standards of transparency.

10 Ministers agree that combating money laundering is a matter of global concern and important to the protection of the integrity of the international financial system. Efforts to combat money laundering should be based on a co-operative strategy involving both developed and developing countries and should encompass not only offshore centers, but also large financial centers where most of the financial flows originate. Ministers caution against the non-voluntary and non-co-operative manner in which the Financial Action Task Force (FATF) 40 Recommendations are currently applied to non-FATF members. They also agree that monitoring of the implementation of anti-money laundering standards should take full account of members' capabilities and stage of financial sector development, and should not be used as a means of diverting legitimate financial resources away from developing countries. Ministers stress the importance of technical assistance to facilitate the effective implementation of anti-money laundering measures. While emphasizing that the focus of the Fund and the Bank should be limited to their respective mandates, they consider that for the Report on the Observance of Standards and Codes (ROSC) and Financial Sector Assessment Program (FSAP) processes, the BWIs will need to work closely with other international bodies. Ministers caution against the BWIs' involvement in the law enforcement aspects of anti-money laundering policies. They also caution against relying on the FATF for ROSC assessments, which should remain the responsibility of the BWIs.

14 November 2001 and 19 April 2002

III *Combating money laundering and the financing of terrorism*

10 Ministers reaffirm their support for international efforts to combat money laundering and the abuse of the international financial

system. They also stress that the IMF's role in combating money laundering and the financing of terrorism should be consistent with its mandate and core areas of expertise. Ministers underline that the IMF is not a law enforcement agency. The abuse of the international financial system through the conduct of illegal activities hurts development prospects and undermines the integrity of financial sectors. In this context, it is important to develop an internationally co-operative strategy, which should encompass not only offshore financial centers, but also large capital-market centers of developed countries where most of the financial flows originate or through which they pass. Ministers welcome the recent UN resolutions in combating terrorism and the ongoing efforts to strengthen the FATF recommendations, and they stress that greater international co-operation among international bodies is needed. It is important that more developing countries are appropriately represented in the FATF and other relevant bodies. Of equal importance, the monitoring of the implementation of internationally-agreed standards must be done on a uniform, co-operative, and voluntary basis, which should take into account the members' capabilities and stage of financial sector development. Ministers stress the importance of additional technical assistance to developing countries to strengthen their financial systems and to help correct deficiencies in members' regulatory frameworks to combat money laundering and financial abuse.

22 September 2002

Anti-money laundering and combating the financing of terrorism

20　Ministers welcomed the progress made by the IMF and the World Bank in advancing the AML/CFT effort worldwide to reduce the abuse of the international financial system. In performing their respective roles, the two institutions should ensure that the co-operative approach that characterizes their interactions with member-countries is upheld. Ministers reiterate that the role of the BWI should be consistent with their mandate and core areas of expertise, and that they should not become involved in law enforcement matters. They emphasize the importance of addressing the resource implications of this endeavor on international financial institutions and member countries' technical assistance needs in a manner that avoids the institutions' effectiveness in other areas. While noting the limited progress achieved in the consultations with the Financial Action Task Force (FATF), Ministers regret that the FATF has not yet totally abolished its non-cooperative approach, as it continues to publish its Non-Cooperative Countries and Territories (NCCT) list, in which many countries believe they have been unfairly included.

Appendix 3.2　List of standards and codes useful for Bank and Fund operational work

Group 1　This is the initial set of areas defined as being within the Fund's direct operational focus when the ROSC pilot was initiated.

Data dissemination　The Fund's *Special Data Dissemination Standard/ General Data Dissemination System* (SDDS/GDDS).

Fiscal Transparency　The Fund's *Code of Good Practices on Fiscal Transparency*.

Monetary and Financial Policy Transparency　The Fund's *Code of Good Practices on Transparency in Monetary and Financial Policies* (usually assessed under the FSAP).

Banking Supervision　Basel Committee's *Core Principles for Effective Banking Supervision* (BCP) (usually assessed under the FSAP).

Group 2　These additional areas are assessed under the FSAP. It is arguable that the Fund's focus on financial sector monitoring under surveillance, and the development of the FSAP as the principal means to conduct that monitoring, combined with the Bank's responsibility for financial sector development, also make these areas of direct operational focus for both institutions.

Securities　International Organization of Securities Commissions' (IOSCO), *Objectives and Principles for Securities Regulation*.

Insurance　International Association of Insurance Supervisors' (IAIS), *Insurance Supervisory Principles*.

Payments systems　Committee on Payments and Settlements Systems' (CPSS), *Core Principles for Systemically Important Payments Systems*.

Group 3　These areas were highlighted as being important for the effective operation of domestic and international financial systems by the Fund Board and are now being assessed by the Bank under the ROSC pilot.

Corporate governance　OECD's *Principles of Corporate Governance*.

Accounting　International Accounting Standards Committee's *International Accounting Standards*.

Auditing International Federation of Accountants' *International Standards on Auditing.*

Insolvency and creditor rights.

Notes

1 In a speech delivered at the Federal Reserve Bank of New York (16 November 2000). The IMF Managing Director made a similar point in his address to the UN Conference on Financing for Development when he stated, 'We are actively promoting rules of the game for the global economy through our work on standards and codes' (Monterrey, 21 March 2002).
2 These eleven areas were carved from an initial list of sixty-four prepared by the Financial Stability Forum (FSF). Note that even the FSF list is restricted to the financial sector, while the international debate on S&C covers a much broader range of activities, including sanitary and phyto-sanitary standards in the WTO context, and a series of additional standards being developed at both industry and firm levels within the private sector.
3 This paragraph is based on IMF News Brief No. 99/58, 21 September 1999.
4 Quotations in this and the preceding paragraph are from IMF PIN No. 01/11 (5 February 2001) reporting on an Executive Board meeting on 12 and 13 December, 2000.
5 Quotations are from IMF PIN No. 01/17 (5 March 2001) reporting on an Executive Board Meeting on 29 January 2001.
6 The FSF was established in February 1999 under the auspices of the Bank for International Settlements in order to bring the banking system and other financial sector regulators into closer liaison with treasury and central bank officials in the major capital-market countries.
7 The Group of 24 (G-24) is the Intergovernmental Group on International Monetary Issues and Development.
8 Typically, these are items that feature on the agendas of the IMF's International Monetary and Financial Committee (IMFC), previously designated as the Interim Committee, and the Joint IMF/World Bank Group Development Committee.
9 Presumably, the reference is to financial institutions in capital-source countries. This is clarified in one of the later communiqués (April 2001), wherein 'Ministers underscore the importance of addressing the existing weaknesses in the regulatory frameworks of the financial sectors of the advanced economies.'
10 The capacity constraint is indicated by a target of twenty-four FSAP exercises to be undertaken per year, set by the BWI Executive Boards.
11 This was spelt out by IMFC chairman, Gordon Brown, in the same New York speech cited in Note 1, when he stated that 'over time – the implementation of the codes should be a condition for IMF and World Bank support'. This position has since been supported by other G-7 leaders.
12 There is a larger governance issue here, as to whether the Executive Boards end up 'rubber-stamping' decisions taken by a sub-set of the membership exercising majority voting power, but this falls outside the scope of this chapter.

13 See the paper by Lilliana Rojas-Suarez on 'International Standards for Strengthening Financial Systems' (Global Development Center document prepared for Conference on Financing for Development: Regional Challenges and the Regional Development Banks, 19 February 2002, mimeo). The paper illustrates the problem of applying the international capital adequacy standard as recommended by the Basle Capital Accord in countries lacking deep and liquid capital markets, and where asset ownership is highly concentrated.

14 A different issue arises in the light of recent revelations about 'creative accounting' by major US corporations, and conflicts of interest on the part of their supposedly independent external auditors as well conflicts within the investment banking community. The ongoing debates underline ethical and other societal values that must be considered when judging performance in all member countries, not only those in the developing world.

15 However, the costs of BWI provision of TA would be borne by developing countries since, *at the margin*, all incremental costs incurred by these institutions are paid for by their borrowing members.

16 In fact, the ongoing Argentine crisis raises larger doubts about the potential lack of effectiveness of the entire standards and codes process. Helmut Reisen, in a Comment on the Lilliana Rojas-Suarez paper (cited in Note 13 above) argues that 'Argentina shows … Gresham's Law in action, paying debts with ROSCs rather than dollars.'

17 The strong private-sector reaction to the concept of an international insolvency regime for sovereign debtors is illustrative of the problem that confronts the BWIs in developing standards in the area of private creditor rights.

18 There is also a broader problem in that the BWI charters have no provisions analogous to those in the WTO Charter under which members deviating or seeking exemptions from observing certain treaty obligations are subject to claims for compensation from other members.

References

Kapur, D. (2002) 'Processes of Change in International Organizations' in D. Nayyar (ed.), *Governing Globalization; Issues and Institutions*, Oxford University Press.

Mohammed, Aziz Ali (2001) *The Future Role of the IMF*, G-24 Discussion Paper Series No. 11, Geneva: UNCTAD, April.

4
The View from India

T. C. A. Anant[1]

The financial crises of the 1990s, with their associated concerns about contagion, have led to discussion on a framework for building a new international financial architecture. While this discussion has been taking place in many forums on a variety of issues, a major focus has been on the initiative to create a framework of international financial standards and codes (S&Cs).

India has been an active participant in this initiative from the beginning, and has advocated a voluntary, equitable and continuous process, taking into account the institutional and legal structure, and the stages of development in different countries. Recognising the importance of this initiative, and in order to examine the status and guide the implementation of these S&Cs in India, the Reserve Bank of India (RBI), in consultation with the Government of India, in December 1999 constituted a 'Standing Committee on International Financial Standards and Codes'. The Standing Committee set up Advisory Groups in ten core subject areas, broadly encompassing the twelve key areas prescribed by the Financial Stability Forum (FSF). These were: transparency in monetary and financial policy; fiscal transparency; insurance regulation; bankruptcy laws; corporate governance; data dissemination; payments and settlement systems; banking supervision; securities market regulation; and accounting and auditing. Later, a technical group from the RBI was formed, to examine the status of India's compliance with the recommendations of the Financial Action Task Force relating to market integrity.

Eminent experts chaired all the Advisory Groups, and the members were similarly drawn from among market participants, academics and other experts. This arrangement gave the Advisory Groups an independent and impartial status, and allowed them to make a critical assessment of the relevance of, as well as the state of compliance with, the S&Cs, and give unbiased recommendations with regard to the feasibility of compliance. These reports provide a valuable internal assessment of a developing country's perspective on S&Cs. All the Advisory Group reports have been published as well as being disseminated on the Internet by posting them on the RBI website (www.rbi.org.in).

In evaluating the work of the Advisory Groups it is useful to keep in mind that reforms in the financial sector were an important element of the package of economic reforms of the 1990s, and furthermore that the process of reform and change is still under way. In pursuance of these reforms, the government has constituted a variety of further advisory groups and committees to work on the same subjects as the original Advisory Groups, which have taken cognisance of their efforts and at times provided inputs to them. In some cases, as we shall see, they provide different perspectives on similar issues. This chapter provides a brief review of the advisory group reports, the aim being not to provide detailed assessments but rather to give a flavour of the process, to outline the nature of the recommendations and their implications for domestic policy, and to use these to draw some lessons for the way in which the framework of S&Cs can be used to further economic reform in India and other developing countries. The next section examines the issue of assessing compliance with S&Cs and the approach of the advisory groups in doing this, after which we look at the implications for policy. The next two sections draw on the reports to highlight the inter-related and dynamic character of the process. The chapter concludes with some lessons which reinforce the traditional position India has taken *vis-à-vis* these S&Cs.

Assessing compliance

The FSF website provides a Compendium of Standards, which serves as a common reference for various standards. The website points out that the key standards vary in terms of their degree of international endorsement, but are broadly accepted as representing the minimum requirements for good practice. It is important to note that the standards were drawn up for use in a number of different ways. The standards on accounting and auditing derive from what are essentially private-sector bodies, whereas the others represent different levels of governmental participation.

The advisory groups examined in detail India's status in each of these critical areas in financial sector governance, in the light of existing law and regulatory practices. Compliance in general is not a simple yes/no scorecard, but a complex assessment based on economic structure, governance practices, and constitutional and other statutory obligations. Further gaps in compliance arise for a complex web of reasons often reflecting the need for interconnected reform measures. This is caused in part by the fact that these standards differ from international treaties in that typically they are not binding to the same degree, but are akin to guidelines or intentions; this has led some commentators to call them 'soft law'. Thus, when seeking to reform the financial sector, such norms can at best be indicative; their application has to take into account the existing legal framework in the country and its economic structure. Therefore it has in general not been possible to relate compliance in terms of some mechanical scorecard. The reports of the advisory groups need to be read in detail and together to get a perspective on the complexity of reform required. On the whole, with the exception of bankruptcy law where we do not as yet have an integrated code in most areas of financial regulation, there is a considerable degree of compliance, with full compliance in data dissemination.

It is difficult to describe all the changes needed in financial sector regulation and management. Some of the key recommendations can be usefully examined to assess the changes required. The advisory group on transparency in monetary and financial policy is of the view that there is a need for transparent setting of monetary policy objectives by the government, and providing the RBI with autonomy to implement these objectives. Providing such autonomy required the group to recognise that this may raise issues of constitutional governance and the possibility of an appropriate amendment. Furthermore, analysing the process of monetary policy formulation, the group observed that there is a strong interaction between the RBI's responsibilities in the areas of monetary policy and internal debt management. This has at times led to a situation where monetary policy has become subservient to debt management. The group also noted that the debt management function puts the RBI in a situation of direct conflict of interest with its objectives on monetary policy. Thus an essential element of reform would require a separation of the debt management function from the monetary policy and regulatory functions of the Reserve Bank.

The advisory group on fiscal transparency noted that, while there is substantial compliance with the code, there are gaps, especially in relation to the quantification of quasi-fiscal activities, contingent liabilities and the overall public-sector balance. The report observed that fiscal practices at the state level generally lagged behind the standards achieved at central level, and suggested measures to help bring these into greater conformity.

The advisory groups focusing on financial supervision (banking, insurance and securities) made a number of recommendations involving legal changes, regulatory guidelines and practices as well as in governance practices with regard to banks and other financial institutions. The overall pattern of compliance is mixed, with very high standards in some areas and considerable gaps in others. Thus, for example, banks have achieved considerable success in loan accounting, transparency and disclosures, but they still need to develop internal practices for better risk management. The gaps occur because of the transitory nature of financial sector development and the earlier history of controls. It should be noted that the reform agenda in place since the early 1990s has been gradualist, and has sought to minimise the costs of dislocation. A number of recommendations at the operational level have either been implemented or are in active discussion among market participants.

The groups on corporate governance, and auditing and accounting, made a number of observations with a likely impact on the functioning of private-sector activities. With regard to auditing and accounting standards, some divergences with corresponding international standards were noted; the group pointed out that, given the divergence between domestic tax and other regulatory laws, and those in other countries, there will always be differences in the corresponding accounting and auditing standards. But to enhance transparency, the group recommended mandatory explanation as a part of the Indian standard, giving the reasons for the departure from the international standard. Further, the group noted that another area of concern was the long gap in time between the issuance of international standards and the adaptation of domestic standards. They further emphasised that the standards under discussion are not fixed over time, either in India or abroad. Thus convergence is a dynamic process in which the relevant standards, both domestically and internationally, are evolving continually. The need to improve and professionalise the standard-setting process was also stressed. These results are merely indicative of the wide range of issues considered by the advisory groups in their process of assessing compliance.

Implications for reform

The recommendations of the advisory groups cover a number of legislative and non-legislative measures. Several legislative measures are already in process, including measures relating to fiscal and budgetary management, public debt, deposit insurance, securitisation and foreclosure, and prevention of money laundering. The agenda for further legal reform, as identified by the advisory groups, include amendments to the RBI banking regulations, regulations of companies, chartered accountants, income tax, bankruptcy, negotiable instruments, contracts, and the Unit Trust of India, among others. The legislative process in a democratic set-up is complex and slow, partly because of the multifarious representative processes and structures. In some cases the legislative intervention has not been fully in consonance with reform expectations. Thus, for example, attempts are being made to amend the bill on fiscal management at the insistence of the Parliamentary Standing Committee on Finance, to delete or dilute the provisions with regard to numerical ceilings as well as the timeframe set for the reduction in revenue and fiscal deficits, the amount of guarantees to be given by the central government, and the total liabilities of the central government. Similarly, the bankruptcy bill is not as comprehensive as might be desired.

However, it is not necessary to wait for legislative developments to bring about or initiate reforms that signal changes in attitudes. The advisory groups have made a number of recommendations which require either executive action or action by the regulators concerned. A variety of these have already been carried out, and others have been recommended and action initiated. Thus, for example, the Institute of Chartered Accountants has decided that a statement explaining the reasons for divergence from international practice should accompany all standards in future. The high-level Committee on Capital Markets has been expanded to include the insurance regulator. And the RBI has recently taken steps to put in place elements of the prompt corrective action (PCA) framework, and so on.

Even with these changes, the process is complex as it involves consultation with and the education of market participants. Furthermore, the regulators need to have an established transparent procedure for making changes. In a number of instances the changes require co-ordinated actions across different regulatory agencies and the government.

Interrelationships and overlaps

The reports of the different groups involve a number of overlapping issues. The overlaps arise because of the inherently interconnected nature of the standards in question. In fact, in a number of places, the groups have noted the overlap and emphasised the need for co-ordinated action. Some of these interrelations are useful to examine.

As already noted, the group on monetary policy emphasised the need to create an independent debt management office to reduce the potential for conflict of interest. However, for this to be done, it is essential that the fiscal balance be brought under greater control; hence the crucial importance of the recommendations to reduce deficits and balance the budget, as envisaged in the original Fiscal Responsibility and Budget Management Bill.

The advisory groups on payment and settlement systems and securities markets had concurrent views on some key issues, in particular on extending electronic funds transfer (EFT) across the country and eliminating the constraint of the lack of a real time gross settlement system (RTGS).

The interrelationship between corporate governance, bankruptcy law and bank performance is too well known to need spelling out. Reforming the bankruptcy law is an important step in reducing corporate moral hazard and improving the balance sheets of banks and financial institutions. Such a reform would require a clearer identification of the stakeholders in a company, and the provision of a transparent and predictable process to reconcile their claims.

The point about these interrelationships is to highlight the importance of reform in a holistic manner rather than in some sort of standard-by-standard approach. In addition to these interrelationships, a number of groups pointed out the need for regulators to co-ordinate their actions, and develop mechanisms to share information and act co-operatively. This becomes particularly important when we add concerns about money laundering and market integrity to the picture. A multiplicity of regulators can lead to both conflicting regulations and regulatory gaps in cases of unclear demarcations of authority. To deal with these problems, the groups' suggestions involved creating some formal mechanism. Thus, the group on payment systems noted the need for an institutionalised problem resolution mechanism when the regulatory burden of the different regulators, for example the RBI, the SEBI and so on impinges on the level playing-field across participants. The group on the securities market was more specific and suggested giving statutory status to the High-level Group on Capital Markets, while the group on banking supervision recommended the idea of a key regulator/supervisor.

Dynamic considerations

The reports of these groups were completed over a longish period spanning almost a year. But even as the advisory groups were formulating their reports, concurrent developments in policy and international events were changing some of the basis for the discussion. In fact, the advisory group on accounting and auditing has pointed out explicitly the inherently dynamic dimension to standards. It is useful to turn to some examples in other areas as well.

The report on monetary policy had recommended the adoption of a single objective, namely, inflation control for the central bank. In recent years some debate has been taking place on the relationship of monetary policy in controlling asset price and exchange-rate movements.[2] While there is virtual unanimity on the centrality of the price objective, there are considerable nuances in its short-term implementation, thus emphasising the importance of flexibility and autonomy for the regulatory institution. The advisory group on data dissemination had noted the virtual compliance with the SDDS standards. Data issues, however, also require us to examine the structure of the system in which data are generated and disseminated, since the needs of effective governance will require a capable institution for data generation. These longer-run systemic dimensions of the statistical system have been dealt with extensively in the report of the National Statistical Commission, which contains some key recommendations relating to the independence of the statistical system and gives it a statutory frame. These recommendations are essential for ensuring the reliability and credibility of the data provided and would also be consistent with the recommendations made by the IMF in evaluating India's observance of fiscal transparency. The point is that compliance should not be viewed in a static manner but rather in a form capable of dynamic sustainability.

The policy on bankruptcy law reform provides one of the most interesting examples of complexity and differences in perception. The advisory group suggested a reform package, which would seek to work within the existing framework of the High Courts but would attempt to strengthen it institutionally by creating a 'trustee' office to manage the process and provide a different procedural law to deal with the problem. Independent of the work of the advisory group, the government had set up a commission under the Law Ministry to examine the problem. They recommended creating a new institution, the National Company Law Tribunal, vested with the powers of the Company Law Board and with the High Courts handling winding-up matters. In principle, both solutions can work, but they represent different assumptions about institutions. The advisory group recommendations were concerned about jurisdictional conflict, constitutional powers and the past experience with tribunals, whereas the proposed bill is concerned with the difficulties associated with reforming the court structure and the need to bring in technical expertise.

Finally, the recent bankruptcy filing by ENRON has raised a number of ethical issues relating to the role of auditors and internal control mechanisms in auditing and accounting firms. In the USA, this has led to some suggestions about revamping their accountability structures. While this is not directly applicable to India, it is an area where we shall need to evaluate our policies in the light of international evidence and developments. This is particularly important, given the rapid convergence taking place in our institutional structures. At present, the focus of international standards and codes relates to the standards as they apply to the market and market participants. Internal mechanisms of governance in the regulator and its self-evaluation have been less emphasised. Thus we shall need to develop effective assessment mechanisms for the regulators as well. While these discussions so far have typically been in the context of the auditing and accounting profession, they could easily be extended to other self-regulatory organisations (SROs) as well.

Lessons

These discussions lead one to identify some underlying common lessons, which may have wider applicability:

1.   The temptation to prescribe universally valid model codes which do not allow for differences in institutional development, legislative framework and, more broadly, different stages of development must be avoided

This conclusion is particularly significant, given the complexity of the reform agenda, which requires legislation and possibly constitutional changes, modifications to regulatory guidelines and practices, education of market participants and the creation of regulatory experience. At the time of writing standards and codes belong to the category of rules, which have been described as 'soft law' (Mario, 2000). The difference between soft and hard relates to degrees of obligation, precision and delegation.

Converting the standards to 'hard law' is fraught with the risk of failure. This is best borne out by assessments of country experiences with legal transplants. The following observation from a multi-country study on law and legal institutions in Asia is highly appropriate:

> A key finding of this research project is that law and legal institutions should not be viewed as technical tools that once adopted will produce the desired outcome. The point that law is embedded in culture has

often been made especially with respect to the Asian economies. We would add that in order to be effective law has to be embedded in the overall economic policy framework. This finding cautions against the blind transplantation of legal institutions without due consideration for the relevant economic framework with which they shall operate. (Pistor and Wellons, 1999: 19)[3]

2. *The accent should be on gradualism rather than a big bang*

The nature of change required, together with its inherent complexity, implies that there will be a considerable process of learning and adaptation associated with such reforms. The timeframe for non-legislative changes would imply a medium-term horizon; the problems of democratic consensus-building required for legislative exercises will extend that horizon easily. In addition to these issues, there are related issues of law reform and improving the functioning of supporting agencies such as the courts, the police and the broader justice delivery system.

This leads us to one of the key questions of this whole subject: should standards and codes be used as part of 'conditionalities'? It is important to note that conditionalities arise in the context of a macroeconomic crisis requiring multilateral intervention. In such a situation conditionalities are good and would be easily acceptable if they were simple, easy to enforce and monitor, and have a direct bearing on improving the macroeconomic balance of the country. But, as we have noted, the implementation and impact of the standards and codes are slow and complex. They require institution building, dialogue and consensus across a variety of market participants. Further, it is true that the adoption of standards and codes of conduct is being viewed as necessary, although certainly not sufficient, to ensure macroeconomic stability. The link between implementation of standards and codes and financial stability is by no means obvious or direct. Even with high standards of compliance and development, systemic problems have been known to arise, as the experience of the developed countries will testify. In view of these facts, it is important that we keep standards and codes in the domain of soft law rather than seeking to harden them by including them in some form of multilateral conditionalities or requirements.

3. *It is important to note that reform is itself a dynamic process requiring institutional support*

The question that arises is how best to further the task of ensuring compliance and continued reform. In addition, the growth of the financial sector is characterised by the blurring of distinctions between banking, securities and insurance activities. Even if we were to compartmentalise the institutions, the nature of linkages has increased the risk of contagion across activities. This has tended to raise the question of whether we should seek to create a single integrated regulator. These issues have been debated and discussed extensively in India.[4] The broad consensus seems to be that, in view of the evolving character of the financial system and the different levels of development in the different segments, it is probably better to retain separate regulators for each sector. However, as has been noted in the advisory group reports, there is a need to co-ordinate the actions of the different regulators. This co-ordination is desirable both from a functional perspective and from the need to promote and direct the process of reform. In view of these considerations it would be useful to highlight the following recommendation made in the synthesis report of the advisory groups and adopted by the standing committee:

> The Reports of the Groups and action cannot be a one-off affair nor can its implementation be made into a strict sequenced process. In view of this, it is desirable that some permanent mechanism be created for monitoring and evaluating follow-up, responding to new developments and co-ordinating with Government, Regulators, SROs and other market participants on a continual basis. Independently, we have noted that a number of Groups have recommended that the High-level Group on Capital Markets be given a formal legal status. The tasks can be merged by assigning this task of evaluation and supervision also to this Group. The analogy of creating a domestic Financial Standards Forum would not be inappropriate. Further, such a group or forum would need some secretariat, which could be located in the RBI, in view of the fact that it has already evolved a small professionally well-equipped group to assist the various Advisory Groups. The responsibility of this establishment would be to monitor both international and domestic developments in this regard and follow up with annual reports. Where required, similar non-official Advisory Groups, involving experts to assess and evaluate change can be set up from time to time. Further, increasingly, our performance under these norms will play an important role in determining the overall risk assessment. In this context, periodic reviews by independent experts will help in providing vital inputs for improved governance.

The overall point is that standards and codes, when viewed as a framework for financial sector reforms, imply a complex web of initiatives requiring considerable flexibility and sensitivity to local cultural and institutional attributes. It reinforces the point that policy-making for economic development is more an art than a science.[5]

Notes

1 I am grateful to Dr Y. V. Reddy, deputy governor, RBI for advice and encouragement in the writing of this chapter and the earlier report on which it is based. I am also grateful to the RBI nodal officers and Shri Arunachalramanan, in particular, for their valuable advice and assistance in this exercise.
2 See White (2001), as an example of this discussion.
3 A more formal version of this result can be seen in Berkowitz *et al.*, 2000.
4 See, for example, Reddy (2001).
5 Since this chapter was written, Parliament has amended company law, creating a tribunal for all company issues, including bankruptcy. A law to create a statistical commission is in process. And an independent pensions regulator has also been mooted.

References

Berkowitz, Daniel, Katharina Pistor and Jean-François Richard (2000) *Economic Development, Legality, and the Transplant Effect*, Working Paper No. 308, Michigan: William Davidson Institute, February.
Mario, Giovanoli (ed.) (2000) *International Monetary Law: Issues for the New Millennium*, Oxford University Press.
Pistor, K. and P. Wellons (1999) *The Role of Law and Legal Institutions in Asian Economic Development 1960–1995*, Oxford University Press for the Asian Development Bank.
Reddy, Y. V. (2001) 'Issues in Choosing between Single and Multiple Regulators of Financial System the Address', Paper presented at the Public Policy Workshop, ICRIER, New Delhi, 22 May.
White, William R. (2001) 'Changing Views on How Best to Conduct Monetary Policy: The Last Fifty Years', Bank for International Settlements Lecture, RBI, December.

5
The View from Mexico

Javier Guzmán Calafell[1]

Introduction

Substantial progress has been achieved to date in efforts aimed at giving a more prominent role to international standards and codes in an attempt to strengthen the international financial architecture. Contrary to the diversity of views that prevailed during the early stages of this initiative, there is general agreement at the beginning of the twenty-first century that widespread use of international standards and codes can contribute to strengthening crisis prevention through several channels. First, they can represent an important element of policy-making in participating countries. Second, the information on progress in implementing standards and codes can improve risk assessments and thereby contribute to supporting investment and lending decisions by market participants. And third, standards and codes can improve the quality of IMF surveillance and decision-making in general in other international institutions. This generalised positive attitude towards international standards and codes has been reflected in concrete facts. In particular, the number of Reports on the Observance of Standards and Codes (ROSC) modules made available rose – nearly fourfold between 1999 and 2002.

Mexico has been an active player in this process. The Mexican authorities formally subscribed to the Special Data Dissemination Standard (SDDS) in 1996. More recently, a Financial Sector Assessment Programme (FSAP) was carried out for Mexico, which included standards and codes assessments in five different areas. Furthermore, following the successful completion of this exercise, two additional assessments were requested. Notwithstanding these positive developments, however, we are still far from a situation in which we could consider that the objectives set for this initiative have been met. In fact, we may have reached a point in which further progress in what was considered by some as 'the most prominent and ambitious item on the architectural agenda' (Eichengreen, 2001) will become increasingly complicated.

This chapter has two objectives. The first is to describe Mexico's experience with international codes and standards, including an explanation of the benefits derived from the assessments carried out, and to provide an analysis of the extent to which concerns frequently heard among developing countries have been relevant in the Mexican case. The second is to evaluate the progress made to date with this initiative at the international level, and the main challenges ahead.

Mexico's involvement with international standards and codes

The participation of Mexico in the initiative leading to a wider adoption of international standards and codes can be separated into three stages:

(i)   participation in the IMF's Special Data Dissemination Standard (SDDS);
(ii) preparation of a Financial Sector Assessment Programme (FSAP); and
(iii) assessment of international codes and standards in other areas after completion of the FSAP.

The rest of this section comments further on Mexico's experience during these three stages.

The SDDS

As may be recalled, much emphasis was placed on transparency issues following the 1994–5 economic crisis in Mexico. The dominant view then was that insufficient transparency in the dissemination of key data by the Mexican authorities had been a major factor behind the problems that the country's economy had experienced in that period. Although many of these criticisms were unfair, the fact is that in the aftermath of the Mexican crisis the international community began to attach much more importance to transparency as an instrument of crisis prevention.

In this context, in April 1995, the Interim Committee called on the Executive Board of the IMF to establish standards to guide members in providing economic and financial data to the public.

The G-7 industrialised countries, which met shortly thereafter in Halifax, Nova Scotia, made a similar request. A year later, in April 1996, the IMF's managing director reported to the Interim Committee that the SDDS had been established, and that invitations to subscribe had been sent to members.

Mexico's decision to participate in the SDDS was naturally influenced by the questions that were raised on the transparency of the country's statistics before the 1994–5 crisis. Thus the authorities accepted the invitation of the IMF to collaborate as a pilot country from the first stage of the SDDS, and a formal application to subscribe was presented in August 1996.

Mexico's subscription to the SDDS was relatively unencumbered, both because of the country's relatively good statistical system and because the institutions involved had already made a good portion of their data-bases available on the Internet. Since June 2000, Mexico has complied fully with the specifications for coverage, periodicity and timeliness of the SDDS, and for the dissemination of advance release calendars. It is also interesting to note that, according to information provided by the IMF, Mexico is among the five most frequently accessed countries on the Dissemination Standards Bulletin Board.

The Financial Sector Assessment Programme (FSAP)

The Mexican authorities' decision to ask for a FSAP in 2001 responded to a combination of objectives:

- With the consequences of the 1994–5 banking crisis absorbed almost completely, the FSAP represented a good opportunity to have a thorough and objective examination of the financial system by a group of outside experts.
- A series of reforms to the financial system was to be sent to Congress, and there was interest in receiving input from the IMF and the World Bank. It was believed that combining the perspectives and expertise of the Fund and the Bank would produce useful feedback.
- A message of transparency would be sent to the international community through this exercise.
- There is a commitment among G-20 member countries to undertake a FSAP.

Following approval of Mexico's request, a joint IMF–World Bank mission visited the country in March 2001. The mission included a team of more than twenty experts, with representatives from the European Central Bank, the US Federal Reserve, the Bank of Spain, the National Commission of Securities Markets of Spain, IOSCO, and the US FDIC and SEC. At that time, this represented the most comprehensive FSAP ever carried out for an emerging market.

Since the Financial System Stability Assessment (FSSA) (the component of the FSAP that the Board of the IMF allows to be released publicly) has been published, there is no need to repeat here the findings of the study (IMF, 2001). Suffice it to say that one of the report's main conclusions was that the sound implementation of macroeconomic policies and the process of bank restructuring and consolidation, among other factors, have made the Mexican economy more resilient to shocks, and provided a favourable background for its continued healthy development. In this context, neither the banking system nor other financial institutions are considered to be a source of systemic risk in the near future.

The overall assessment under the FSAP had, as important inputs, reports on the observance of standards and codes, and good practices of transparency in the following areas: monetary and financial policies, payments systems, banking supervision, IOSCO objectives and principles of securities regulation, and IAIS insurance supervisory principles. Three general observations stand out from Mexico's experience in this regard:

(i) The evaluations made in the different ROSC modules were frank and objective. They point to the problems faced and express clearly whenever the standards are not met. There is a lot of progress in this regard in comparison with previous practices, since many assessments performed in the early stages of this initiative can be criticised on the grounds that they are neither very deep nor very critical.

(ii) In general, no major disagreements with the authorities' views were observed. In fact, most of the problems stressed in the FSAP had already been identified. In a number of cases, the authorities had begun to take action, or planned to do so, to sort out these difficulties before the FSAP was asked.

(iii) Involvement in the design of codes and standards was very useful for the authorities to identify areas of weaknesses before the FSAP was begun. As will be seen below, the case of the payments system is illustrative in this respect.

Was the FSAP useful for Mexico? The answer is affirmative, for the following reasons. First, the FSAP represented an input for the financial reform measures that were introduced in 2001. Discussions with the FSAP team allowed the authorities a useful exchange of views and the opportunity to confirm that the path chosen was the correct one. Second, self-assessments performed by each institution as background for the FSAP compelled them to review the strengths and weaknesses of the financial system on the basis of an international point of reference. Third, misunderstandings on a number of issues were clarified. And, finally, Mexico's commitment to a policy of transparency was confirmed. This last is crucial for any country, as the international community attaches great value to transparency. But it was even more important in the case of Mexico, given the major crisis that was experienced in the country a few years earlier and, as already explained, the prominent role that was attached to insufficient transparency as a factor behind the crisis.

The proposal to use international codes and standards as an instrument to strengthen crisis prevention has not been free of questions. In particular, many developing countries have expressed concerns about the appropriateness of the existing standards and codes for their stage of development. Similarly, doubts have arisen regarding their institutional capacity to apply the recommendations emanating from standards and codes, and many countries have noted that, if standards and codes assessments were to be based on a pass/fail approach, market uncertainty could be the end result, with the consequent costs for the economies under evaluation.

These concerns are understandable, and devoting a lot of energy in alleviating them is clearly warranted. Fortunately, they were not a source of major difficulties in the Mexican FSAP. The use of standards inconsistent with the stage of the country's development was not a problem. Inadequate technical expertise or support to perform the mission's recommendations was not an issue either. In addition, it could hardly be argued that the evaluations followed a pass/fail approach. In fact, in some cases the opposite argument could be made – namely, that the assessments under the FSAP in some cases lacked clarity in the final judgement.

A word of caution is needed, however. The fact that ownership of the standards and codes did not pose major problems in the case of Mexico must not be taken to mean that ownership was not important for the country. On the contrary, in fact. An example may be useful. Mexico participated actively in the design of the core principles of transparency for payments systems. This gave rise to at least two benefits. On the one hand, the views of Mexico and other emerging markets were taken into account in developing the principles and this helped greatly to balance the final outcome. And on the other, this process allowed the authorities to make an adequate diagnosis of the problems faced by the domestic payments system before the FSAP exercise was carried out.

What, then, are the challenges that deserve to be noted from the Mexican experience? Two are worth highlighting. First, to be useful in the medium and long term, exercises such as the FSAP need to be updated frequently. However, capacity constraints make this unlikely to happen. Under current circumstances, it is difficult to expect that the IMF and the World Bank will be in a position to repeat the FSAP exercise for Mexico with an adequate periodicity. Second, it is not clear whether markets are taking into account sufficiently the evaluation made by the IMF and the World Bank under the FSAP. We have only partial evidence, and neither of these institutions provides such information. This is a missing element in the standards and codes initiative that should be tackled promptly.

Other international standards and codes

An objective way of evaluating the importance attached by the Mexican authorities to the outcome of the FSAP is to take a look at the actions taken by them after this exercise was completed. The information speaks for itself. Two more ROSC modules have been requested: an evaluation of the transparency of public finances has been finalised and published, and the data module of the ROSC will be completed in the short term.

The international experience

A lot of progress has been made over the period 1999–2002 in making international standards and codes a more relevant instrument of crisis prevention in the world economy. As shown in Figure 5.1, the number of ROSC modules published trebled between 1999 and 2001, and the trend continued in 2002. Naturally, the quantity of resources involved in this process is huge.

Notwithstanding these positive developments, it is too early to take the above information as a sign of success, since the road ahead looks extremely complicated. For example, as at 31 December 2002, ROSC modules had been published for 68 out of 184 IMF member countries that is, for only 37 per cent of the membership. In the case of the industrialised countries, the corresponding figure is 50 per cent, for Latin America, 26 per cent, and for other developing and emerging-market countries, 29 per cent (see Figure 5.2). Furthermore, the average number of ROSC modules for the 68 countries mentioned above is only four per country. The magnitude of the effort still required is more evident, if it is recalled that the Financial Stability Forum has recommended that countries focus on the adoption of twelve key standards.

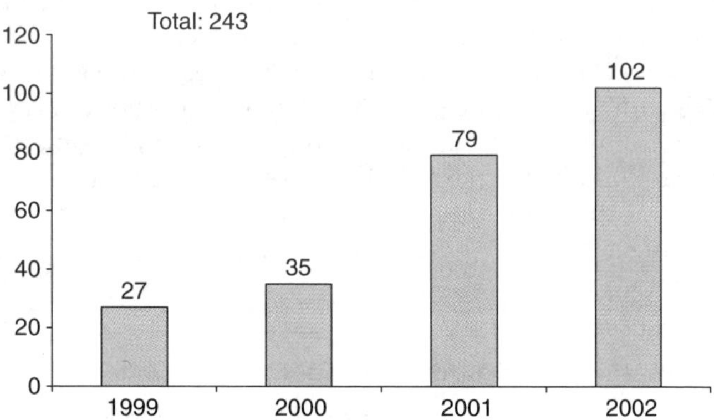

Figure 5.1   ROSC modules made available by IMF/World Bank (as at 31 December 2002)

Source: International Monetary Fund.

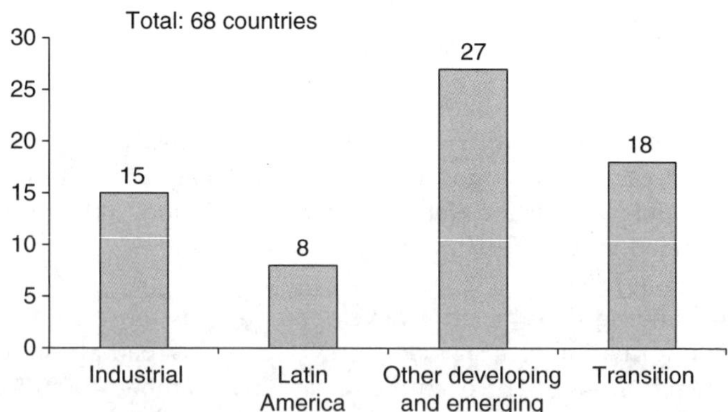

Figure 5.2   Countries for which ROSC modules have been completed and published (as at 31 December 2002)

Source: International Monetary Fund.

ROSC modules have been classified under three broad categories: data disclosure and transparency (data dissemination, fiscal transparency, and monetary and financial policy transparency); regulation and supervision (banking supervision, insurance regulation, securities regulation, and payments systems); and market integrity (corporate governance, accounting and auditing, and insolvency and creditor rights) (see Table 1.1 on page 2). Although it has received more emphasis lately, the number of modules in the field of market integrity is well behind that of data disclosure. This can be seen clearly in Figure 5.3, which presents the number of ROSC modules published by subject as at 31 December 2002. It must be clarified, on the other hand, that in some cases (for example, corporate governance) the number of completed modules (twenty-two as at 31 December 2002) is well above that for published modules.

The challenges faced in attempting to give international standards and codes a more prominent role in the international financial architecture look even greater when further hindrances to this initiative are considered: these originate on both the supply and demand sides, and are mainly related to resource constraints, limitations on the capacity to provide technical assistance to countries in need, reluctance on the part of some countries to implement international standards and codes, and insufficient market use of the information provided by these assessments.

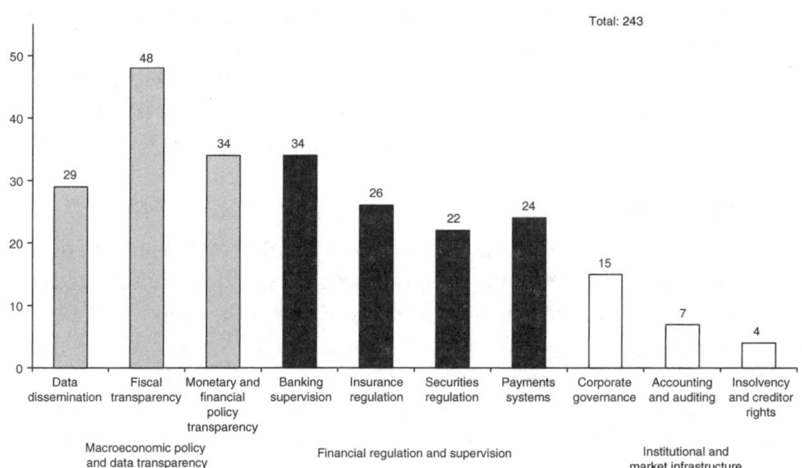

Figure 5.3   ROSC modules completed and published by subject (as at 31 December 2002)

Source: International Monetary Fund.

Resource constraints

The preparation of ROSC modules involves significant resource costs. The IMF estimates that under current arrangements it would take up to eight years before an average of four ROSC modules could be prepared for the entire membership (IMF and World Bank, 2001). The situation is even worse in the case of the World Bank: it is estimated that Bank staff could assess countries with lending arrangements every twenty-three years. As explained earlier, to be useful, standards and codes must be seen as a dynamic concept. In other words, they have to be updated frequently. The above information provides an idea of the limitations that are faced in this respect. Not surprisingly, progress to date on this front is not very encouraging. As at 31 December 2002, only ten countries revealed published ROSC modules that had been carried out more than once.

Technical assistance

For many countries, implementing the recommendations emanating from standards and codes assessments is simply impossible without the support of technical assistance. Resource limitations here are also important, both regarding financing and the availability of experts. And there is an additional problem worth noting. The international institutions report important ripple effects of the standards and codes initiatives on their technical assistance programmes. However, the information available publicly is insufficient to make an adequate evaluation in this respect. Indeed, the international institutions should make extra efforts to estimate and publish this impact, which would be an important factor in evaluating the usefulness of this initiative.

Country reluctance

Despite repeated efforts on several fronts, the opinion of many national authorities remains that the development of standards and codes in some areas has not given sufficient recognition to the views of developing and emerging-market countries. In fact, this is one of the most frequently heard complaints when the issue of standards is discussed. The reluctance of some countries to demand international standards and codes assessments is far more understandable when this is taken into account. In the absence of developing country involvement in the design of standards, there is a much greater danger that requirements are set at a level that is unattainable for them; also, the merits of adopting the standards are more difficult to see in so far as a country does not participate in their design. Lack of political will within the governments and parliaments of some countries has also represented an obstacle to further progress in the adoption of standards and codes.

Market response

One area of the standards and codes initiative where progress is less evident relates to the attention paid by market participants to these assessments. Perhaps the best source of information in this connection is the most recent report of the Financial Stability Forum (2001). The group's survey among market participants shows an increased understanding and awareness of the key standards. However, the degree to which this information is used in risk decisions is uneven across institutions and financial centres. Furthermore, many market participants indicate that they rely largely on in-house arrangements and refer to ROSCs only occasionally.

A number of measures have been proposed, and some of them implemented, to deal with this problem, such as a more intense dialogue with market participants, their more active involvement in the design of standards and codes to foster ownership, and so on. These are clearly steps in the right direction. But there is another more modest yet still important action worth considering. We do not at present have a source of information that can allow us easily and systematically to know the extent to which markets are using the information provided by standards and codes. Although surveys and seminars are useful, and have allowed us to realise that market participants are not using standards extensively as an input for decision-making, this evidence is sporadic and based on relatively small samples. For these reasons, it would be useful to ask the IMF and the World Bank to monitor and make available information of this nature. To this end, they could, for example, use information they already have, such as the number of hits per web page containing country information on ROSCs, and disaggregate it further to identify whenever a market participant is the user. This would serve as a thermometer allowing knowledge of whether efforts are yielding positive results. In any event, in this area, as in many others, in order to be able to solve a problem it needs to be known how serious it is in the first place.

Final remarks

Mexico's case is a good illustration of the benefits that can be derived from a more intensive use of international standards and codes. After participating in the IMF's Special Data Dissemination Standards, the Mexican authorities in 2001 requested a Financial Sector Assessment Programme that included evaluations under five different international standards and codes. The exercise was considered to be useful by the Mexican authorities, as it represented an input for policy decisions under consideration, forced the different institutions involved to perform self-assessments that allowed them to review the strengths and weaknesses of the financial system, allowed them to exchange views with experts in the different fields, served to clarify misunderstandings in a number of areas, and confirmed Mexico's commitment to a policy of transparency. Perhaps the clearest evidence of the usefulness attached by the Mexican authorities to these actions lies in the fact that new evaluations under additional standards and codes have already been requested.

Self-interest was the main force behind the Mexican decision to participate more actively in international standards and codes assessments. However, the potential merits of this initiative go beyond its beneficial impact on the countries subjected to these reviews. They could provide useful information to support investment and lending decisions by market participants, as well as being of help to the surveillance activities of the IMF and, in general, to decision-making at other international institutions.

Unfortunately, progress in profiting from these different dimensions has been uneven. Perhaps the area where progress is least evident relates to the attention paid by markets to standards and codes. This is unfortunate, since one of the main incentives for countries to adopt international standards is to see these assessments reflected in market decisions. We lack a systematic and updated source of reliable information in this respect. The IMF and the World Bank ought to fill this gap and, perhaps on the basis of data they already have, begin the release of information on markets' use of codes and standards.

Of course, the challenges faced by the standards initiative go far beyond the insufficient attention paid to them by markets. Resource costs, constraints on the capacity to provide technical assistance, reluctance by countries to request assessments or to implement the recommendations derived from them, and so on, are other important obstacles to further progress. The sum of resources that have been invested in the development and implementation of standards is substantial, but much more will be needed if there is to be a relevant contribution from this source to international financial stability. The challenges faced are so huge that the only possibility of achieving this objective is through a joint effort of all the parties involved: governments, international institutions and market participants.

Two final observations are worth making. First, as already explained, it is natural to expect that the information provided by standards assessments will be fed into IMF surveillance. Otherwise, an important piece of information for the institution will be wasted. However, the voluntary nature of the participation in ROSCs has to be preserved. In view of the obstacles faced by the adoption of standards and codes, such as the implementation capacity of many countries and the limitations on the availability of technical assistance, it would be extremely risky to incorporate them as an element of conditionality in international institutions.

Second, even under the assumption that a substantial effort is made, it seems difficult to expect that sufficient resources will be available to undertake ROSCs for all or even most members of the IMF and the World Bank, and to update these studies as needed. Self-assessments, though useful, will not take us very far, since there is a natural tendency for countries to be benevolent with themselves. Priorities will therefore have to be set. The next question is how these priorities should be defined. It seems clear that our main concern at this stage should be to try to enhance the stability of the world economy by all possible means. From this perspective, priority should be assigned to those countries that pose the risk of a larger impact worldwide. Although this may be to the detriment of the smallest countries, it has to be recognised that, by fostering a more stable world economic environment we are working to the benefit of all. It makes sense to allocate our scarce resources to the areas where the greatest risks are found. As these risks are reduced or eliminated, resources will be freed for other countries of less systemic importance.

Note

1   The opinions expressed herein are the sole responsibility of the author and do not necessarily coincide with the views of the Bank of Mexico.

References

Eichengreen, Barry (2001) 'Strengthening the International Financial Architecture: Open Issues, Asian Concerns', Paper prepared for the IMF/KIEP Conference on Recovery from the Asian Crisis, Seoul, May.

Financial Stability Forum (2001) *Final Report of the Follow-up Group on Incentives to Foster Implementation of Standards*, August.

IMF (2001) *Mexico: Financial System Stability Assessment, including Reports on the Observance of Standards and Codes*, Washington, DC: IMF, 25 October.

IMF and World Bank (2001) *Assessing the Implementation of Standards – A Review of Experience and Next Steps*, Washington, DC: IMF, 11 January.

6
Implementation in East Asia

Andrew Walter[1]

Introduction

International standards and codes moved to the top of the reform agenda in East Asia after the crisis of 1997–8. To understand why, we need to consider the debate over the causes of the crisis. Initially, two explanations of the 1997–8 Asian crisis dominated the literature: an international explanation and a domestic one. The former located the origins of the crisis in unregulated and volatile international capital flows (Radelet and Sachs, 1998; Wade and Veneroso, 1998). The domestic explanation focused on the ways in which cronyism, corruption and generally poor domestic governance exacerbated problems of moral hazard (Corsetti *et al.*, 1998; Krugman, 1998). The latter explanation predominated in official circles in the developed world and played an important role in the design of the structural reform packages attached as conditions of the IMF-led rescue packages (Blustein, 2001).

Since then, there has been some convergence between these polarised positions (Eichengreen, 2000; Hamilton-Hart, 2000; Krugman, 1999; Noble and Ravenhill, 2000; Rosenbluth and Schaap, 2002; Stiglitz, 1998). This emerging consensus accepts elements of both of the early explanations. It accepts that failures in domestic governance cannot explain why and when the crisis began, since such failures had persisted for some time before the crisis. However, domestic-level factors rendered financial liberalisation a much more dangerous proposition.[2] Thus most commentators have largely accepted the core of the domestic explanation. In the context of financial liberalisation and deregulation, weak prudential regulation and institutions created substantial vulnerabilities in various developing countries. As an IMF review in 2000 stated, 'financial sector vulnerability was at the root of the Asian crisis'

(Boorman *et al.*, 2000: 5). The moral hazard problems associated with a politically and economically important banking sector may be increased by financial liberalisation that erodes bank profitability. In other words, greater competition may lead banks to take greater risks to sustain levels of profitability previously ensured by government restrictions on competition in the banking sector. Consistent with this argument, studies on banking and currency crises have found previous financial liberalisation to be a significant predictor of future crises (Demirgüç-Kunt and Detragiache, 1998; Glick and Hutchison, 1999).

The proposed solution, touted by the leading developed countries and the international financial institutions, is also essentially domestic in character: it demands the upgrading of the domestic economic governance framework in key emerging-market countries via convergence on international 'best practice', as outlined in the various standards and codes. A key objective of government policy, and a core element of the IMF packages, has been to facilitate a move from a 'relational-patrimonial' system of financial regulation towards a (Western-style) 'rules-based' system of prudential regulation and supervision. In the meantime, the process of financial liberalisation begun in the 1980s in the crisis countries has been entrenched and accelerated by the IMF programmes of the late 1990s. The conspicuous exception, in the early post-crisis phase, was Malaysia, which reversed its pre-crisis levels of financial openness. More recently, however, even Malaysia appears to be converging on this broad approach.

It is argued in this chapter that the main problem with this reform strategy is that it underestimates the likelihood of implementation failure in reforming countries. Formal convergence on standards and codes is the easy part; failures in real implementation mean that prudential regulation will lag the process of financial liberalisation dangerously. Contrary to the intention of the standards and codes, regulatory forbearance remains chronic in a number of East Asian countries. The result is that policy sequencing remains perverse in most East Asian countries, essentially for political economy reasons. This creates ongoing financial vulnerabilities for them. I also argue that, despite the desire of the IFIs to promote the implementation of financial governance reforms in East Asia, there are reasons to doubt that they have a strong interest in exposing the degree of implementation failure in the region. This, in turn, casts doubt on their role as 'enforcers' of standards and codes.

The next section outlines how, until the Asian crisis, both the academic literature on sequencing and policy practice in the region paid insufficient attention to the prudential regulatory preconditions of financial liberalisation. The third section discusses the important role of regulatory failures at the level of implementation, which can be a key source of perverse sequencing. It focuses on the specific area of regulatory forbearance relating to bank capital adequacy in Indonesia, Korea and Thailand. The fourth section attempts a rough estimation of real bank capital in these three countries, noting how non-transparent real bank capital is even in the best case (Korea). The fifth section outlines how implementation failures occur when politicians may have strong incentives to supply the regulatory forbearance that weak banks and debtors demand. The concluding section discusses the implications for the standards and codes exercise.

Financial liberalisation: sequencing arguments and the Washington consensus

The sequencing literature

There is a substantial literature on the appropriate sequencing of capital account liberalisation that goes back to McKinnon (1973) and Shaw (1973).[3] The broad policy conclusion was that financial sector 'repression', common in developing countries, should be removed gradually, and then only in the wake of other policy reforms. In particular, fiscal consolidation/tax reform and price stabilisation should precede and facilitate domestic financial liberalisation (raising real interest rates to encourage savings to flow into the banking sector). Exchange-rate reform should precede the liberalisation of the current account (trade). External financial liberalisation should come last. As McKinnon (1973: 4) warned, 'the absorption of substantial amounts of foreign capital during the [trade] liberalisation process may … be a serious mistake'. McKinnon was especially critical of the Latin American strategy of maintaining substantial trade restrictions while allowing in foreign direct investment, holding out the opposite Japanese strategy (which included controls on FDI as well as portfolio capital inflows) as a more appropriate model for developing countries.

There were important weaknesses in this literature. First, it said little about why, in practice, so many countries diverged from optimal sequencing. The assumption was that appropriate sequencing was essentially an intellectual problem to be solved by economists and then applied by governments. Second, the role of prudential regulation of the domestic banking sector was barely mentioned in this early literature. This was an important gap since, as various financial crises would later show, the upgrading of the financial regulatory framework was arguably another essential prerequisite of financial sector liberalisation.[4]

Arguments about the optimal sequencing of reforms were swept aside in part from the late 1980s by the triumph of the ideology of market liberalism. Poland's 'big bang' liberalisation of 1990, to cite the most prominent example, effectively liberalised everything at once, well in advance of the construction of robust governance institutions appropriate to a market economy. McKinnon's later (1993) book, firmly in the gradualist camp, argued that this kind of strategy was misguided, and that gradual sequencing, with foreign bank entry and capital account liberalisation in particular coming last, was essential (McKinnon, 1993: 4–10). He made some passing remarks about institutional preconditions, such as the need to establish a framework of enforceable commercial law before the financial sector was liberalised (ibid.: 7). In chapter 7 of his book, he argued that an effective prudential regulation framework is especially crucial in countries experiencing macroeconomic instability.[5] Although he accepted that effective prudential supervision was necessary even in macroeconomically stable countries, the emphasis on macroeconomic instability as a key source of financial sector misbehaviour was consistent with the dominant view of the time.

This dominant view was embodied in the so-called Washington Consensus on appropriate development policy of the early 1990s. The emphasis was firmly upon the combination of macroeconomic stabilisation, and trade and financial liberalisation, with less attention paid to appropriate sequencing (Naim, 1999). However, there was little attention paid to the institutional/governance requirements of financial openness, with the possible exception of the now standard recommendation of central bank independence in monetary policy. Before and after the Asian crisis, the US government was also pushing financial liberalisation for its own purposes, though it continued to argue that financial liberalisation had welfare benefits for the countries involved (US Treasury, 2000). As Lawrence Summers, then America's deputy Treasury Secretary argued in 1997, 'Financial liberalisation, both domestically and internationally, is a critical part of the US agenda.' The IMF itself, with its limited institutional knowledge of banking sector regulation, was also guilty of myopia.[6]

Since the Asian crisis, the emphasis on institutional and governance reforms, including the upgrading of prudential regulatory frameworks, has, of course, been much greater. In October 1998, the G-7 countries commissioned Mr Tietmeyer, the former President of the German Bundesbank, to recommend various reforms to promote international financial stability. The Tietmeyer report of February 1999 advocated little in the way of reform to the existing international architecture besides more co-ordination among the key international and national authorities involved in financial sector stability. The main emphasis was on formulating and disseminating a set of international 'best practice' standards and codes for financial-sector governance. The Financial Stability Forum, established in April 1999 by the G-7, was put in charge of this task. Its various working groups, which have included developing-country representatives, in turn placed most emphasis not on the regulation of international financial flows, but on reforms to domestic regulatory governance.[7]

Consistent with this approach, the G-7 finance ministers, reporting to the heads of government meeting in Cologne in July 1999, prioritised strongly the importance of domestic institutional reform *in emerging-market countries*. The promotion of global financial stability, they argued:

> does not require new international organizations. It requires that all countries assume their responsibility for global stability by pursuing sound macroeconomic and sustainable exchange rate policies and establishing strong and resilient financial systems. It requires the adoption and implementation of internationally-agreed standards and rules in these and other areas. It requires the existing institutions to adapt their roles to meet the demands of today's global financial system: in particular to put in place effective mechanisms for devising standards, monitoring their implementation and making public the results; to have the right tools to help countries to manage crises; and to take steps to enhance their effectiveness, accountability and legitimacy. It also requires the right structure of incentives for all participants in the international financial system: national authorities as well as the private sector. (G-7 Finance Ministers, 1999)

This chapter must leave aside the interesting question as to why many of the major emerging-market countries have apparently signed up to this agenda. For present purposes, it is important to note that the new emphasis on domestic financial governance reform has not entailed the rejection of the Washington Consensus. On the contrary, the consensus has merely been supplemented. Financial liberalisation continues to be promoted as welfare-enhancing, with the additional proviso that an effective prudential regulatory framework is in place. Larry Summers' well-known airline metaphor captures the dominant view nicely, which is that financial liberalisation is worth having despite the risks, and that the solution is to build a (domestic) regulatory infrastructure that can support it.[8]

In keeping with this 'enhanced' Washington Consensus, recent literature has recognised explicitly effective prudential regulation as a necessary precursor to financial liberalisation (Williamson and Mahar, 1998). In this view, the appropriate sequence is now macroeconomic stabilisation, enhanced prudential supervision, and only then capital account liberalisation. Barry Eichengreen (2000: 184) makes a similar argument:

> problems in these areas [bank regulation, corporate governance, accounting, insolvency codes, etc.] are too pressing to do nothing. If the Asian crisis has taught us one thing, it is that countries cannot restore exchange rate and balance of payments stability without rectifying deficiencies in their domestic financial systems…The particulars of these arrangements can differ – countries can reach these goals by different routes – but any country active in international financial markets must meet internationally accepted standards.

If it is suggested that the costs of regulatory upgrading may be too great, the standard response is that the required reforms are 'necessary' in any case, and that their benefits extend well beyond the financial sector. However, it is difficult to find serious assessments of the costs of domestic governance reform. Perhaps even more remarkably, there is little evidence linking the level of compliance directly with the various international standards and codes, on the one hand, and financial efficiency and stability on the other (Jordan and Majnone, 2002: 21).

It is worthwhile enumerating just how extensive the 'governance requirements' of the new consensus have become. Mishkin (2001) argues that, in order for financial liberalisation to work and to make financial crises less likely, various institutional/governance prerequisites are necessary, including: (i) adequate prudential supervision; (ii) high accounting and disclosure standards; (iii) effective legal and judicial systems; (iv) the facilitation of market-based discipline through entry and exit policies, competition policy and so on; (v) reduction of the role of state-owned financial institutions; and (vi) elimination of too-big-to-fail in the corporate sector. These are in addition to the standard macro- and microeconomic requirements of the early 1990s. This vast new agenda was reflected clearly in the various structural conditionalities attached to the IMF-led rescue packages for Thailand, Indonesia and Korea (Goldstein, 2001; Kapur, 2001).

**Prudential
supervision standards**

| | Low | High |

		Prudential supervision standards	
		Low	High
Financial liberalisation	Low	I 'Profit-padding' regulation	III Excessive protection
	High	II Moral hazard danger	IV Competitive regulatory environment

Figure 6.1 Combining prudential supervision and financial liberalisation
Source: Adapted from Rosenbluth and Schaap, 2002: 8.

The consensus is summarised in Figure 6.1. In the standard scenario, countries that move from quadrant I to II create moral hazard problems and greater financial fragility in the process. A number of the so-called 'systemically important' emerging-market countries, particularly in East Asia, went through this process in the 1980s and 1990s. In the past, extensive restrictions on the financial sector, including barriers to entry, legal limits on the ability of financial firms to offer different financial services, the regulation of interest rates, branching limits and so on may have served as a form of prudential supervision (quadrant I). By raising bank profits, they may reduce incentives for banks to engage in risky lending (Hellman *et al.*, 2000). Banks in such regulatory environments typically constitute a kind of protected oligopoly; their centrality to the domestic financial and political system ensures that they are too important to fail (Rosenbluth and Schaap, 2002). Close relationships between banks and bank regulators are common, and regulation is more relationship-based than rules-based. The moral hazard implications of such protective prudential regimes may require substantial limits on the operating freedom of banks. Once these kinds of restrictions on the operating freedoms of banks are removed, competition intensifies and relationship-based regulation breaks down. Since risk-taking by banks may become excessive, optimal sequencing would require a preceding or simultaneous move towards enhanced regulation via a 'rules-based' regulatory framework (quadrant IV).

Sequencing in practice

Rosenbluth and Schaap (2002: 8) argue that quadrant II is such a dangerous combination that it is rare and unlikely to persist for long. On the contrary, however, it is clear that many countries, developing and developed, have moved blithely from quadrant I to II in recent years, apparently in disregard of the high costs of financial crises (Barro, 2001). Perverse sequencing, far from being rare, is arguably the norm and it can persist in particular cases for long periods. Indonesian financial liberalisation, which began in the early 1980s, was followed by some (largely ineffective) efforts to raise prudential standards only in the early 1990s. Thailand, and to a large extent Korea, fit the same pattern. Dramatic improvements to prudential supervisory frameworks may follow rather than precede crises. Prime examples are the new FDIC Act of 1991 in the USA after the Savings and Loan crisis and the extensive reform programme of many East Asian governments in the wake of the regional financial crisis of 1997–8.

Thus we confront the standard political economy question as to why countries tend to delay upgrading prudential financial supervision and indulge in perverse sequencing. One reason, at least in the years prior to the new consensus, could be imperfect technical knowledge concerning optimal sequencing. However, even before the Asian crisis, there were clear indications that policy-makers in various countries perceived the need to improve prudential supervision at the same time as proceeding with financial liberalisation. There were attempts in Thailand and Indonesia, for example, to impose new limits on related party lending by banks in the early 1990s. Korea had recently formulated a financial governance reform plan when the crisis struck, and had introduced some new financial regulations in the pre-crisis period. Many developing countries adopted the Basle capital adequacy ratios (CARs) in the early and mid-1990s, including all the major East Asian ones. Thus, it seems possible that policy-makers were more aware than academic authors of the need for enhanced prudential supervision.

A practical reason for perverse sequencing is that financial liberalisation is simply much easier to implement than is enhanced prudential supervision. The former requires minimal institutional capacity, since it only involves removing pre-existing controls. Thus, in countries with weak government, deregulation is the easier option, producing a potentially perverse outcome (as quadrant II, in Figure 6.1). The simple matrix of Figure 6.1 does not allow us to make a cost–benefit calculation about the net benefits of shifting from quadrant I to quadrant IV, not least when economists dispute the growth benefits of financial liberalisation.[9] The institutional investment costs of moving to quadrant IV (or quadrant III) may be sufficient to discourage policy-makers from attempting to raise prudential standards in the first place, or to undertake financial liberalisation first in the hope that stronger prudential rules and enforcement may be achievable in the longer term (particularly if they estimate the risks of this strategy to be limited). There is evidence that this strategy was indeed pursued by technocrats in various countries.[10] However, resource constraints are very unlikely to be the only explanation, particularly in parts of East Asia.

A third reason is that political institutions can allow vested interests to block reform. It is sometimes argued that democratisation has hampered the institutional reform process in East Asian countries, notably in Thailand before the crisis, and in Thailand and Indonesia since then. In Thailand and Indonesia, there has been a sharp increase since 1997–8 in the number of veto players, who may block reform at key points in the political process (see Table 6.1). The post-crisis constitutional reforms in Thailand have created a system of checks and balances that has weakened substantially the ability of the central government to achieve reform. The result has been a prolonged delay in key legislative reforms, including a proposed new companies act, Bank of Thailand independence, and the elimination of outstanding weaknesses in the bankruptcy code. Thus, in the Thai case, veto players have so far prevented the wholesale reform of regulatory institutions and law. Consistent with this view, in Singapore and Malaysia the existence of fewer veto players has made reforms politically easier.

A related possibility is that electoral laws may affect the incentives for elected politicians to undertake prudential reform. Rosenbluth and Schaap (2002) discuss how centrifugal and centripetal electoral systems create tendencies for politicians to cater, respectively, to the preferences of the median voter or to narrow electoral interests. Politicians in centripetal electoral systems tend to resist raising prudential standards because doing so might undermine the position of banks, which are often substantial contributors to political financing and play important roles in local economies.[11] Proportional representation (PR) rules, in particular, tend to create weak parties, with politicians appealing to organised interests rather than the median voter. PR in Indonesia and Thailand has reduced party discipline and promoted rampant money politics. Consistent with Rosenbluth and Schaap, limited deposit

Table 6.1   Political-institutional characteristics, selected East Asian countries

	Constraints on executive: XCONST (Polity IV, 2002, 0–7 range, global mean 3.6)	Electoral system (Beck et al., 2001)	Dominant ownership structures (Claessens et al., 1999)	Regulator statutory independence
Indonesia	XCONST = 6	PR (closed list)	Families, state (banks)	Yes (BI); plans 'FSA'
Thailand	XCONST = 7	PR	Families, state (banks)	Not yet (BoT)
Korea	XCONST = 6	Mixed	Families, companies, state (banks)	Yes? (FSS/FSC)
Malaysia	XCONST = 4	Plurality	Families, state (banks)	No (BNM)
Singapore	XCONST = 3	Plurality	Families, state (banks)	No (MAS)

insurance schemes have yet to be introduced in these countries. However, this could simply reflect the post-crisis difficulty of removing the blanket guarantee on banks without precipitating further bank runs.

The problem with all the above explanations is that they are less helpful for explaining why formal regulatory upgrading and regulatory forbearance can occur together. In the Indonesian case, for example, formal regulatory upgrading since the crisis has been extensive. Indeed, this is true in all the major East Asian countries, with the partial exception of Thailand, where key new legislation has been blocked. In Indonesia, despite the fact that a more powerful Parliament since the crisis has also complicated the reform process, key pieces of legislation were forthcoming in 1998–2000. No one who reads the various documents relating to financial regulatory reform in Indonesia can fail to be impressed at the degree of formal change that has occurred. However, as argued below, implementation failure is chronic here and elsewhere.

Implementation failure: capital adequacy rules

Implementation failure rather than the blocking of key reform legislation is the main obstacle to the upgrading of financial sector governance in much of East Asia at the time of writing. To make a counterfactual argument, even if Thailand had achieved the same degree of formal regulatory reform since 1997 as many of its Asian neighbours, implementation failures would still have minimised its practical effects. In Indonesia, formal reform success has simply meant that opponents have concentrated their efforts on undermining the implementation of the new prudential rules. This outcome might be described as *formal regulatory upgrading with continued regulatory forbearance*. This can give the impression of regulatory upgrading, while keeping badly-run banks and related debtors alive.

To illustrate this point, let us consider the specific case of the Basle bank capital adequacy framework of 1988 which all major East Asian countries have adopted. This is a central aspect of one of the most important standards and codes, the twenty-five Basle Core Principles for Banking Supervision (1999). Naturally, regulators in the crisis-hit countries deny strenuously that they are engaged in regulatory forbearance. They claim that they implement strictly new rules relating to loan classifications and provisioning for non-performing loan (NPLs), and that regulator discretion is effectively ruled out by new automatic prompt corrective action (PCA) rules.[12] However, the ambiguity of the rules, not least in calculations of bank capital, facilitates forbearance, as does the fact that regulatory interpretations of the rules are often hidden from public view. There is nothing specific in the Basle Core Principles regarding the problem of dealing with undercapitalised banks (Asian Policy Forum, 2001: 12). This allows considerable discretion to supervisors in this area: supervisors and banks may reach agreement on appropriate actions and any penalties. Such collusion can result in apparent rather than real convergence in capital adequacy ratios (CARs).

Loan accounting rules

Countries account for NPLs very differently, though there has been some convergence in loan accounting standards in recent years towards the US system.[13] Loans typically are defined as under-performing when an outright default occurs, and when repayments are classified as 'overdue'. However, the time period by which such loans are judged to be overdue can make a great deal of difference. In Korea and Japan before the crisis, loans were judged to be non-performing if repayments were overdue for more than six months, compared with the US standard of ninety days. Most countries in the region have, since the crisis, converged on the ninety-day standard.[14]

Ambiguity arises in the application of this rule, however. Loans with concessional terms (those that have been restructured via extended maturities or reduced interest rates) may or may not be included in the definition. This can have a big impact in crisis countries. The definition of concessional terms may also be more or less strict. In Indonesia today, both the banks and the regulator (Bank Indonesia – BI) classify as 'pass' many loans that have been restructured. The IMF has forced BI to include a separate line for restructured but passed loans in its monthly reporting requirements for banks, so that in principle one can add these back into official NPLs. However, the relatively small numbers of restructured loans reported by Indonesian banks (see Table 6.3 on page 127) raises questions as to whether this requirement encourages banks not to report some restructured loans.

In Thailand after the crisis, debt classified as doubtful or a loss was reclassified as substandard when a debt restructuring agreement was signed. Debt classified as substandard or special mention remained in that category until three months of repayments or three instalments were fulfilled, after which it was upgraded to the pass (accrual) category. This less conservative standard (compared with the USA, which requires six months of repayments) was further relaxed on 10 April 2000, allowing the immediate reclassification to accrual status of restructured loans that satisfy certain criteria. However, Thai banks, unlike their Indonesian counterparts, are not required to report the total amount of such restructured debt in accrual status. We can see, however, from the high levels of 're-entry NPLs', reported to and by the Bank of Thailand (BoT), that many restructured loans continue to turn bad again (see Table 6.2).

In Korea, the adoption since 1999 of US-style 'forward-looking criteria' (FLC) for loan classification has possibly provided it with a stricter classification system than those in South-East Asia. FLC systems rely heavily on credit-rating skills within banks and on the part of ratings agencies. In less developed countries such as Thailand and Indonesia, skills like these are often lacking, and few firms have credit ratings. Even in Korea, only the largest firms are rated, so that banks must also rely on backward-looking criteria (credit history) in loan classification. Thus the difference between Korea's system and those of Indonesia and Thailand may in practice be less than it first appears. Furthermore, in contrast to loan classification systems that rely only on a borrower's repayment history, FLC systems introduce an element of judgement and hence room for regulatory discretion.

Provisioning rules

Banks typically are required to set aside 'loan loss provisions' against outstanding loans. The US system requires different percentages of

Table 6.2 Thailand: increase in NPLs by financial institution, 2002 (baht m) – classified by the Financial Institution Group

	Jan.	Feb.	Mar.	Apr.	May	June	July	Aug.	Sep.
Private banks	4082	4717	6504	6076	6895	7490	6213	4709	5432
State-owned banks	2011	3926	2606	3156	1553	5037	1872	1152	1486
Foreign banks (full branch)	603	167	765	156	146	5309	399	190	921
Finance companies	134	115	131	168	430	525	352	344	249
Total	6830	8925	10006	9556	9024	18361	8836	6395	8088
Re-entry NPLs									
Private banks	13843	8138	17774	14748	16686	9972	14558	10361	13986
State-owned banks	10168	1073	4723	5976	8740	5180	1608	2116	8102
Foreign banks (full branch)	18	7	455	78	229	424	13	49	59
Finance companies	271	204	374	530	888	408	348	492	92
Total	24300	9422	23326	21332	26543	15984	16527	13018	22239
Total increase in NPLs	31130	18347	33332	30888	35567	34345	25363	19413	30327

Source: Bank of Thailand, http://www.bot.or.th/BOThomepage/databank/Financial Institutions, accessed 11 December 2002.

total loans to be set aside as provisions, depending on the classification of each loan according to the accounting rules. Similarly, the new Thai system requires the following percentages of loan loss provisions for each category of loan: normal, 1 per cent; special mention, 2 per cent; sub-standard, 20 per cent; doubtful, 50 per cent; loss, 100 per cent. Thus, lax loan accounting rules will overstate real capital by the total amount that would, under stricter rules, be set aside as additional loan loss provisions.

Furthermore, regulators in Thailand and Indonesia allow banks to deduct from required loan loss provisions the value of collateral (up to 75 per cent of such value in Indonesia, up to 90 per cent in Thailand) attached to each non-performing loan. In doing so, they do not necessarily diverge substantially from international best practice; indeed, there is little evidence of convergent practice regarding the treatment of collateral in the G-10 countries, and most allow collateral to play some role in loan classification or provisioning requirements (Song, 2002: 18). Where this is done, it assumes that, in the event of default, the bank could collect the assumed value of the collateral. Of course, this may not be the case, depending on the nature of the collateral, the country's bankruptcy code and judicial system, and how the collateral is valued. In cases such as Thailand and Indonesia, where most collateral is in the form of illiquid real estate, and when the foreclosure regime is dysfunctional, a best-practice (conservative) approach would be not to allow such netting practices regarding required provisions.[15]

In the case of Thailand, the BoT defines the market value of collateral as 'the probable price on the date of the collateral asset valuation or appraisal under normal market conditions with no transaction costs (nor taxes)'.[16] The 'normal market conditions' clause, and the poor quality of valuation firms in Thailand, suggests that collateral is often overvalued, and banks therefore comparatively under-provisioned. Indonesia has a slightly more conservative policy relating to collateral. However, as in Thailand, the ability of banks to collect attached collateral through the court system in a timely manner is poor, casting doubt on the value of such collateral to banks. In Korea, as in the USA, collateral is taken into account when classifying loans as sub-standard or below, though it is not deducted explicitly from the provisioning requirement (Comptroller of the Currency, 2001: 37; KorAm Bank, *Annual Report 2001*: 41–2; Song, 2002). However, the outsider is largely in the dark as to how this classification is done.

Deferred taxes

Companies, including banks, are often allowed to carry forward losses as assets that can be offset against taxes in future years. These deferred tax assets often have value for a limited period (say, three or five years), but their value depends on the assumption that the bank will enjoy future taxable profits sufficient to utilise the value of the asset. If not, assets will be overstated and their value may need to be written down subsequently, thus reducing capital. In Japan, for example, where losses can be carried forward for five years, Fukao (2002: 5) argues that the likely unprofitability of Japanese banks going forward makes deferred tax assets another source of overstatement of Japanese bank CARs. In the USA, by contrast, banks can only claim deferred tax assets of the lesser of the amount that is expected to be claimed within one year, or 10 per cent of Tier I capital.[17] The much laxer rule in Japan is another source of inflated bank capital calculations compared with the USA.

Sources of capital

A bank's liabilities, such as shareholder equity and subordinated debt, make up its core capital. However, cross-shareholdings, which are common in a number of Asian (and European) countries, may reduce the real level of capital. If a bank is part of a corporate group, related companies may provide a significant proportion of its equity capital. Supervisors are attempting increasingly to ensure that they oversee financial institutions on a consolidated basis, to ensure that capital is not double-counted in this way. However, not all regulators (including those in Thailand and Indonesia) have such authority as yet, though they claim to ensure that such cross-shareholdings are taken into account in calculating CARs.

Other problems arise over the inclusion of non-equity instruments in bank capital. In Indonesia, recapitalisation bonds issued by the Indonesian Bank Restructuring Agency (IBRA) form the bulk of Indonesian banks' reported CARs. If such bonds are held on a bank's investment book, as most are, they are valued at par (on the argument that they are risk-free). If they are held on the trading book they must be marked-to-market, but this can be difficult because of the illiquidity of Indonesia's secondary bond markets. In Thailand, regulators allowed banks to issue expensive hybrid debt instruments, so-called CAPS and SLIPS, and to include these in Tier I capital, as long as maturities were at least ten and five years, respectively.[18] The Bank of Thailand claims these are Basle-compatible, but officials at the BIS are doubtful.[19] This makes the official Tier I CAR in

Thailand incomparable with those of other countries. In Japan, Fukao (2002: 5–6) argues that real bank capital is overstated systematically because related life insurance companies hold substantial proportions of banks' subordinated debt (and in turn, the banks hold much of the life companies' debt). The Japanese Ministry of Finance, and subsequently the FSA, have also exercised forbearance regarding required capital for these insurance companies, which are often chronically weak.

Unrealised capital gains and losses

Basle rules permit regulators to allow banks up to 45 per cent of unrealised capital gains as Tier II capital; in fact, many developing countries allow up to 100 per cent. This, and how much of unrealised losses banks are required to deduct from capital, can vary. In the case of Thailand, 70 per cent of land and 50 per cent of building revaluation values can be incorporated into Tier II capital. In Indonesia and Korea there is no such provision. Although the Japanese authorities tightened the loan loss provisioning rules in 1998, simultaneously they loosened the rules relating to unrealised capital gains and losses, allowing banks to include unrealised gains from real estate assets.

Weak auditors

Regulators are often dependent on external auditors discovering problems relating to bank loan accounting and provisioning practices. Even when regulators have a permanent on-site supervisory presence in large banks, which is increasingly common, they may not have the capacity to monitor all accounting decisions. Auditors, who can provide another form of supervision, have often been found to be incompetent, or willing to collude with banks, and not just in East Asia. In a number of East Asian developing countries, international accounting firms tended to franchise their name to local auditors without being concerned about staff quality. And, of course, even international accounting firms have sometimes failed to live up to their reputation.[20]

Estimating real bank capital in Indonesia, Korea and Thailand

For all the above reasons, bank capital ratios should generally not be compared either across time or across countries. A further consideration reinforces this conclusion. In much of East Asia, where lending is often to related parties, the quality of assets may be low when compared with those of banks in other countries (Asian Policy Forum, 2001: 12; Rojas-Suarez, 2001; Shirai, 2001a: 59–60). In such circumstances, the required CARs should arguably be higher than for banks in advanced countries. Indeed, some East Asian countries, including Hong Kong and Singapore, require CARs to be considerably higher than the 8 per cent Basle minimum. However, the Basle Committee has given no guidance as to how much higher these requirements need to be in the case of emerging-market countries, presumably in part because of the political sensitivity of the issue.

Some suggest abandoning CARs and other traditional ratios altogether when analysing emerging-market countries, recommending greater reliance on alternative market-based indicators. These include banks' interest-rate spreads, deposit rates, inter-bank rates and loan growth (Rojas-Suarez, 2001; Shirai, 2001: 60). Others try to recalculate CARs using more conservative accounting. For example, Fukao (2002: 6) estimates that, if the Japanese regulatory authorities adopted conservative definitions in the above areas, the real level of capital of Japanese banks would have been less than 1 per cent in September 2001, compared with the official level of 10.7 per cent.[21] Many private-sector analysts think even Fukao's estimate is optimistic.

At the end of the first quarter of 2002, the average risk-based Basle CAR of the top twenty-five US banks was 12.4 per cent.[22] On the face of it, Asian banks have converged towards this level: Thai banks' average CAR was 13.1 per cent, while that for Korean and Indonesian banks was 10.8 per cent and 19.3 per cent, respectively. For some Indonesian banks, official CARs are in excess of 30 per cent. There is little doubt, given the above considerations, that this (over-)convergence is more apparent than real. As a first cut towards comparing East Asian developing country CARs with those in the USA, we simply focus on pure equity capital, given the evident problems with the definition of capital in the Basle regime. The (unweighted) average for the top twenty-five US banks' equity capital to total asset ratio was 7.9 per cent. On this measure, officially Asian banks score worse than US banks, but not disastrously so (see Table 6.3). Indeed, Indonesian and Thai banks appear to be better capitalised than Korean banks, which is not in accordance with market opinion.

But there are good reasons to believe that even this picture is misleading, particularly for Indonesian and Thai banks. As noted above, their ability to deduct the value of allowable collateral from provisioning requirements may inflate equity capital artificially. If such collateral is overvalued and/or uncollectable within a reasonable timeframe, this

Table 6.3   Adjusted equity-to-asset ratios for Indonesian, Korean and Thai banks

Country	Bank	Equity: Asset ratio (2002, Q1) (%)	Official CAR (%)	Official NPLs/ loans (%)	Extra provisions required assuming collateral value = 0 (as at 12/2001)	Restructured: Pass	Restructured: Precautionary/ Special mention	Restructured: loan provision @ 20%	Adjusted equity: Asset ratio (%)
Thailand	BBL	3.6	11.2	16.2	162 439 754 530	–	–	–	–9.3
Thailand	BoAyudhya	3.5	–	15.4	–	–	–	–	–
Thailand	TFB	3.7	12.9	12.1	47 393 673 000	–	–	–	–2.3
Thailand	DBS–TDB	4.4	12.4	5.8	2 758 009 560	–	–	–	1.6
Thailand	TMB	3.7	12.2	11.4	–	–	–	–	–
Thailand	SCommB	8.8	16.6	19.0	66 210 493 000	–	–	–	–0.3
Thailand	TB	19.9	3.4	3.4	–	–	–	–	–
Thailand	KTB	6.4	15.7	7.7	58 179 757 000	–	–	–	0.9
Thailand	BT	4.5	–	3.1	–	–	–	–	–
Thailand	SCityB	3.4	–	2.6	–	–	–	–	–
Thailand	W. AVERAGE	5.0	–	11.6	–	–	–	–	–2.3
Korea	Cho-Hung Bank	4.5	10.4	6.9	–	–	–	–	–
Korea	Woori Bank	3.9	11.3	7.6	–	–	–	–	–
Korea	Seoul Bank	2.9	9.2	9.6	–	–	–	–	–
Korea	KEB	3.3	11.0	7.2	–	–	–	–	–
Korea	Kookmin Bank	5.7	10.2	4.2	–	–	–	–	–
Korea	Shinhan Bank	6.4	12.0	2.0	–	–	–	–	–
Korea	KorAm Bank	4.0	11.2	6.3	–	–	–	–	–
Korea	Hana Bank	4.6	10.3	3.4	–	–	–	–	–

Table 6.3   (*Contd.*)

Country	Bank	Equity: Asset ratio (2002, Q1) (%)	Official CAR (%)	Official NPLs/ loans (%)	Extra provisions required assuming collateral value = 0 (as at 12/2001)	Restructured: Pass	Restructured: Precautionary/ Special mention	Restructured: loan provision @ 20%	Adjusted equity: Asset ratio (%)
Korea	W. AVERAGE	4.8	–	5.6	–	–	–	–	–
Indonesia	BCA	10.0	40.1	11.3	–	1 640	0	311.6	10.0
Indonesia	Lippo	12.1	25.4	8.6	–	333 926	532 156	143 269.3	11.5
Indonesia	Mandiri	4.0	26.4	15.4	–	0	0	0	4.0
Indonesia	BNI	7.8	15.6	28.7	–	416 595	9 899 115	1 564 020	6.6
Indonesia	BRI	4.2	13.7	13.7	–	648 310	2 983 585	570 716.7	3.5
Indonesia	BTN	3.2	13.8	12.4	–	13 275	2 427	2 886.3	3.2
Indonesia	Danamon	8.7	38.8	3.8	–	47 626	271 767	49 813.99	8.6
Indonesia	BII	1.7	−14.6	20.2	–	100 360	885 730	151 927.9	1.3
Indonesia	Niaga	3.7	17.5	15.1	–	0	0	0	3.7
Indonesia	Universal	1.6	2.2	11.9	–	844 439	69 102	170 808.7	0.3
Indonesia	Pan Indonesia	18.6	36.9	10.6	–	918 570	447	174 595.4	17.6
Indonesia	Buana Indonesia	9.1	23.2	1.3	–	1 194	1 170	402.36	9.1
Indonesia	Mega	3.9	11.4	0.3	–	43	188	36.37	3.9
Indonesia	W. AVERAGE	6.2	–	14.3	–	–	–	–	5.9

will require additional provisions in the future, reducing equity capital. As a worst-case calculation, I assume the value of such collateral is zero. Second, there is a widespread concern that Indonesian and Thai banks have engaged in superficial restructuring of problem loans. If so, restructured loans classified as 'passed' or merely precautionary/special mention should attract a higher provision than the small amounts usually required. Here, I assume these restructured loans should attract a 'sub-standard' provisioning requirement of 20 per cent (which is not especially conservative), and subtract from equity capital the increased provision that would result from such a reclassification.

A further possibility would be to assign an extra provisioning requirement to all related party loans, but this is difficult to do, since data on how much of such loans is already provisioned for is generally unavailable. Indeed, data availability is a real problem generally, calling into question the claims made by regulatory authorities in these countries that their financial sector accounting is now fully transparent. Thai banks are required to provide figures on the value of collateral that may be deducted from provisioning requirements, but they do so infrequently, often only in annual reports. Furthermore, they do not provide data on the (re-)classifications of restructured loans. The opposite situation prevails in Indonesia. As for Korea, the regulatory authority requires banks to apply an apparently more sophisticated procedure for loan classification based on FLC, but in practice the manner of loan classification (and the role that collateral may play in mitigating credit risks) is non-transparent. We must simply take the word of the authorities that such standards are applied as rigorously in Korea as in the USA, and a number of bank analysts in Asia dispute this.

Lacking key data for each country makes comparison very difficult. Furthermore, the figures for adjusted equity by individual banks shown in Table 6.3 may be misleading in particular cases, since much depends on the conservatism of individual banks' management. However, the overall weighted averages should be indicative of the overall levels of capital in each country's banking system. Generally, there is little doubt that real (unweighted) equity-to-asset ratios among banks in these countries are much lower than for US banks, and in some cases may be negative. On US criteria it is likely that a number of Thai and Indonesian banks remain at least 'significantly undercapitalised' and in some cases 'critically undercapitalised' (Comptroller of the Currency, 2001: 13ff). In the USA since 1991, this would trigger a mandatory requirement for a capital restoration plan, which, in the Thai and Indonesian context, would require either bank closure or further injections of state funds into banks.

Thai banks

For the Thai banks that have provided recent information on their deductible collateral, subtracting it from equity capital reduces the weighted average equity-to-asset ratio of Thai banks from +5 per cent to −2.3 per cent. The Bank of Thailand and the Thai banks would no doubt claim that this is wholly unreasonable, but in a system where collection of collateral may take years, where valuations are questionable, and where the BoT itself remains under the ultimate control of the Ministry of Finance, outsiders may reasonably suspect that current rules inflate the real equity base of the banking system. Furthermore, if superficial NPL restructuring is still going on in Thailand, accounting for it would further reduce the real equity bases of Thai banks.

Indeed, it may be much worse than the calculations in the table suggest. More evidence of the vast gap that remains in loan classification standards between Thailand and more developed countries is given by DBS (Singapore) Group's consolidated accounts for 2001. This group has a Thai subsidiary, DBS–Thai Danu Bank. DBS Group is required by the Monetary Authority of Singapore to note in these accounts that Thailand's loan classification standards are much laxer than those in Singapore, and that if Singapore loan classification standards were used instead of Thailand's, Thai Danu Bank's NPLs would be much higher than as reported in Thailand.[23] According to Singapore's loan classification standards, Thai Danu Bank's NPLs at the end of 2001 were 27.7 per cent of total loans, whereas by Thai classification standards they were merely 5.8 per cent. The resulting translation loss accrued by the parent group more than offsets Thai Danu Bank's 2001 profits. If we multiply the official NPLs of other Thai banks by 4.8 times (the amount of 'understatement' of Thai Danu Bank's NPLs), the picture is rather gloomy. The weighted average of official NPLs as a percentage of total loans of Thai banks in early 2002 stood at 11.6 per cent. By this rough estimate, real Thai NPLs (based on Singapore classification standards) could be over 55 per cent of total loans. This, in turn, suggests that the Thai banking system remains massively under-provisioned.[24]

Indonesian banks are required to submit monthly information to BI, which then publishes some of the data on the BI website. This does not include information on the value of collateral attached to loans, but does include data on the reclassification of restructured loans. Perhaps the surprising thing about the latter is that the numbers are so small, even though many private-sector analysts claim that the practice predominates in Indonesia (it is important to remember that the majority of Indonesian corporations remain effectively bankrupt).[25] As noted earlier, Indonesian transparency in this regard may give banks incentives to understate restructured loans. If so, the published figures may underestimate the impact of any loan misclassification on banks' equity-to-asset ratios. Furthermore, given the extent of the problem of realising collateral in a dysfunctional legal system, if this were fully accounted for, it is likely that real bank equity-to-asset ratios would be much lower than those published. Finally, the apparently healthy published bank equity-to-asset ratios in Indonesia reflect as much the collapse of bank intermediation in the Indonesian economy since the crisis as anything else.

All this is not to argue that all is well with Korean banks. Some argue that the government has continued to put pressure on banks to lend to important companies in difficulty, such as Hynix Semiconductors, and that the regulatory authorities have exercised forbearance on these loans. Hynix loans were often classified until late 2001 as 'precautionary', requiring a relatively low 2 per cent provisioning requirement (subsequently, Korean bank creditors were required to write down substantial values of these loans). This and other cases raise concerns as to whether the full extent of problem loans in the Korean banking system has been recognised, though official NPLs are now little more than 2 per cent of total loans. In general, the difficulty of assessing whether real bank capital in Korea is as high as the official figures suggest casts doubt on the extent to which the practice of 'transparency' significantly reduces uncertainty in financial markets.

Explaining implementation failures

Why do serious implementation failures occur even when formal reforms are achieved? One explanation focuses on legal frameworks. Most notably, the common legal frameworks inherited from Britain by Malaysia and Singapore appear to have left these countries with much more effective corporate law (in general, see La Porta *et al.*, 1998a, 1998b). Bankruptcy systems in particular are much more effective in the former British colonies than in other Asian countries.[26] This may counterbalance two other institutional factors that Singapore and Malaysia share with most East Asian countries, and that otherwise tend to bode poorly for effective prudential supervision: ownership structures dominated by families and the state; and politically subordinate supervisory institutions (except, in theory, Bank Indonesia since 1998) (see Table 6.1).

A basic problem with the legal origin hypothesis is that it does not specify why countries so 'burdened' with civil law frameworks do not simply change them to re-balance the law in favour of creditors. Explaining this may require attention to electoral rules, veto players, vested interests and so on. Taking the case of bankruptcy laws, for example, it was evident in many Asian countries before the crisis that these were dysfunctional, typically being chronically biased in favour of the debtors. Although, as in Thailand, reform of the bankruptcy and foreclosure system had been considered in the early 1990s, there was little political support for this. Creditors were not over-concerned, because rapid growth and connected lending meant that even poorly managed firms rarely went bankrupt; and long delays in foreclosing on assets could even work to the benefit of creditors in an economy with asset price inflation. Furthermore, debtors had a strong incentive to organise to oppose such reforms, and they sometimes occupied positions of influence or veto power in the political system. Thus, for fundamentally political reasons, the legal regime often exhibited a strong degree of inertia.

Another theory that addresses both legislative and implementation failure focuses explicitly on distributional factors and sectoral interests. Hamilton-Hart (2000: 110) argues that financial liberalisation typically precedes the enhancement of prudential supervision for a simple reason: the benefits of financial liberalisation are concentrated (among borrowers and some financial sector firms), while the costs are diffuse and often delayed. Conversely, the benefits of prudential supervision (preventing crises) are diffuse, while the costs are concentrated. This means that financial-sector lobbies have strong incentives to push for financial-sector liberalisation, but they have little interest in pushing for enhanced prudential supervision, the costs of which might fall mainly upon them. Large borrowers may also oppose stricter prudential regulation if this raises the costs of finance. In countries such as Indonesia, Thailand and Korea, where company groups often used related banks and non-banks as a source of intra-group financing, the costs of imposing and enforcing new rules limiting related lending and single/group lending limits were particularly costly for powerful lobbies.

This helps to explain why prudential regulation was limited, or weakly enforced, in these countries before the crisis, and why sequencing was perverse. It also helps to explain why enhancements to prudential supervisory frameworks sometimes follow crises, since if the median voter bears much of the cost of perverse sequencing when crises hit, governments may come under general electoral pressure to raise prudential standards. However, what the theory does not tell us is why in some countries financial-sector interests are less successful than in others in blocking the implementation of enhanced prudential standards.

One reason for this could be differential external pressure. The IMF required Indonesia, Thailand and Korea to make regulatory upgrading a key priority. Furthermore, the IMF's requirements also became, in part, a stamp of approval for private capital markets. However, in spite of such clear (and similar) external pressure, implementation failures continue in these countries, though much less so in Korea.

Another factor is corruption. The weaker elements of the financial sector and major debtors have a powerful incentive to demand regulatory forbearance. Although most commentators would mention Thailand and Indonesia in this context, Korea's new Financial Supervisory Service has also suffered at least one case of bribery.

Severe fiscal constraints may mean that even uncorrupt politicians and officials have an incentive to supply the private sector with the regulatory forbearance they demand (see Figure 6.2 on page 134). When the banking sector is burdened with high NPLs, raising prudential standards (such as CARs) may also raise the short-term fiscal (and hence electoral) costs of crisis resolution, if this in turn requires the government to recapitalise banks. Thus, after severe financial crises, the costs of raising prudential standards may be high for the financial sector itself, and for heavily indebted firms and sectors, as well as for the median voter. This, in turn, might unleash a political struggle over the distribution of resolution costs. In turn, such a political struggle would tend to lead governments to delay the realisation of such costs, even if this raised the ultimate cost of resolving the financial sector problems. Delay can be achieved by regulatory forbearance, increased debt issuance rather than current taxation, and so on. But since the ability of governments in developing countries to issue debt is usually constrained, this is rarely the whole solution. Were Indonesia and Thailand, or for that matter Japan, to converge fully with US regulatory standards, the required recapitalisation of the banking system this would require would have major fiscal consequences.

Since 1997, politicians in Asian countries have come under considerable pressure from voters and the IFIs to be seen to raise prudential standards. Furthermore, large debtors and banks have found it much more difficult to oppose such reforms compared with the pre-1997 period. However, there is no easy way out for governments when the banking sector is burdened with high NPLs. Politicians may try to square the circle by raising formal prudential standards while encouraging the financial supervisory authorities to forbear in terms of their implementation, even if this raises the ultimate fiscal cost of resolving financial sector problems.

Whether banks themselves favour full recognition of NPLs and government recapitalisation, or continued regulatory forbearance, depends on the relative costs of these strategies. When the supply of funds for bank recapitalisation is limited, bank owners tend to favour forbearance in the hope that either future government support may be forthcoming or that the cost of new equity will eventually fall so as not to dilute their control.[27] Korea, with its relatively developed capital markets and taxation system, was able to sustain the fiscal cost of bank recapitalisations much more successfully than were Thailand and Indonesia. Furthermore, its more robust economic recovery has enabled it to implement reforms more vigorously than elsewhere. Consistent with this interpretation, the stalling of Korean economic recovery in 2000 did

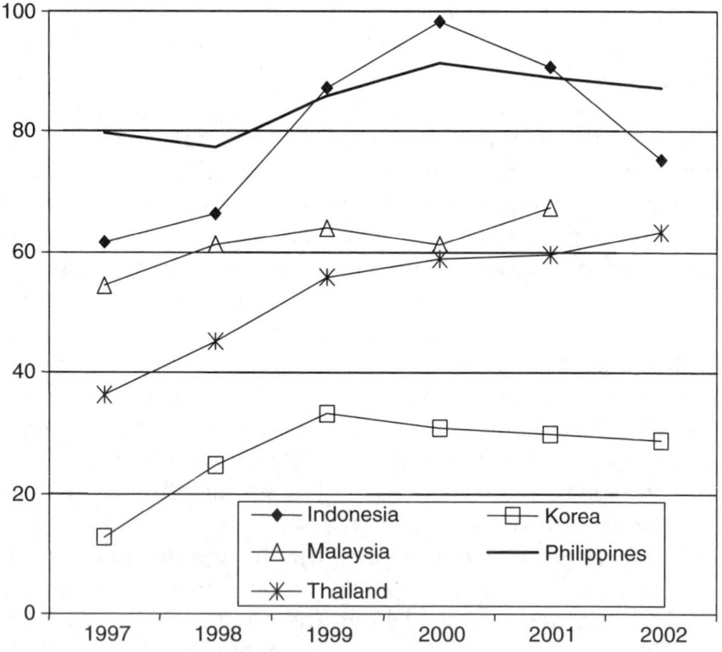

Figure 6.2   Public sector debt, 1997–2002 (% of GDP)

Note: Indonesian and Korean figures are for central government; estimates for 2002.

Source: World Bank (2002): 12.

delay temporarily the second stage of reform, in part because of concern that stricter prudential regulation had exacerbated the credit crunch.[28]

Conclusion: implications for the standards and codes exercise

As we have seen, the problem in post-crisis East Asia is that a number of countries, having accepted the task of convergence on the major standards and codes, have then found it difficult to implement them in practice. It is unlikely that East Asian countries are alone in this. Thus, the standards and codes exercise risks creating a large 'forbearance gap' between formal rules and regulatory practice.

Implementation failures can mean, as suggested by the case of bank CARs, that countries never quite make it to quadrant IV (competitive regulatory environment) and may remain stuck in quadrant II (moral hazard dangers) (see Figure 6.1). Many economists, and the IFIs, might be accused of blithely recommending deep political and bureaucratic reform without understanding adequately the difficulties involved in achieving successful reforms of this kind. The demand for regulatory convergence places an enormous burden on the governance capabilities of the state. It requires dramatically enhanced monitoring capabilities (such as in bank supervision) and enforcement capabilities (given that the number of explicit rules has been increased greatly). At the same time, the need for government recapitalisations of banks has led to a great accumulation of financial and non-financial assets in the hands of government agencies. Although this was intended to be temporary, in many cases the sale of state assets has been delayed because of slower than expected growth, ongoing difficulties in resolving NPLs and corporate restructuring, and weak bankruptcy regimes. The result is that this has created additional opportunities for rent-seeking and political patronage.[29]

To the extent that continued governance failures are recognised by the IMF, the FSF and other agencies, this tends to lead to the conclusion that greater 'market discipline' is a necessary supplement to strengthened prudential regulatory standards. In practice, this has bolstered the case for further financial deregulation and (in principle) a government withdrawal from active intervention in the financial markets. Remaining controls on interest rates have typically been removed, and capital controls have been discouraged.[30] However, if the argument presented here is correct, the result may sometimes be a growing gap between financial liberalisation and weak prudential regulation.

This may matter less in an environment in which banks have been very unwilling to make new loans to corporations, as in Indonesia and Thailand, but this is hardly an adequate basis for long-term financial stability.

Therefore, not only does the standards and codes exercise *not* ensure global financial stability, it may even make it worse. It could be argued that 'transition problems' are inevitable, and that the standards and codes exercise will eventually produce beneficial outcomes. Who, after all, can argue with the desirability of implementing regulatory 'best practice'? This chapter suggests that this view is complacent and does not take into account the political economy factors that are likely to produce a continued forbearance gap in many developing (and developed) countries.

There are a few further implications. If implementation failures are likely to continue to be chronic, the best solution for particular countries may be to remain in quadrant I ('profit-padding' regulation). That China and Taiwan, which both suffered far less than other Asian countries during the crisis, also maintained capital controls of various kinds, suggests that financial openness for some of the others was premature and counterproductive.

It is also important to note that the IFIs, which have the responsibility to monitor and enforce the implementation of the standards and codes, may have mixed incentives to do so in practice. Is it in the interest of the IMF and World Bank, or their respective executive boards, to argue that Indonesian and Thai banks might still need massive recapitalisations? This could trigger bank runs and require fiscal infusions that the governments are not in a position to make. Notably, the IMF, in the case of Indonesia, continues to gloss over implementation failures in continuing to extend its lending programme to Jakarta. And none of the East Asian countries, with the exception of Hong Kong, have published ROSCs relating to financial-sector governance. Finally, nor have private capital markets been any more successful in enforcing real convergence. A strong implication of this chapter is that domestic political and institutional factors are more important than external factors in explaining the degree of real convergence in regulatory governance.

Notes

1   I wish to thank Benu Schneider, Jonathan Di John, Ngaire Woods, and various seminar participants for helpful comments on an earlier draft of this chapter. I also wish to thank the Institute of Defence and Strategic Studies, NTU, Singapore, for generously providing me with a visiting fellowship in 2001–2 when I was on leave from the London School of Economics.

2 One prominent line of argument in the debate over the Asian crisis was that the IMF was mistaken in requiring so-called 'structural' reforms in the Asian countries, and that its conditionality should have concentrated only on its core areas of expertise in monetary and fiscal policy (Feldstein, 1998). However, this was less a disagreement concerning the importance of an adequate financial regulatory framework than about the legitimacy and appropriate scope of IMF conditionality.

3 More recent work in this area includes Diaz-Alejandro (1988), McKinnon (1993) and McKinnon and Pill (1996).

4 However, Diaz-Alejandro (1988, originally published 1985) argued that the Chilean crisis of the early 1980s was caused by a combination of premature financial liberalisation and lax prudential regulation.

5 This is because macro instability creates positive covariance of default rates among bank borrowers, providing banks that have deposit bases guaranteed by the government with an incentive to bet on favourable macro outcomes by overlending (McKinnon, 1993: 90).

6 This is the position of an IMF-commissioned independent review of IMF surveillance; see IMF, 1999.

7 For example, the emphasis of the report of the working group on capital flows is on the costs imposed by 'distortions that may arise from national policy measures or international regulations biasing capital flows towards forms that can generate greater volatility or risk' (Financial Stability Forum, 2000).

8 A related line of argument is that financial openness combined with trade closure renders economies especially vulnerable to financial crisis (such combinations are most marked in Latin America). Again, the recommended solution is greater trade openness rather than financial closure (IMF, 2002: 108).

9 For recent discussions, see Klein and Olivei, 1999, and Arteta *et al.*, 2001.

10 Confidential author interviews, Thailand, March 2002, and Indonesia, May 2002.

11 One example is Japan, where local banks have been heavy lenders to *nokyo*, or private agricultural co-operatives, which are electorally influential (Amyx, 2000: 139). The centrifugal–centripetal dimension of electoral laws is not the only possible relevant one. The way in which electoral boundaries are drawn may also affect policy choices, such as that favouring rural constituencies in Japan.

12 Author interviews, various East Asian financial regulators, 2000–2002. Typically, such rules have been closely adapted from those of the US FDIC models which were rewritten in 1991 in the wake of the S&L crisis.

13 This system classifies loans as pass, special mention (sometimes 'precautionary'), sub-standard, doubtful and loss (see Comptroller of the Currency, 2001: 36–7).

14 Only in March 1998 did the Japanese authorities adopt rules defining banks' NPLs similar to those adopted by the US SEC (that is, defaulted loans, and loans in arrears for more than 90 days, or loans with concessional terms). Indeed, before March 1996, the definition of NPLs in Japan was simply 'defaulted loans and loans in arrears'. From 1996–8, the definition was modified to specify NPLs as loans in arrears for more than 180 days, and loans with concessional interest rates below the official deposit rate. See Fukao, 2002.

15   For precisely these reasons, the Czech National Bank in July 1998 disallowed the previous practice of allowing banks to subtract the value of collateral from the provisioning requirement on loans overdue by more than 360 days (Song, 2002: 21).

16   BoT, 'Regulations for Collateral Valuation and Appraisal,' http://www.bot.or.th/bothomepage/notification/fsupv/2541/thtm/RCVA.DOC, accessed 1 April 2002.

17   Comptroller of the Currency, 2001: 69. In October 2002, the newly appointed head of the FSA suggested that the US system should be adopted by Japan from 31 March 2004 (IDEAglobal, 'Takenaka battles old-guard, surprise from the BOJ?', accessed from www.ideaglobal.com, 30 October 2002).

18   Such capital must also be fully amortised in its last five years of maturity. Early redemptions are not permitted without BoT permission, which is a problem, as the cost of such capital is currently very high, with coupon rates between 5 and 23 per cent. This makes it likely that BoT permission for redemption will be granted after 5 years 1–1 that is, in 2004.

19   Author interviews, Hong Kong, April 2002, and Thailand, March 2002. In the USA, approved subordinated debt instruments are only allowable as Tier II capital (Comptroller of the Currency, 2001: 40).

20   Thai and Indonesian officials now complain that auditors have become excessively conservative since the crisis.

21   Source: Japanese Bankers Association, http://www.zenginkyo.or.jp/en/stat/index.html, accessed 12 June 2002.

22   Data from FDIC, *The 25 Largest Banking Companies*, FDIC Research Staff publication, 1st quarter 2002, available at: http://www.fdic.gov/bank/analytical/largest/2002may/top251st2002.pd.

23   DBS Group, *Annual Report 2001*, notes to the consolidated financial statements, p. 126.

24   Another Singapore-owned Thai bank, UOB–Radhanasin Bank, also estimates in its group accounts that Radhanasin Bank's NPLs are 1,996 million baht. This compares with the 407 million baht of NPLs Radhanasin reported to the BoT. The factor of difference is very close to the TDB case at 4.9 times. (UOB Group, *Annual Report 2001*, and UOB–Radhanasin Bank monthly reports to the BoT, available at http://www.bot.or.th/bothomepage/databank/financial_institutions/np-fi/254412/ecb.htm.)

25   Various interviews, Jakarta, May 2002.

26   In Thailand, the backlog in the commercial court runs up to 10 years; in Indonesia, despite the new bankruptcy framework, IBRA (the state-owned bank asset management agency) has yet to win a case in the commercial court. Most commentators argue that such outcomes are due to a combination of incompetence and high levels of corruption.

27   The severity of the conditions attached to bank recapitalisations will also affect bank incentives.

28   Confidential author interview, senior Financial Supervisory Commission official, Seoul, September 2000.

29   For a general discussion of this 'grabbing hand' view of prudential regulation, see Barth *et al.* (2001). They contrast this political economy view of regulation with the standard 'helping hand' view of government assumed by most economists.

30 Hellman *et al.* (2000) argue that simply introducing new capital requirements (which many emerging-market countries made the centrepiece of
their regulatory policies in the 1990s in the wake of the Basle I accord) may
have the perverse effect of eroding the franchise value of banks, providing
them with further incentives to gamble. They argue for the retention of
deposit interest-rate ceilings in the interim before enhanced prudential
regulation is achieved.

References

Amyx, Jennifer (2000) 'Political Impediments to Far-Reaching Banking Reforms
in Japan: Implications for Asia', in Gregory W. Noble and John Ravenhill (eds),
The Asian Financial Crisis and the Architecture of Global Finance, Cambridge
University Press.

Arteta, Carlos, Barry Eichengreen and Charles Wyplosz (2001) *When Does Capital
Account Liberalisation Help More than It Hurts?*, NBER Working Paper No. 8414,
Cambridge, Mass.: NBER, August.

Asian Policy Forum (2001) *Designing New and Balanced Financial Market Structures
in Post-Crisis Asia*, Tokyo: APF/ADB Institute, October.

Barro, Robert J. (2001) *Economic Growth in East Asia Before and After the Financial
Crisis*, NBER Working Paper No. 8330, Cambridge, Mass.: NBER, June.

Barth, James R., Gerard Caprio, Jr. and Ross Levine (2001) *Bank Regulation and
Supervision: What Works Best?*, Working Paper, Washington, DC: World Bank,
December.

Beck, Thorsten, George Clarke, Alberto Groff, Philip Keefer, and Patrick
Walsh (2001) 'Database of Political Institutions', Washington, DC: World Bank,
(second version).

Blustein, Paul (2001) *The Chastening: Inside the Crisis that Rocked the Global
Financial System and Humbled the IMF*, New York: Public Affairs.

Boorman, Jack, *et al.* (2000) *Managing Financial Crises – The Experience in East Asia*,
IMF Working Paper No. 00/107, Washington, DC: IMF, June.

Claessens, Stijn, Simeon Djankov and Larry Lang (1999) *The Separation of
Ownership and Control in East Asian Corporations*, World Bank Working Paper,
Washington, DC: World Bank, November.

Comptroller of the Currency, Administrator of National Banks (2001) *An
Examiner's Guide to Problem Bank Identification, Rehabilitation, and Resolution*,
Washington, DC: Office of the Comptroller of the Currency, January.

Corsetti, Giancarlo, Paolo Pesenti and Nouriel Roubini (1998) 'Paper Tigers?
A Model of the Asian Crisis', Working Paper, December.

Demirgüç-Kunt, Asli and Enrica Detragiache (1998) *Financial Liberalisation and
Financial Fragility*, IMF Working Paper, No. 98/83, Washington, DC: IMF, June.

Diaz-Alejandro, Carlos F. (1988) 'Good-bye Financial Repression, Hello Financial
Crash', in Andres Velasco (ed.), *Trade, Development and the World Economy:
Selected Essays of Carlos F. Diaz-Alejandro*, Oxford: Basil Blackwell.

Eichengreen, Barry J. (2000) 'The International Monetary Fund in the Wake of
the Asian Crisis', in Gregory W. Noble and John Ravenhill (eds), *The Asian
Financial Crisis and the Architecture of Global Finance*, Cambridge University
Press.

Feldstein, Martin (1998) 'Refocusing the IMF', *Foreign Affairs*, vol. 77, no. 2, March/April.

Financial Stability Forum (2000) *Report of the Working Group on Capital Flows*, Basle: FSF, 5 April.

Fukao, Mitsuhiro (2002) 'Barriers to Financial Restructuring: Japanese Banking and Life-Insurance Industries', Working Paper; Keio University, 25 February.

Glick, R. and M. Hutchison (1999) 'Banking and Currency Crises: How Common are Twins?', in Reuven Glick, Ramon Moreno, and Mark Spiegel (eds), *Financial Crises in Emerging Markets*, New York: Cambridge University Press.

Goldstein, Morris (2001) *IMF Structural Conditionality: How Much Is Too Much?*, Institute for International Economics Working Paper, available at www.iie.com.

Hamilton-Hart, Natasha (2000) 'Indonesia: Reforming the Institutions of Financial Governance?', in Gregory W. Noble and John Ravenhill (eds), *The Asian Financial Crisis and the Architecture of Global Finance*, Cambridge University Press.

Hellman, Thomas F., Kevin C. Murdock and Joseph E. Stiglitz (2000) 'Liberalisation, Moral Hazard in Banking, and Prudential Regulation: Are Capital Requirements Enough?', *American Economic Review*, vol. 90, no. 1, March; pp. 147–65.

Huntington, Samuel (1968) *Political Order in Changing Societies*, New Haven, Conn.: Yale University Press.

IMF (1999) *External Evaluation of IMF Surveillance: Report by a Group of Independent Experts*, Washington, DC: IMF.

IMF (2002) *World Economic Outlook: Trade and Finance*, Washington, DC: IMF, September.

Jordan, Cally and Giovanni Majnone (2002) *Financial Regulatory Harmonization and the Globalization of Finance*, World Bank Policy Research Working Paper No. 2919, Washington, DC: World Bank, October.

Kapur, Devesh (2001) 'Expansive Agendas and Weak Instruments: Governance Related Conditionalities of International Financial Institutions', *Journal of Policy Reform*, vol. 4, no. 3, pp. 207–41.

Klein, Michael W. and Giovanni Olivei (1999) *Capital Account Liberalisation, Financial Depth and Economic Growth*, NBER Working Paper No. 7384, Cambridge, Mass.: NBER, October.

Krugman, Paul (1998) 'What Happened to Asia?', Unpublished paper, Cambridge, Mass.: MIT, January.

Krugman, Paul (1999) 'The Return of Depression Economics', *Foreign Affairs*, vol. 78, no. 1, January/February.

La Porta, Rafael, Florencio Lopez-de-Silanes and Andrei Shleifer (1998a) *Corporate Ownership Around the World*, Harvard Institute of Economic Research Paper, No. 1840, Cambridge, Mass.: Harvard Institute of Economics, August.

La Porta, Rafael, Florencio Lopez-de-Silanes, and Andrei Shleifer (1998b) 'Law and Finance', *Journal of Political Economy*, vol. 106, no. 6, pp. 1113–55.

McKinnon, Ronald I. (1973) *Money and Capital in Economic Development*, Washington, DC: Brookings Institution.

McKinnon, Ronald I. (1993) *The Order of Economic Liberalisation: Financial Control in the Transition to a Market Economy*, 2nd edn, Baltimore, Md: Johns Hopkins University Press.

McKinnon, Ronald I. and Huw Pill (1996) 'Credible Liberalizations and International Capital Flows: The Overborrowing Syndrome', in Takatoshi Ito and Anne O. Krueger (eds), *Financial Deregulation and Integration in East Asia*, Chicago: University of Chicago Press, NBER East Asia Seminar on Economics, vol. 5.

Mishkin, Frederic S. (2001) *Financial Policies and the Prevention of Financial Crises in Emerging Market Countries*, NBER Working Paper, No. 8087, Cambridge, Mass.: NBER, January.

Naim, Moises (1999) 'Fads and Fashion in Economic Reforms: Washington Consensus or Washington Confusion?', Paper prepared for the IMF Conference on Second Generation Reforms, Washington, DC, 26 October.

Noble, Gregory W. and John Ravenhill (2000) 'Causes and Consequences of the Asian Financial Crisis', in Gregory W. Noble and John Ravenhill (eds), *The Asian Financial Crisis and the Architecture of Global Finance*, Cambridge University Press.

Radelet, Steven and Jeffrey Sachs (1998) *The Onset of the East Asian Currency Crisis*, NBER Working Paper No. 6680, Cambridge, Mass.: NBER, April.

Rojas-Suarez, Liliana (2001) *Rating Banks in Emerging Markets: What Credit Rating Agencies should Learn from Financial Indicators*, Institute for International Economics Working Paper, 01-6, available at http://www.iie.com/CATALOG/WP/2001/01-6.pdf, accessed 3 May 2002.

Rosenbluth, Frances and Ross Schaap (2002) 'The Domestic Politics of Banking Regulation', Working paper, Yale/UCLA, February.

Shaw, Edward S. (1973) *Financing Deepening in Economic Development*, New York: Oxford University Press.

Shirai, Sayuri (2001) *Searching for New Regulatory Frameworks for the Intermediate Financial Market Structure in Post-Crisis Asia*, ADB Institute Research Paper No. 24, Manila: Asian Development Bank, September.

Song, Inwon (2002) *Collateral in Loan Classification and Provisioning*, IMF Working Paper WP/02/122, Washington, DC: IMF, July.

Stiglitz, Joseph E (1998) 'Sound Finance and Sustainable Development in Asia', Speech to the Asia Development Forum, Manila, 12 March, available at: http://www.worldbank.org/html/extdr/extme/jssp031298.htm, accessed 21 May 2002.

US Treasury (2000) *Report on IMF Reforms*, Washington, DC: US Treasury, available at: http://www.treas.gov/press/releases/docs/imfrefor.pdf.

Wade, Robert and Frank Veneroso (1998) 'The Asian Crisis: The High Debt Model versus the Wall Street–Treasury–IMF Complex', *New Left Review*, no. 288, March/April.

Williamson, John and Molly Mahar (1998) 'A Survey of Financial Liberalisation', *Princeton Essays in International Finance*, no. 211, November.

World Bank (2002) *East Asia Rebounds, But How Far?*, Washington, DC: East Asia Update, Regional Overview, April.

Part II

Developed-country Perspectives

7
Standards and Codes: A G-7 Countries Perspective

Alastair Clark

Introduction

The standards and codes programme is an important part of current efforts to reinforce the international financial system. In terms of the conventional crisis prevention/crisis resolution distinction, it sits most naturally on the crisis prevention side of the fence, although some standards – for example, relating to insolvency arrangements – are very relevant to the process of crisis resolution.

Before commenting on the implementation of standards in the G-7 economies, and on the standards and codes programme more generally, let me begin with the question of why setting out international benchmarks of good practice has moved so sharply up the agenda in recent years. A number of factors are involved.

One is globalisation. National economies are increasingly interlinked, so that problems in one can have rapid and significant knock-on effects in others. Put differently, as countries integrate themselves more closely into the global economy, their national economic and financial policies become more of a concern to other members of the international 'club'. These other members want reassurance that everyone is playing by broadly the same rules, or at least is not exposing the club as a whole to unreasonable risks.

Second, international capital flows have expanded greatly. Since the late 1980s, cross-border bank lending, as measured by the Bank for International Settlements, has increased about sevenfold, and there has probably been even faster growth in other kinds of cross-border financial claims. This compares with increases of 150 per cent in nominal world GDP, and 200 per cent in nominal world trade. Large financial exposures mean that shocks are transmitted faster, and are likely to be more damaging, than when trade linkages were the main transmission channel.

Third, there is increased emphasis on private markets. Not only has the overall value of capital flows risen, but the private-sector component has also increased sharply. This is true of flows between the developed economies. But a marked shift from public to private is also evident in the external borrowing of some developing countries and many emerging markets. One result is that more attention is now being paid to the efficient functioning of private financial markets, and in particular to the availability of accurate and timely information – that is, to 'transparency'.

Fourth, there is recent experience. The concern about knock-on effects is not just theoretical; since the early 1980s, country debt problems have on several occasions threatened to cause wider systemic damage. From Mexico in 1982 through the other Latin American debt crises of the 1980s, to Mexico again in 1994 and 1995, the East Asian debt problems of 1997 and 1998, Russia in 1998 and Brazil in 1999, and now to Argentina and Turkey – all have led to intervention, and the provision of substantial amounts of cash, by the international financial institutions. At the same time, so far as the G-7 countries are concerned, it is very clear that the overall health of the world economy depends crucially on their prudent conduct of macroeconomic and financial policy.

Adherence to standards and codes cannot be a complete response to these issues. Many factors underlie poor economic performance and/ or the emergence of debt crises. But typically, where problems have arisen, there have been areas where policy fell rather obviously short of recognised good practice, or where a country's financial infrastructure – for example, the financial regulation regime – left the financial system excessively vulnerable, or where there was simply not enough reliable information for lenders and borrowers to make a proper assessment of risk. The position has differed from country to country. But the different cases have had enough in common to allow some general lessons to be drawn, and the current work on standards and codes is partly aimed at capturing those lessons. What it amounts to is a broad effort to improve the quality and transparency of economic and financial policy in all countries – in the emerging markets but also in the G-7.

What standards?

The label 'standards and codes' does not convey a very specific agenda. As we all know, it does not, in the present context, mean international, legally enforceable rules. There would be very little legal machinery to enforce such rules. And even if the machinery did exist, a legalistic approach might not be desirable, for all sorts of reasons. An informal approach, on the other hand, leaves open a number of questions, such as 'How far can flexibility in the interpretation of standards reasonably extend without undermining the credibility of the standard?' and 'What happens when a country fails to meet a standard?'

Standards and codes have been drawn up in many areas of financial policy. Depending on how they are counted, upwards of seventy have been set out so far. We shall not say anything about individual standards here, but only make one general observation. Standards and codes are addressed mainly to three broad areas: transparency of monetary and financial policy; sound institutional and market infrastructure; and effective financial regulation. The nature of the standards in these three areas differs somewhat. The focus in terms of monetary and financial policy is not on the *substance* of policy but on *transparency* – the quality and quantity of the publicly available information about policy. This is an important distinction, and it has caused some to question how valuable compliance with standards and codes really is as an indicator of financial robustness. Good information about bad policy may be better than no information at all; but good policy would be better still. So far as institutional and market arrangements are concerned, the standards are more prescriptive in terms of the substance, but at the level of broad principles rather than detail. As for regulation, the standards cover both substance and process.

Standards and the G-7

Formulation

The drawing-up of international standards has sometimes been portrayed as just another example of financial imperialism. The tablets, designed in the context of developed economies, are brought down from the G-7 or G-10 mountain and the rest of the world is expected to implement them without proper recognition of the different circumstances of different countries. We do not think that this is now – even if it ever was – a justified criticism; and we believe, in particular, that the need for some flexibility in implementation at the notional level is well recognised.

So far as the *formulation* of standards is concerned, the two arguments that are perhaps most commonly made concern manageability and ownership – and they tend to pull in opposite directions.

Securing agreement among a group of sovereign states with genuinely different preferences or interests is seldom easy. The process just about works in groups such as the Basle Committee on Banking Supervision, which has thirteen formal members. We shall discover how satisfactorily it works in an expanded European Union with perhaps twenty-five members. But there is considerable nervousness about the manageability of any process for developing standards that requires the agreement of several dozen countries before it can move forward. On the other hand, I believe there is now ready acknowledgment that it would be an empty exercise if a large proportion of the countries to which standards are supposed to apply resist their implementation because they have had little or no input in their formulation. Moreover, this non-participation means, it is suggested, that the standards eventually decided upon are not well adapted to an emerging-market environment.

We do not believe that these two concerns – manageability and ownership – are irreconcilable, at least to the extent of providing wider opportunities for comment at an earlier stage in the development of standards. But clearly this is an issue that the standard-setting bodies themselves need to consider, and indeed have already begun to address.

We believe that the question of 'suitability' is also capable of being addressed satisfactorily, provided that the structure and hierarchy of standards taken as a whole are well designed. That hierarchy might start at the top level with a relatively small number of standards setting out broad principles for the major areas of policy. Such principles should be of general relevance, at least to countries which seek to establish an open, market-based economy. Under each of them, however, it should then be possible to 'drill down' to progressively greater levels of detail, relevant to increasingly developed economies and markets. This is indeed very much the approach that has been adopted in practice, reflected, for example, in the identification by the Financial Stability Forum of twelve key standards. But it may be possible to go further in organising the remaining standards in a more clearly structured way.

Implementation

At one level, many of the issues that arise in the *implementation* of standards and codes are the same for the G-7 countries as for most emerging markets. There is typically the need to introduce or adapt legislation covering the relevant area of economic, financial or commercial policy; there is the need to establish or modify institutional arrangements so that there is a clear assignment of responsibilities for implementation; and there is the need to have effective monitoring arrangements to ensure continuing compliance. Monitoring will be discussed further below. There are nevertheless clear differences in the demands placed on emerging markets or developing countries, as opposed to developed economies, in the process of implementation. Often, however, these may be more of degree than kind, or of practice rather than principle. First, the so-called 'developed economies' are, at least in relative terms, just that. Their financial sectors, in particular, are typically larger, more complicated and more sophisticated. The corollary is that a wider range of standards and codes are likely to be relevant in developed economies than would be true of most emerging markets.

Second, there is the question of priorities. Even where a range of standards may be relevant to a particular country's situation, there are likely to be some that merit closer attention than others. For many emerging markets, it may be more sensible to focus on fuller implementation of key standards rather than to devote resources to partial implementation of more detailed standards. For developed economies, on the other hand, where implementation of the key standards may be more complete, it may be reasonable to devote effort to the detail.

Third, because, as a matter of fact and whether desirable or not, the form of many standards reflects what has emerged as best practice in the major developed economies, implementation may involve relatively minor changes to their existing arrangements. This is not always the case, however, because in some areas, for example, there have been significant differences in practice among the major economies, and any international standard has therefore implied significant change for at least some of them. Moreover, even where relatively minor changes may be indicated, there can often be considerable resistance to change, because existing practice is deeply embedded. In sum, therefore, while implementation of standards may in certain respects be relatively less demanding for developed countries, the arguments are not all one-way.

Finally, for most developed economies there is no material issue about the resources needed to implement standards. By and large, they are readily available. The same is often not true, however, of emerging markets and developing countries. Indeed, this question of how to make adequate resources available to support the standards and codes programme has, it seems, still not been resolved satisfactorily.

Monitoring

So far as the monitoring of compliance with standards is concerned, for most developed countries until recently this has been implicit rather than explicit. There have, however, been some cases of peer review covering the implementation of certain areas of financial policy. These have sometimes been of value; but the experience has not always been a happy one, perhaps in part because the process has often lacked a consistent or agreed framework. Reviewers have therefore tended to interpret standards according to their own practices, which leaves the potential for wrangling about what constitutes a reasonable norm.

Recently, as is now well known, a number of G-7 countries have undertaken or committed to undertake IMF ROSCs (Reports on the Observance of Standards and Codes) and FSAPs (Financial Sector Assessment Programmes). The UK has participated fully in this initiative and the results of its FSAP were to be published in Spring 2003. Some other countries, notably the USA, have published self-assessments. These are also useful, although the procedures under which they have been conducted are clearly less transparent than in the case of formal ROSCs and FSAPs.

There are those who doubt the value of applying the FSAP process to G-7 countries, partly because they do not judge that these countries are likely to be a major source of financial instability, and partly because, given the considerable resources involved both for the IMF and the country concerned, they do not believe that it is time and money well spent. The argument for undertaking such reviews is twofold. First, there is genuine value for the country concerned in going through the exercise. Certainly, in the UK case, we have learned a lot. But second, and perhaps more importantly, it helps to avoid the charge that the G-7 countries are not prepared to take their own medicine. In any event, the effort to assess the compliance of G-7 countries with the key standards has been helpful to the IMF in developing its own approach and techniques for the FSAP process.

Concluding remarks

One further message has emerged from recent experience. As noted previously, the implementation of standards can involve a substantial resource cost. The same is true of monitoring through ROSCs and FSAPs, both for the country concerned and for the IMF. There may be a danger that the best becomes the enemy of the good, and that a streamlined version of the FSAP procedure, which delivered a large part of the diagnostic benefit at substantially less resource cost, would be worth considering. There are understandable concerns about rigour and consistency; but such an approach might nevertheless deliver a worthwhile overall benefit.

Finally, three general observations. First, it is worth emphasising that the main rationale for the implementation of standards and codes is the contribution it can make to improved economic performance. In that sense, virtue is its own reward. As a corollary, however – although the link is by no means immediate or complete – it should also mean that countries can obtain access to finance in international markets on more favourable terms.

Second, we devote a lot of attention to the behaviour of borrowers. But it seems at least important, both in substance and in terms of providing the right incentives, to consider the behaviour of lenders and investors. They need to be persuaded that assessing compliance with standards and codes can make an important contribution to their risk management; and that they should reflect differences in compliance in the terms of the finance they provide. For a variety of reasons, we are still some way away from achieving this objective.

Finally, it seems important to have a realistic timetable. The standards and codes programme is not something that can be delivered overnight, within a few months or even within a year or two. It is bound to require a sustained effort. The important thing is to keep going.

8

The View from Germany: Standards and Codes – Important Cornerstones for Financial Crisis Prevention

Axel Nawrath

Importance of external assessment versus self-assessment and further updating of standards and codes

Self-assessments of compliance with standards and codes are an important first step in detecting gaps in the domestic regulatory framework and in providing guidance for prioritising implementation efforts. But self-assessments cannot replace external assessments by neutral parties, especially the IMF and the World Bank. Such external assessments normally take into account the views of a broad range of experts, which helps in enhancing the quality of the guidance given.

Clearly, standards and codes have to reflect the structural developments of financial markets and hence are open to improvement. In deciding whether there is a need for the updating of individual standards, a wide range of views should also be taken into account during the updating process, including – as in the past – the views of national regulators, market participants and the international financial institutions. For the time being, updates should be the exception rather than the rule, because implementing standards is a time-consuming and resource-intensive process. The scarce resources available should not be overstretched by a continuous process of implementing updated standards. Priority should be given to updates for countries with significant financial sectors, large deficiencies identified in previous assessments and a lack of compliance with the forty recommendations of the Financial Action Task Force (FATF) on money laundering and the eight recommendations on the financing of terrorism. The 40 + 8 recommendations are also taken into account in all Financial Sector Assessment Programmes (FSAP) of the IMF.

It is important that standards and codes are reviewed by the same bodies that established them (see, for example; *Core Principles for Effective Banking Supervision* by the Basle Committee) to make best use of the scarce expertise available and to ensure consistency.

Public and private sector information: how to bridge the different needs?

The gap that exists between the type of information the official sector is (willing and) able to supply, and the format in which the private sector wishes to receive it can in the last analysis only be closed by the private participants themselves. Some private firms (for example, eStandardsForum, PricewaterhouseCoopers, Standard and Poors) have already stepped forward to fill this gap in the market: eStandards, for example, analyses publicly accessible information on the observation of the standards and codes by every country and makes it available to private participants for a fee.

In spite of certain reservations regarding the objectivity and accuracy of the assessments made by private firms, the official side should not attempt to curb such initiatives. We can assume that, ultimately, market forces will take effect here, too, and that competition between the private suppliers of information will ensure the reliability of that information.

Response of market participants and prioritisation of standards and codes

The public availability of Reports on Observation of Standards and Codes (ROSCs) for a broad range of countries provides the basis for the development of a general willingness among market participants to search for and take into account ROSCs when analysing the financial sector of individual countries. ROSCs could also become an important source of information for rating agencies when they assess the financial sectors of countries. If necessary, discussion with rating agencies should ensure that ROSCs are used appropriately.

The Financial Stability Forum (FSF) follow-up group on the implementation of standards repeated in 2001 a survey on how market participants view standards and codes. This investigation of financial institutions in the members' countries confirmed that, in the private sector's view, the practical usefulness of information on the observance of standards is still limited, since:

- external assessments have not been made for all countries;
- there are still problems with translating the qualitative analyses of the IMF's Reports on the Observance of Standards and Codes (ROSCs) into the simple, quantitative ratings which some institutions prefer and need for their internal country risk evaluation models; and
- the lack of benchmarks makes it hard to compare the implementation of standards and codes across countries.

Additional IMF and World Bank outreach seminars could be organised to further enhance the awareness of market participants on the role of standards and codes, and the availability of ROSCs. Furthermore, publication of ROSCs should become the usual practice after external assessments by the IMF and the World Bank have been completed.

The twelve key standards identified for financial stability by the Financial Stability Forum provide only general guidance for prioritising the implementation of standards and codes. This guidance needs to be adapted to the specific circumstances of individual countries. The FSAPs of the IMF can play an important role in this process. FSAPs serve to identify gaps in financial sector regulation and transparency practices; furthermore, they give guidance on reform and development needs. Therefore, FSAPs can help to direct countries' efforts in implementing standards to areas with the greatest benefit for financial stability.

Empirical evidence for the importance of standards and codes

Empirical evidence provided by the Institute of International Finance shows that borrowing costs are lower for countries that comply with the SDDS transparency standard. However, further research is necessary to prove the positive effects of the compliance with other standards and codes.

There is further evidence at the IMF that:

- countries are changing policies in response to the lessons of the emerging-market crises – for example, releasing data more frequently, taking steps to improve their observance of standards and codes; and
- investors are becoming more discriminating in their investment decisions (in part as a result of greater transparency through ROSCs).

But one has to keep in mind that ROSCs have not been completed, for all countries and all standards and codes, and that the whole process is still rather new for countries and market participants. Given the usual transmission period for the introduction of a complex evaluation system such as the standards and codes effort, it is quite certain that empirical evidence will be provided in the near future, and this will be a strong positive incentive to improve the voluntary observance of standards and codes.

Germany complies fully with the key standards and codes for financial stability

Germany is confident that it has implemented fully all major financial standards and codes. A fiscal ROSC was conducted in Autumn 2002 and a FSAP was to be conducted in spring 2003.

Part III

Private-sector Perspectives

9
Effects of Standards and Codes on Country Risk Ratings

Lionel Price

Over the last few years, policy-makers and regulators have been putting a great deal of work into developing and implementing the set of standards and codes developed by a number of international bodies. But the European Central Bank has suggested that awareness of the standards is not widespread among market participants, including rating agencies, so this process is not yet having much effect on market incentives (*ECB Monthly Bulletin*, February 2002). This chapter looks at whether implementation of the standards and codes is helping sovereign borrowers, and particularly at whether it has had any identifiable impact on sovereign ratings.

The standards and codes

The IMF set the ball rolling in 1996 with its opaquely titled *Dissemination Standards Bulletin Board*. The Basle Committee followed in 1997, with its more transparently named *Core Principles for Effective Banking Supervision*. These efforts to encourage countries to apply high standards in statistical and supervisory fields were given more political focus by the Asian and Russian sovereign debt crises, and this led to the establishment in April 1999 of the Financial Stability Forum. The FSF is now working with the IMF, World Bank, and other organisations to promote the twelve standards listed in Table 1.1 on page 2.

There is little doubt that adherence to the various standards will generally aid creditworthiness. Of course, cost-effectiveness is important too. Regulation can be costly and may distort market forces. In some cases, the risks being addressed will be too small to merit building elaborate defences, but this aspect has been recognised in decisions to avoid judging implementation of the standards as a matter of 'pass' or 'fail'.

Instead, Reports on the Observance of Standards and Codes (ROSCs) detail the ways in which countries do not meet them, so that a view can be taken on whether a deficiency needs to be addressed, and if so, how quickly.

For the creditworthiness of sovereign governments themselves, the key standards are potentially those on data, fiscal transparency, banking supervision, and transparency in monetary and financial policies. These are the fields where failures are most likely to lead to sovereign debt problems, and we shall be concentrating on these in this chapter.

Weaknesses in other fields, such as corporate governance or accounting, can harm a country's creditworthiness by reducing potential growth and direct investment or permitting bad debts to accumulate, but are less likely to be the proximate cause of a sovereign crisis. This is not to say that they are unimportant for a rating agency. The transparency and reliability of a company's accounts can have a great bearing on a corporate rating, as do judgements on the quality and objectives of the management. And reports on a country's implementation of the core supervisory principles for insurance can provide useful information for rating that country's insurance companies, just as the effectiveness of banking supervision is germane to bank ratings.

Data standards

When first launched, the IMF's Data Dissemination Standards seemed to offer a lot of jargon and few new numbers. But the statistical gaps revealed by the Asian crisis, together with the explosion of internet access, have provided the incentive and the means for great improvements in data provision. First, the links provided from the IMF's own website are now often the quickest way to find up-to-date economic statistics from unfamiliar national sources. Second, dozens of countries have been persuaded to publish more frequent, timely, complete and internationally comparable data in key fields. In particular, the Asian crisis reminded analysts to look more closely at a country's external liquidity position, and emphasised the need for data on private external debt as well as public borrowing. Third, a more recent initiative to assess the quality of data is helping make the greater amount of information now being published also more reliable.

As Table 9.1 shows, there are two Data Dissemination Standards specifying the data that countries should provide, their frequency and their timeliness. In June 2002, fifty countries, all except one rated by Fitch, had signed up for the more demanding Special Standard. A further forty

Table 9.1 Data Dissemination Standards (as at June 2002)

Investment grade countries				Others*	
Special DDS					
Australia	France	Latvia	S. Africa	Argentina	Philippines
Austria	Germany	Lithuania	Spain	Brazil	Slovakia
Belgium	Hong Kong	Malaysia	Sweden	Colombia	Turkey
Canada	Hungary	Mexico	Switzerland	Costa Rica	
Chile	Iceland	Netherlands	Thailand	El Salvador	
Croatia	Ireland	Norway	Tunisia	India	
Czech Republic	Israel	Poland	UK	Indonesia	
Denmark	Italy	Portugal	USA	Peru	
Estonia	Japan	Singapore			
Finland	Korea	Slovenia			
General DDS					
China				Azerbaijan	Panama
Kuwait				Bulgaria	Romania
Malta				Kazakhstan	Venezuela
Not subscribing to DDS					
Aruba	Greece			Iran	Turkmenistan
Bahrain	Luxembourg			Lebanon	Ukraine
Bermuda	New Zealand			Moldova	Uruguay
Cyprus	San Marino			PNG	Vietnam
Egypt	Taiwan			Russia	

Note

* Countries with lower Fitch ratings. Of countries not rated by Fitch in June 2002, Ecuador subscribes to the SDDS, and 31 other countries to the GDDS.

countries, nine of them rated by Fitch, were committed to meeting the less demanding General Standard. Investment-grade countries are significantly more likely[1] than lower-rated countries to be applying the Special Standard, but nearly a quarter of them do not. Among investment-grade countries not subscribing to either standard have been some that issue debt on international markets (Egypt and Greece) as well as a number of international banking centres (notably Luxembourg and Bahrain). Analysis of these countries is hampered by poor data. In contrast, almost half of the countries with lower ratings are applying the Special Standard. Among their number is Argentina, an assiduous supplier of information on its external position – even on a daily basis – in 2001, but this was not enough to save it from default.

A key part of the Special Standard is a template for publishing data on international reserves and liquidity. This has required more disclosure, not only from developing countries but also from industrial countries that previously kept their forward and other operations secret. The extra cost of publishing these data is minimal, but the need for more transparency was plain when it became clear in late 1997 that Korea's published foreign-exchange reserves were not available to meet the outflow of short-term funds from the country. Much of the central bank's 'reserves' were in fact claims on Korean banks' head offices, which had already used the counterpart assets. A little earlier, Thailand had shown what could happen to a central bank that secretly supported its currency in the forward market (a practice with a costly precedent in the United Kingdom, among other countries). South Africa, in contrast, published a full account of its heavily oversold forward position. It is not easy to judge whether views on the country's creditworthiness were, on balance, strengthened by the Reserve Bank's transparency, or weakened by the disclosure of the size of the position. The reserves template shows not only how and where spot and forward foreign exchange is held, but also credit-lines and contingent claims on the reserves. So we can see, for example, that Korea's official reserves no longer include any deposits with Korean banks, and that Mexico has available undrawn unconditional credit-lines of US$6.6 billion. In contrast, a few industrial countries are still including in their reserves deposits with resident banks. By far the largest such holdings are in Japan, where as much as US$60 billion of the official reserves is deposited with banks in Japan, and three-fifths of that with Japanese-owned banks.

In sovereign rating analysis, one of the trickiest areas to obtain comprehensive up-to-date data has been external debt. That task has become less difficult, as two-thirds of the countries we rate now publish an international investment position (IIP). Data provided in this standard format for a country's external balance sheet are not always complete, but usually provide a good starting point for analysis. Countries have been encouraged to provide annual IIP data within six months of the end of the year, and this became a requirement for SDDS countries from mid-2002. To meet the demands of investors for timely information, four industrial countries and ten emerging markets are now publishing a quarterly IIP, but many industrial countries are slow to produce even annual data. National statistical offices in countries with good access to capital markets are often reluctant to give much priority to this activity, perhaps understandably preferring to devote resources to domestic demands for social and economic data.

In the August 2001 edition of *International Financial Statistics (IFS)*, eleven industrial countries showed their IIP only up to end-1999 and two only until 1998. Some of these countries may possibly have already published their IIPs for 2000 elsewhere. Indeed Korea, whose latest IIP figures in *IFS* are for 1994, is putting a lot of effort into investor relations and sends emails to analysts giving quarterly updates of external assets and liabilities, though not in the same format. As *IFS* – itself now available on the internet – is a key data source for analysts around the world, it is strange that Korea does not ensure its data can be seen promptly there by those wishing to make comparisons between countries.

Although publication in *IFS* is not itself required under the standards, the timely availability of data there is an indication of the effort being put into implementing the standards in a useful manner. If national and IMF statisticians were together achieving the timeliness specified in the standards, the February 2002 edition (Table 9.2) of *IFS* should have shown balance of payments (BoP) data for the third quarter of 2001, and IIPs for

Table 9.2   Latest data available in IFS, February 2002

For 73 rated countries	Balance of payments	International investment position
September 2001	18*	1*
June 2001	22	10*
March 2001	7	1*
December 2000	17	31*
June 2000	1	0
December 1999	3	6
December 1994	0	2
No data	5	22

Note
* Meets the encouraged timeliness standard.

December 2000. Of the seventy-three countries then rated by Fitch, only eighteen in fact showed such up-to-date BoP data, though another twenty-two did show second-quarter figures. All except eight of the fifty-one rated countries publishing IIPs in IFS met the less demanding expectation of providing data for December 2000.

Despite these deficiencies, there is no doubt that, thanks to the work done to implement the data standards, analysts now have easier access to more consistent and timely information. When credit analysts do not have access to information, they will tend to assume the worst; potentially, therefore, better data could lead to higher ratings. However, it is difficult to find evidence that this has been the case. As has already been mentioned, defaulting Argentina has been a keen provider of data. At the other end of the scale, there are highly-rated countries such as Bermuda and San Marino that do not offer much data.

Comparisons of different characteristics (such as to which data standard they subscribe, or whether they publish an IIP) of countries that have been upgraded or downgraded over the previous three years[2] also show little in the way of a pattern. The only significant result, even at a fairly undemanding 10 per cent level, is that countries unable to provide BoP data are more likely to have been downgraded. But that result hinges on Lebanon and Turkmenistan featuring among the eight downgrades, and there was no shortage of other reasons for these countries being downgraded.

ROSCs and ratings

Outside the data area, the potential impact of countries' efforts to implement the various standards and codes is often restricted by their reluctance to be transparent about the process. Some countries, such as India, are following a largely 'home-grown' approach with limited outside assessment or peer review, and reporting on the process mainly domestically. The likelihood that independent analysts will quickly become aware of improvements in banking supervision, for example, is much greater where the country agrees to the IMF or another international agency publishing a ROSC on the subject. Other countries have been reluctant to agree to publication of reports that would highlight their remaining deficiencies. From the point of view of Fitch Ratings, we are usually already aware of important deficiencies. Without publication, what we miss hearing about are the steps being taken to remedy them.

One of Fitch Ratings' sovereign analysts explains how useful she has found the reports:

> I make a point of reading every one that appears on the countries I cover. While they rarely include issues I was not already aware of, they can give far more background on a topic than is available elsewhere. The fiscal reports for example may contain information on off-budget activities or problems with local government data. More generally, the reports can indicate the key questions to pursue during rating visits, and better knowledge of the background makes our discussions with the authorities more productive.
>
> Banking reports can be particularly helpful as most authorities will claim that their standards are in line with international rules, but these reports give an independent assessment of the extent to which that is true and indicate what progress is being made in remedying any deficiencies. In one case, I was able to draw on the financial system assessment report to support my point that earlier banking problems had been resolved, thereby helping convince the rating committee of the case for an upgrade.

But only 72 per cent of the ROSCs completed by the end of April 2002 had by then been published, though this proportion can be expected to rise over time, for two reasons. First, some countries can take many months to agree to publish a report, so some of those completed earlier may yet be released. Second, the attitude to publication has been changing with experience. Over half of the reports have been produced under the financial system assessment programme (FSAP) launched by the IMF and the World Bank in 1999. There was initially no intention to publish these reports, and publication of the overall assessments (though not of the component modules) was actually banned until majority opinion on the institutions' Boards was convinced of the benefits. Even now, Fund staff stress that the purpose of the FSAP is to assess financial system health and to improve countries' resilience to financial sector problems, rather than to improve transparency *per se*. They point out that countries' decisions to participate in the programme may not necessarily be motivated by a desire for transparency.

As might be expected, the reluctance to publish reports seems to be greatest among the least creditworthy countries. Of the 116 reports published before March 2002 on Fitch-rated countries, only twenty related to countries below investment grade. Of these, seven were for Bulgaria, largely reflecting the country's participation in the FSAP. Another four resulted from a pilot FSAP for which Argentina had volunteered in 1999. Even though several other sub-investment grade countries are known to have been participating in the financial system programme, the results of these endeavours have not seen the light of day, and all except three of the remaining reports for these lower-rated countries were on fiscal transparency.

Of the global total of thirty-nine reports on fiscal transparency completed by April 2002, as many as thirty-five had then been published. Evidently, those responsible for this work have succeeded in persuading countries to publish the results even where they pointed to serious weaknesses. But ironically, only twenty-four of the thirty-nine reports produced on transparency in monetary and financial policy had been released. The figures for reports on banking supervision were also twenty-four published out of thirty-nine completed. We hope to see more reports published in future, and while they are still fresh. Interim reports can be useful in providing information while work is still in progress.

In practice, there has been a highly significant relationship between the publication of ROSCs and changes in sovereign ratings over the period December 1998 to February 2002 (see Table 9.3). Of course, it is difficult to disentangle cause and effect. The relationship could arise because countries undertaking reforms that possibly are consistent with their rating being upgraded are more likely to be willing to see reports published. Alternatively, it may be that publishing details of assessments and reforms helps to increase the chance of an upgrade. Both influences are probably at work, but our belief is that transparency is more likely to enhance creditworthiness than to damage it. Acknowledging problems, even though they may still take some time to tackle, itself reduces some of the doubts about how the country will behave in future.

The strongest relationships between publication of ROSCs and rating changes are for reports on banking, insurance and securities regulation. Again, this could partly reflect the reluctance of countries weak in these areas to see assessment findings published, but we do know from our own experience that some upgrades have been directly supported by evidence of a strengthening of a country's banking system and its supervision.

The link between publication of reports on fiscal transparency and upgrades has been much weaker. Three of the nine countries downgraded – Argentina, Japan and Turkey – have serious fiscal problems but still agreed to the publication of fiscal ROSCs. But it was not the publication of the three reports that led to the downgrades. These countries' fiscal problems were already well-known and it was, if anything,

Table 9.3   Numbers of published Reports on the Observance of Standards and Codes, classified by rating change

Rating Change[a] 12/98–2/02	Totals		Topic							
	Countries	*Reports*	*Data*	*Fiscal*	*Monetary*	*Banking*	*Insurance*	*Securities*	*Payments*	*Corporate*
Upgrades	20	54	7	9	8	9	7	7	6	1
No change	44	55	6	11	9	8	5	5	5	6
Downgrades	9	7	1	3	1	1	0	0	0	1
Total	73	116	14	23	18	18	12	12	11	8
χ^2 test		0.6%[b]	10.6%	27.7%	14.6%	4.2%	2.2%	2.2%	6.2%	59.1%

Notes

[a] Upgrades and downgrades are determined by comparing a country's long-term foreign currency rating at 28 February 2002 with the rating at 31 December 1998 (or the initial rating, if later).

[b] Calculated treating ROSCs on Banking, Insurance, Securities and Payments as a single report as they are usually joint parts of an FSAP. (Treating them as if they were independent events would give a significance level of one in a million.)

helpful to their cases to see that at least some of the problems were being recognised and tackled.

ROSCs and market access

Several industrialised countries, including Australia, Canada, Finland, France, Ireland, Luxembourg, Sweden, Switzerland and the United Kingdom, have shown themselves to be willing to participate in the standards and codes exercise and publish ROSCs – in part apparently to encourage others to do the same. Japan has eventually been persuaded to embark on a financial sector assessment, but the USA seems unwilling to set an example itself.

For a number of developing countries, participation has accompanied broader efforts to improve relations with investors and the information they make available to them. Perhaps predictably, the countries that have shown themselves most likely to publish ROSCs are the emerging-market borrowers that appear to have found the primary market less welcoming in 1998[3] but are now issuing international bonds again. Of twelve such sovereigns, nine (Brazil, Croatia, Lithuania, Mexico, Panama, Poland, South Africa, Tunisia and Turkey) have published one or more ROSCs. Only Kazakhstan and Venezuela have not published any, though Kazakhstan has been undertaking an FSAP. None of the three other previous sovereign issuers that have stayed away from international markets since 1998 (Indonesia, Moldova and Thailand) has published a ROSC.

Almost all other active emerging-market borrowers – that is, those whose issuance did not shrink in 1998 – have been, or are being, assessed under the FSAP, but only slightly more than half of them have so far published ROSCs. Evidently, to these borrowers the need for transparency appears somewhat less urgent than it does to those that faced problems in 1998. Two large countries appear to have felt little or no urgency. Russia and China have been notable absentees from the whole process – data standards, the FSAP and publishing ROSCs – though China has subscribed recently to the GDDS.

Conclusion

That some important borrowers have not felt impelled to participate more actively and transparently in implementing the standards and codes does give some support to the European Central Bank's contention that this channel of market incentives is not yet working effectively. It is none the less clear that an improved flow of information is resulting from the process, and this enables investors and rating agencies to make assessments that are better informed. Although it is not entirely possible to disentangle cause and effect, the positive association between ratings upgrades and the publication of Reports on the Observance of Standards and Codes does suggest that the combined effect of working to improve implementation of the standards and codes, and publishing information about this, can strengthen a country's credit rating. But governments that undertake reforms without permitting publication of reports risk losing the potential beneficial impact on perceptions of their country's creditworthiness.

Notes

1   At 2 per cent level on a $\chi2$ test.
2   Upgrades and downgrades are determined by comparing a country's long-term foreign currency rating at 28 February 2002 with the rating at 31 December 1998 (or the initial rating, if later).
3   As indicated by smaller issuance in the international bond markets in 1998 (in most cases, nothing) than a country's average in the previous two years. (This definition fails to capture Russia.)

10
Do We Need to Go Beyond Disclosure?[1]

Michael Metcalfe and Avinash Persaud

Introduction

Following crises in Asia, Argentina and more recently the weakness in global equity markets after the US accounting scandals, there would appear to be a stronger case than ever for better standards regarding the disclosure and quality of information. Yet this assumption is based on the notion that these market failures are caused by the lack of information, and that improvement in the quality and dissemination of information will therefore help to avoid future crises. We shall consider a variety of recent crises to deduce the extent that they could have been prevented by better disclosure, or whether the warning signals were simply ignored as asset market bubbles developed. And we discover that, while, in general, stronger data standards will help market efficiency, it is questionable whether they are the panacea that is often assumed. Indeed, there are some forms of disclosure that might even increase financial instability.

Background – a new model

As is often the way with the debate on crisis models, the Asian crisis has pushed the debate on reforming the international financial system in a new direction. The debt crisis in Mexico, for example, suggested that crises resulted primarily from governments' running persistent budget deficits and at the same time using a limited stock of reserves to peg the exchange rate. This, in turn, pointed policy towards promoting fiscal discipline. Later models following the ERM crises were related more directly to policy credibility. These were based around the principle that governments chose whether or not to defend an exchange rate by weighing the trade-off between short-run macroeconomic flexibility (higher interest rates and unemployment) and longer-term credibility. The Asian crisis, however, did not fit these earlier crisis models very well. On the eve of the Asian crisis, the governments were more or less in fiscal balance, they were not engaged in runaway monetary expansion, and their inflation and unemployment rates were relatively low. A new explanation was required.

The stylised version of the Asian crisis suggests that risky lending by unregulated financial intermediaries created asset (not goods) price inflation. This created a virtuous circle under which widespread risky lending drove up the price of risky assets, in turn making the financial condition of the intermediaries seem sounder than it was. Once the asset price bubble burst, this circular process reversed and falling asset prices made the insolvency of intermediaries visible, forcing them to liquidate their portfolios and driving asset prices down even further. So why was the bubble not spotted? The Asian crisis, perhaps more than any other, it might be argued, was the result of the fragility of the financial sector in these countries, which in turn was argued to be a function of a lack of transparency and inappropriate market standards.

This has produced an interesting shift in the crisis prevention debate towards the importance of information. There are two possible theoretical links between information provision and crisis. The first is the 'skeleton in the cupboard' theory. Rather than looking at the 'wrong' variables, the information inputs into efficient markets to forewarn of a crisis are either not available, not accurate, and/or not timely enough. When this information is revealed, or finally becomes apparent, a crisis ensues.

The second is that an environment of sub-optimal information will encourage investors to herd, thereby increasing market volatility. Incomplete information, whereby smaller investors use price action to deduce the actions of larger players who are assumed to be better informed, is only one rationalisation of herding behaviour. This rationalisation of herding is known as 'informational cascades' in the literature. In theory, if this is the main driving factor behind herding, greater provision of information should, generally speaking, result in less herding and fewer crises.

A longer-run perspective

If we take a very long-run perspective of crises, the evidence that better information would reduce the incidence of crises is minimal. There can

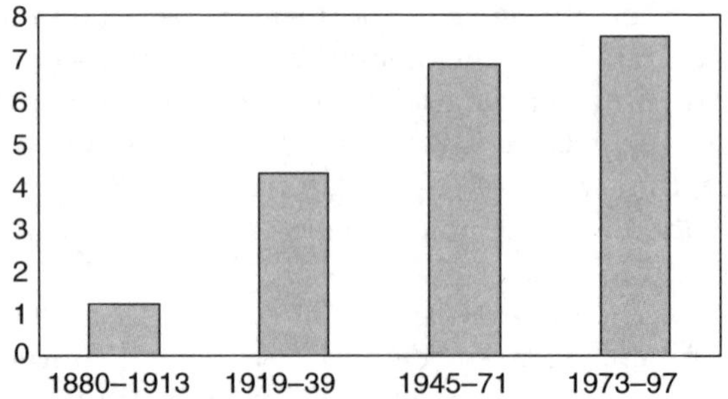

Figure 10.1   Probability of a currency crisis (1880–1997)
Source: Eichengreen and Bordo (2002).

be little debate that access to information improved over the course of the twentieth century, and particularly in the 1990s through the Internet. Yet a study by Barry Eichengreen and Michael Bordo (2002) shows that the probability of a currency crisis, defined as the abandonment of a fixed currency regime or a large move in either the exchange rate, interest rate or reserves (defined as a move in either variable by more than one standard error away from the mean), in fact increased over the twentieth century. Of course, the historical example is far from perfect, given the greater number of floating currencies in the current market, and the fact that capital markets have now been liberalised. However, it is still worth noting that the liberalisation of markets has not brought greater stability, as promised. Some commentators would go even further and suggest that greater access to information has in fact increased the risk of crisis (see Figure 10.1).[2]

If the flow of information has improved, albeit still far from perfect, this goes back to the principal flaw of the original models of crisis prevention: 'Are we simply ignoring the warning signs?' To analyse this question more thoroughly we shall take three diverse examples of recent crises: the Asian crisis of 1997–8; the NASDAQ bubble; and Argentina 2001–2.

A necessary, but not sufficient, condition

There are three main reasons why improved information flows are a necessary, but not sufficient, condition to prevent crises. First, market myopia, where information is available but the market chooses to focus on other variables. Second, the provision of 'bad news': it is important to remember that improved delivery and clarity of information provides no guarantee that investment flows will become less volatile. Third, the release of some forms of information may in fact make markets more volatile if they contribute to the tendency of investors to herd.

Market myopia

With respect to the Asian crisis, there are clear specific examples of where low data standards disguised the risks of the impending crash. For example, South Korea revised its foreign debt figures upwards constantly, while the Bank of Thailand did not indicate that a substantial share of its foreign reserves was committed to forward market transactions. Such factors clearly exacerbated the crisis. It would, however, be wrong to suggest that there was no information at all on the excessive lending position of a number of emerging Asian countries. Data on international bank lending was available from the BIS well before the crisis.[3] Just as the crisis was taking hold in July 1997, the BIS report using data up to the end of 1996 showed that short-term banking loan volumes to emerging markets were at a record, as Figure 10.2 illustrates. The five Asian crisis countries – Thailand, Malaysia, South Korea, Indonesia and the Philippines – between them received US$47.8 billion in foreign bank loans in 1996, only for international banks to withdraw nearly US$30 billion in the following year.

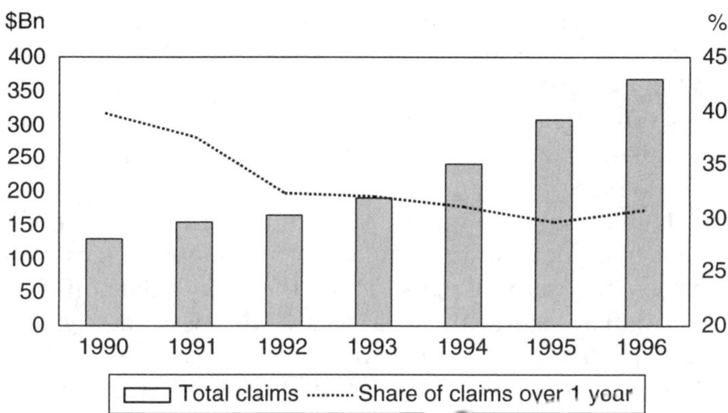

Figure 10.2   International bank lending to Asia – a retrospect

Source: Bank for International Settlements.

These warning signs, however, were largely ignored. Less than two months before Thailand abandoned its exchange-rate peg, most commentators and international agencies were still optimistic about the region: 'Despite gloomy forecasts that Asia's environment will worsen, a new policy model holds promise for an improved environment' (Asian Development Bank, 1997). This 'new model' had been extolled throughout the 1990s as a more flexible form of capitalism dependent on 'trust-based implicit relationships', a 'magic' ingredient that later became termed 'crony capitalism'. This highlights an underlying problem that better information cannot solve. We move rapidly through assertions that the world has changed and that there is now an entirely different model. At its limit this boils down to the issue of whether markets are rational, or whether they are subject to bouts of significant irrational overshoots.

It is difficult, for example, to look at what happened also in the US equity bubble, and more recently in the rash of accounting scandals, and conclude that valuations were rational. In 2000, the USA in general, and practices in corporate America specifically, would have been the benchmark for codes of corporate governance and transparency. Indeed, the USA was one of the first countries to initiate a self-assessment of the twelve key international standards and codes identified by the Financial Stability Forum. Yet in the specific case of accounting scandals, the checks and balances put in place in supposedly the world's most liberal economy were not sufficient to prevent the creation and subsequent destruction over only a few years of companies worth as much as US$60 bn. At first glance, the equity market bubble and the accounting scandals would appear to heighten specifically the need for better disclosure and accounting standards, but at the same time they also highlight their limitations. The current emphasis on transparent accounting standards should ensure that markets are better informed to reward sound companies rather than doubtful ones, which should go some way to preventing a re-run of an ENRON-style affair. However, even without doubts about the quality of reported earnings, we should not ignore that traditional measures of equity valuations such as P/E ratios had been sending warning signals about US equity valuations for some time. In a similar vein to the Asian crisis, what warning signals there were were dismissed on the presumption that the US equities were an entirely different model. So, while disclosure in general should be a good thing, it is only effective if markets use the information efficiently.

No news is bad news … but more news doesn't have to be good news

Even if markets do focus on the 'correct variables', a second point is that better information provision alone does not shelter a country from crisis. The limitations of simple disclosure are best highlighted by the recent collapse of the Argentine exchange-rate regime. Here the problem was more political, to the extent that the government was not prepared, or able, to take the tough domestic choices about taxing and spending rather than one of transparency *per se*. An IMF report of 1999 suggested that Argentina had already made some progress in this regard: 'Transparency is generally high in each of the four areas assessed here – data dissemination, fiscal, monetary and financial policy transparency, and the disclosure aspects of banking supervision' (IMF, 1999). Indeed, by the end of 1999, four Reports on the Observance of Standards and Codes (ROSCs) covering data dissemination, fiscal transparency, monetary transparency and banking supervision had been produced on Argentina, more than on most emerging markets at the time. The lesson, it seems, is that improved information flows are one thing, but there is no guarantee that more information will always mean that markets will be treated more or less favourably by capital markets.

More generally, we find that the example of Argentina is not isolated, although a recent paper by the IMF (Gaston Gelos and Shang-Jin Wei, 2002) found that on average emerging-market funds tended to hold more assets in more transparent markets. We used State Street's database on institutional investor portfolio flows, which covers approximately US$6.3 trillion in assets, to assess the impact of the publication of ROSCs on the volatility of cross-border equity flows for a range of twenty-three emerging market countries.[4] Although there are a number of transparency measures currently being developed,[5] as yet there are no dominant private-sector benchmarks being developed. As a consequence, we used the number of published ROSCs for each country to ascertain whether this has any impact on reducing the short-term volatility of cross-border equity flows.

As Figure 10.3 shows, there appears to be some negative relationship between the number of ROSC modules published and the volatility of gross (purchases plus sales) cross-border equity flows measured in basis points of market capitalisation.[6] More formally, a simple panel regression of volatility of cross-border flows during 2001 2 on ROSC scores yields an R-squared of only 0.01 (see Appendix 10.1). Further, while the sign on the number of ROSC publications measure is negative (that is,

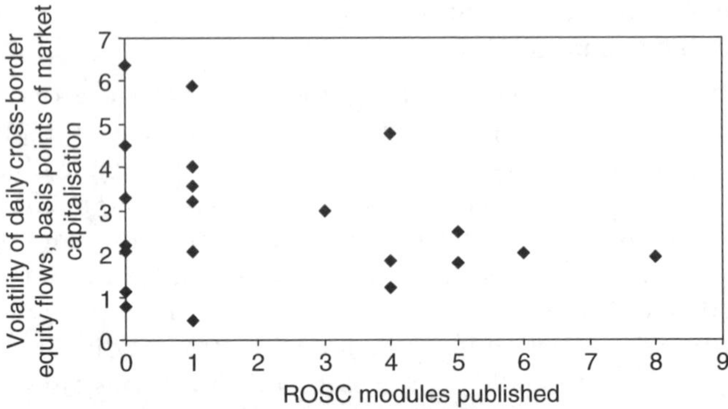

Figure 10.3   ROSC and the daily volatility of cross-border equity flows in 2001

ROSC publication reduces volatility of flows), it is statistically insignificant at the 10 per cent confidence level, even if we add another variable to control for GDP per capita. Given that the publication of ROSCs is still a relatively new (3-year at the time of writing) phenomenon, it is possible that our study, looking at flows in 2001 and 2002, does not allow sufficient time for the publications to have an impact on investor behaviour. At present, however, the best that can be said is that the argument that the publication of ROSCs reduces the volatility of cross-border equity flows is unproven.

Can too much news be destabilising?

An even deeper concern to be addressed is the possibility that some types of disclosure might even have a detrimental impact on financial stability. Some markets exist because they can pool risks efficiently. However, this pooling of risks might not occur if there was a greater degree of disclosure. In the medical insurance market, for example, if the insurers and the insured knew exactly when someone was about to fall ill, it is unlikely that the market would even exist. In a similar vein, liquid financial markets exist in part because of differing opinions based on, among other things, agents' different access to, or interpretation of, information. In this case, the publication of some information, such as positioning data, might simply exacerbate herding and/or discourage investor diversity.

Here it is useful to consider an alternative rationale for herding activity other than the informational cascades theory discussed earlier – the compensation of fund managers. Given that managers are rewarded on the basis of relative performance, it is often costly (quite literally) for them to go 'against' the market. In such cases, the release of information on the positions of other players in the market, or even from which positions, could be detrimental. It would merely make it easier to become 'part of the crowd', thereby increasing the tendency to herd, which in turn might actually increase market instability. This is not to argue that disclosure is in some way a bad thing, but at its limit some informational asymmetries may not be the negative factor they are often assumed to be.

Going back to the example of Argentina, for example, some might even argue that the level of disclosure was excessive. As Avinash Persaud (2000),[7] notes, the publication of daily reserves can often add to the dangers of herding behaviour on the part of investors. Falling reserves simply signal to market participants that other investors are leaving the country. In the specific case of Argentina, it is interesting to note that, using ten years of historic data, we find that the volatility of percentage changes in published monthly reserves has become significantly greater since the central bank also began to publish its reserves on a daily basis in 1996. This is an avenue of research we intend to explore further.

Conclusion

Improved information flows have enabled, and will continue to enable, investors to allocate capital more efficiently. This, however, does not appear to warrant the central role of information in crisis prevention. First, markets are as prone to crisis now as they ever were, even though there has undoubtedly been some improvement in information flows. Second, markets can sometimes turn 'a blind eye' to information during bubbles. And finally, at its limit, if better disclosure ultimately reduces the diversity of investor opinion, this could actually contribute to greater financial instability.

Appendix 10.1

The equation below presents the results of the following panel regression:

$$Vol_{it} = Constant + ROSC_{it}$$

where Vol_{it} is the volatility of foreign demand for country I's equities at time t and $ROSC_{it}$ is the number of ROSCs published by that country at time t:

$$Vol_{it} - 3.33 - 0.081\ ROSC_{it} \qquad\qquad R\text{-squared } 0.01$$

(9.86) (−0.73) T–Statistics in parenthesis

Notes

1 This chapter expresses the views of the authors alone and not of State Street Bank and Trust Company.
2 For example, Shiller (2000: 71) writes, 'The history of speculative bubbles begins roughly with the advent of newspapers. Although the news media … along with their outlets on the Internet present themselves as detached observers of market events, they are themselves an integral part of these events.'
3 For further details on methodology, see Bank of England, 'Financial Stability Review' December 2001, box 3.
4 Argentina, Brazil, Chile, Colombia, Czech Republic, Hong Kong, Egypt, Hungary, India, Indonesia, Israel, Korea, Malaysia, Mexico, Pakistan, Peru, Philippines, Poland, South Africa, Taiwan, Thailand, Turkey and Venezuela.
5 Such as the Opacity Index developed by PriceWaterhouseCoopers which is intended to measure transparency in accounting, regulation, the legal system, economic policy and bureaucratic corruption.
6 By measuring cross-border flows in this way, we overcome the potential bias that large markets will receive greater inflows.
7 Winner of Jacques de Larosière award for *Essays on Global Finance*.

References

Asian Development Bank (1997) *Emerging Asia: Changes and Challenges*, Manila: Asian Development Bank.

Eichengreen, Barry and Michael Bordo (2002) *Crises Now and Then: What Lessons from the Last Era of Financial Globalisation?*, NBER Working Paper 8716, Cambridge, Mass.: NBER.

Gaston Gelos, R. and Shang-Jin Wei (2002) *Transparency and International Investor Behaviour*, IMF Working Paper, Washington, DC: IMF.

IMF (1999) *Experimental Report on Transparency and Practices: Argentina*, Washington, DC: IMF.

Persaud, Avinash (2000) 'Sending the Herd off the Cliff Edge', in A. Persaud, *Essays on Global Finance*, Washington, DC: Institute of International Finance.

Shiller, R (2000) *Irrational Exuberance*, Princeton, NJ: Princeton University Press.

11
Filling the Information Gap: The Role of the Private Sector

Michael Bates

Introduction

The straight response to the question; 'Can the provision of information by the private sector fill the gap?' is 'No'. The private sector can provide the vehicle for conveying large amounts of complex information in a user-friendly form, but it cannot on its own fill the information gap. Ultimately, it is only through a commitment to transparency and disclosure by governments that information on the implementation of standards and codes can be made more widely available.

Indeed, it was this gap in the availability of reliable information that precipitated the series of financial crises in the 1990s – most notably as far as standards and codes are concerned, the Asian crisis. In 1997, rumours circulated in the capital markets of previously undisclosed foreign-exchange liabilities which, if true, would have led to a complete erosion of foreign-exchange reserves. The resulting loss of confidence and panic accelerated capital outflows and magnified the financial crisis of the country concerned, resulting in regional and global contagion effects. Weak regulation and lack of transparency of national financial systems, particularly relative to commercial banks, caused insolvencies, requiring massive government bailouts (for example, in Korea, Japan, Indonesia, Thailand and Brazil). The consequent cessation of normal bank credit and financial services flows to businesses and individuals caused severe domestic recessions (Vojta, 2001).

It was against this backdrop of a severe lack of market confidence in the reliability of information in developing countries and emerging markets that, on 15 September 1999, the Financial Stability Forum established an *ad hoc* Task Force on the Implementation of Standards under the chairmanship of Andrew Sheng. While the purpose of the task force initially was to look at strengthening systems in emerging and developing economies with a view to encouraging the engagement of the private sector in providing market incentives, only four of the 22-member Task Force represented emerging markets, and there was no private-sector representation. In their *Issues Paper* prepared for the Meeting of the Financial Stability Forum on 25–26 March 2000, the following observations were made:

- A strong sense of country ownership – including political commitment – is critical for fostering successful implementation. That ownership must extend beyond governments and central banks. Implementation can be encouraged but not enforced from outside.
- Substantial human and financial resources will be required from the official sector national authorities, international financial institutions such as the World Bank and the International Monetary Fund, and standard-setting bodies to support the implementation effort.
- Disseminating information on progress in the observance of standards is critical if there is to be any prospect of making market or official incentives work.
- Standards are not an end in themselves but a means of promoting sound financial systems and sustained economic growth.

Official sector information flows

While 2001–2 have seen considerable efforts by the Reports on Observance of Standards and Codes (ROSC) teams at the Bank and Fund to undertake assessments, as of May 2002 only fifty-three countries out of the 180 member countries had been assessed. Moreover, the majority of these assessments have focused on the three macroeconomic fundamentals: standards of data dissemination; monetary transparency; and fiscal policy transparency. Of the 141 modules published by May 2002, seventy-two fell into these three subject areas. Conversely, only ten modules had been published in the standard areas of insolvency and creditor rights, accounting and auditing, and corporate governance. In the wake of the ENRON and WorldCom scandals in the United States, these standards of institutional and market infrastructure have taken on an even greater significance for private-sector investors and official regulators.

Timeliness of information is critical for private-sector confidence. The lack of 'substantial' resources identified as necessary by the FSF is a constraint to the wider consideration of information on standards and codes by the private sector. Even if the Bank and the Fund were to publish 100 modules per year, it would still take them eighteen years to complete all ten module areas (twelve standards and codes) for each of their 180 member countries. Part of this gap is being addressed by publishing more Financial Sector Assessment Programme (FSAP) reports. Moreover, the current rota system leaves some glaring anomalies – for example the last set of ROSC modules to be conducted for Argentina covering banking supervision, data dissemination, fiscal transparency, and monetary and financial policy transparency are dated 15 April 1999. The response to this 'timeliness gap' may rest with the private sector, but a more feasible solution might involve the member countries themselves undertaking self-assessments on an annual basis. These self-assessments could then be audited by the international financial institutions and in some cases by the standard-setting bodies.

The role of the private sector

It is appropriate to mention certain concerns that exist between the private and the official sectors, on the one hand, and the developed and the developing economies, on the other. The initial discussion paper from the FSF Task Force rightly stressed the need for a sense of ownership in the global financial system. It is assumed that a robust global financial system that is less vulnerable to shocks is in the interests of both the private and the official sectors, and developed and developing countries alike. Each will therefore have an interest in advancing the adoption of financial standards and codes. Their motivations may be, at the same time, both enlightened self-interest and a global common interest. For example, a developing country may seek to adopt international standards and codes as a means of promoting sound domestic financial systems and sustained economic growth. As the British Chancellor of the Exchequer, Gordon Brown (2001) put it:

> Having worked to establish a framework of codes and standards, it is essential that we work closely with developing and lower income countries to help them meet the benchmarks and access international capital markets from a solid foundation. Technical assistance and support is crucial to assure that no country is left behind in our efforts to raise standards globally.

Undoubtedly, in the field of standards and codes we are likely to witness swifter adoption and implementation if the emphasis is placed on the 'self-interest' side of the equation. Moreover, while developed countries have promoted this path as a means of insulating their financial systems from currency crises in emerging markets, the loss of confidence by investors in accounting standards in the USA, banking standards in Japan, and corporate governance standards in the European Union, means that the dividing line of adherence to standards and codes does not run conveniently between the developed and developing world.

The private sector continues to express some reservations about the timeliness and transparency of data. For example, under the ROSC programmes, countries must volunteer to be assessed and then have the right to edit, or indeed block publication of, the final report. This is no criticism of the Bank–Fund staff but rather reflects the fact that the Bank and Fund consist of the member countries.

Meanwhile, as the official sector continues to monitor the activities of the private sector with a wary eye, the FSF Task Force (2000) report articulates these concerns.

While it would be useful to leverage private sector expertise given official resource constraints, there are several issues to be addressed:

- In some areas, the willingness of national authorities to undergo assessments by internationally recognised bodies may not extend to private-sector experts or institutions for confidentiality reasons.
- The private sector's ability to assess observance of standards, particularly those dealing with policy transparency, and supervision and regulation, is limited at this stage due to the evolving nature of most international standards and codes.
- Private-sector involvement poses difficult issues related to conflicts of interest and privileged access to information that could result in unfair market advantage.

The concerns expressed by the private and official sectors are legitimate. However, the private sector needs the official sector because of its access to information and knowledge of particular standards and codes. And the official sector needs the private sector to provide a market incentive for the implementation of standards and codes through differentiated credit ratings, borrowing spreads, asset allocations, and other lending and investment decisions. Moreover, it could be argued that under the second point above concerning the private sector's ability to assess the observance of standards and codes, this may be the case in so far as macroeconomic fundamentals are concerned, but in areas relating to institutional and market infrastructure the standard-setting bodies and the private sector might be better placed to undertake assessments.

If the adoption of standards and codes is to achieve the FSF's ambition of spreading beyond governments and central banks, then the private sector must become increasingly involved. If this is to be the case, then the 'governance gap' in the current operation of standards and codes needs to be addressed by establishing a body which engages with the private sector and standard-setting bodies on the basis not of consultation but of real partnership and trust. Such a body could receive flows of information from the private sector which may be used to augment official-sector self-assessments and target better technical assistance. An international body could be replicated at national level to provide symmetry in the new financial architecture.

eStandardsForum

Project background

eStandardsForum is a private company organised and funded by George Vojta, recently retired vice-chairman of Bankers Trust and president of the Financial Services Forum. In 1999, Vojta envisaged a private-sector resource that would provide a comprehensive database of information on how individual countries were performing with regard to the observance of the twelve international standards and codes identified by the FSF. During a career in international finance stretching over forty years, he had become convinced of the need for reform of the international financial architecture towards greater transparency across internationally agreed standards and codes.

eStandardsForum identifies, aggregates and interprets third-party assessments in order to provide a single and easy-to-use source of information on standards implementation. The database, which has been created in a strategic partnership with Oxford Analytica, now contains eighty-three completed country assessments across all twelve international standards and codes recommended by the FSF. The emphasis has been placed on creating a user-friendly site which enables the user to drill down from a summary of the country's overall position to the actual document on which the assessment is based.

The Internet and transparency

The importance of the Internet to the eStandardsForum project, and to improving the transparency of information on financial governance, cannot be overstated. Most countries now have well developed central bank websites into which self-assessments and announcements can be placed. For the small number of least developed countries whose central banks do not have functioning websites, this should be the first target of international technical assistance. Although more contentious, wherever possible there should be an English-language version of documents relating to financial standards and codes.

Methodology

The methodology adopted for the eStandardsForum project established from the outset the importance of using only publicly available information sources as the basis for assessment. Markets will always have a degree of suspicion if assessments are based on off-the-record verbal assurances of intent or adherence. Moreover, the potential for inaccurate assessments is increased when verbal briefings are used. Therefore the ability to provide the user not only with an assessment but also with access to the actual documentation on which it is based, be it from the country itself or from the report of an international standard-setting body, is a key strength of the database.

Because the sole purpose of the country assessments is to convey accurately to the user the current situation regarding the twelve international standards and codes, a key part of the methodology involves the distribution of draft versions of the assessment to the central bank and Ministry of Finance of each country concerned. It has been our experience that the vast majority of countries approached have taken these assessments seriously, and in many cases this has led to previously private information being released into the public domain to confirm assessments.

Addressing private-sector needs

It is important for the eStandardsForum project to address the timeliness requirement of the private sector. As such, central banks, standard-setting bodies, regulators and international financial institutions are encouraged to include eStandardsForum in the distribution of announcements relating to standards and codes. Since its inception, eStandardsForum has circulated to subscribers a weekly report that carries notification of changes in country assessments, and of regulatory developments as they relate to standards and codes. The increase in the scope and quantity of material included in the weekly report over the period 2000–2 is evidence of the heightened level of activity in this area, as well as the drive towards implementation. It is also worth noting the expansion in the number of routine announcements made by developing countries on matters relating to the implementation of internationally agreed standards and codes.

While standards and codes are an important indicator of market health and transparency, they must be placed in context. It is for this reason that the database includes a substantial section looking at 'qualitative factors', which include a country's economic model, foreign-exchange regulations, foreign-investment law, trade regulations, the tax regime, bankruptcy indicators, international dispute settlement, the political environment and stability, the corruption level, the adherence to global labour standards, and sovereign credit ratings. It is the view of eStandardsForum that only through a combination of indicators will a user be in a position to develop a coherent picture of risk in each country.

At this stage, eStandardsForum has resisted market pressures to produce a rating based on the extensive data collected in the site. While official-sector clients have welcomed the depth and comprehensiveness of the coverage, the private sector has expressed the view that the qualitative judgements cannot easily be incorporated into quantitative risk models. The view held by eStandardsForum is that the lack of thorough market diligence has contributed to poor investment and lending decisions which have, in turn, exacerbated international financial crises. The preferred solution to this problem would be that the rating agencies, investment managers and credit risk managers incorporate more qualitative information into their risk assessments.

A tool for developing countries

While eStandardsForum is a private-sector initiative, the database carries significant value as a tool for developing countries:

Assessing financial system strength

First, the database can be used to assist countries in assessing the overall strengths and weaknesses of their domestic financial systems, and their macro-policy framework. This is important, not only to increase the amounts of portfolio or foreign direct investment in the country concerned, but also to increase domestic confidence in the integrity of the financial system. There is considerable evidence that capital from wealthy individuals in developing countries is transferred to banks in the West because of a lack of confidence in domestic savings and banking arrangements. The first step in development must be to secure the confidence of the resident population, as this source of capital is likely to be less volatile.

Benchmarking

Second, the database can be used for peer review. Much is made of the downside of international standards and codes being a 'one-size-fits-all' solution for financial governance. By using the database to benchmark country performance against a group of similar economies, a fairer measurement of progress can be achieved.

Determining technical assistance needs

Third, the database can be used to target technical assistance. By being able to view the progress of a region in the implementation of standards or codes, it should enable providers of technical assistance to ensure that resources are better targeted. In addition, there could be economies of scale by providing technical assistance jointly to groups of countries within the same region with similar needs. The role of eStandardsForum as a tool for providers of technical assistance to developing countries was a principal objective in its establishment.

Conclusion

Few would suggest that progress towards the globalisation of financial markets is likely to slow or retreat in the next decade. If there is to be a further expansion of global trade, there will be a further expansion of global finance to facilitate it. The more integrated the financial markets become, the greater the demand for internationally agreed standards and regulation. If developing countries fail to participate in the move towards international standards and codes, the gap between rich and poor will continue to widen.

The recent UN conference in Monterrey highlighted the role of private finance in achieving the Millennium Goal of reducing by half the proportion of the global population living on less than one dollar a day by 2015. Optimistically, official development assistance may rise to US$50 billion. On the other hand, net private capital flows (direct investment, portfolio investment and bank lending) to emerging markets in 2001 amounted to US$160 billion (Institute of International Finance, 2002), while trade in goods and services amounts to around US$1.5 trillion annually.

Such figures point to the inability of official sector assistance to fill the financing gap. If this problem is to be addressed effectively, then it will be through developing countries putting in place transparent local markets and robust governance. Such moves will strengthen the confidence of the domestic population in the integrity of their financial systems and governments, assist government authorities to prepare credible development strategies, and increase the confidence of international business, international capital and international institutions.

The private sector has a strong interest in the overall stability of the global financial architecture. The private sector also requires timely and authoritative information. Where there is no information, participants are more likely to listen to rumour and conjecture. Initially, it must be individual countries that take the lead in reforming their domestic markets and governance systems out of enlightened self-interest. The secondary responsibility is to make information available in a timely way under guidance from the standard-setting bodies and the international financial institutions.

References

Brown, Gordon (2001) Speech by UK Chancellor of the Exchequer, IMF/World Bank Spring Meeting.

FSF Task Force (2000) *Issues Paper on Implementation of Standards*, Washington, DC: IMF, 15 March.

Institute of International Finance (2002) *Capital Flows to Emerging Market Economies*, Washington, DC.

Vojta, George J. (2001) 'Global Standards: The Path to an Improved Financial System', *Central Banking*, August.

12
Standards and Codes: Firing at the Wrong Target?

David Lubin

The intense level of activity regarding standards and codes that can be seen in the official sector is not especially evident in the private sector. Among private-sector investors and analysts there is, by and large, a rather high degree of indifference or ignorance about the standards and codes (S&C) effort. Should anyone be bothered by this ignorance? After all, one might argue that there are plenty of official-sector initiatives, aimed at building a stronger infrastructure for international capital markets, of which the private sector is barely aware, and that is just how it should be. The driver of a car, after all, needs to know little about the underlying engineering that makes the vehicle move efficiently. The question then, is whether the private sector's ignorance of S&C is any different from this. If not, fine. If it is different, it might be worth asking why the private sector chooses not to embrace the S&C exercise more enthusiastically.

Although it is quite likely that some of the private sector's ignorance about standards and codes is the same as the ignorance of the car driver, there are a couple of other explanations which suggest that the private sector's disregard for S&C may reflect some underlying problems with the initiative. In the first place, it is possible to argue that the standards and codes do not help the private sector do its job properly. In order for international capital to be allocated efficiently, what is required is that private investors assess risk correctly, and the private sector's interest in S&C is likely to depend on how the initiative helps it to achieve this. Supporters of standards and codes will argue that the initiative is designed precisely to help improve the assessment of risk – for example, by encouraging countries to improve data transparency. The idea here is that S&C will not only help to improve the private sector's ability to assess risk by offering more information to the market, but will also help to improve countries' creditworthiness, by making it more difficult for policy-makers to hide bad policies. Yet the relationship between transparency and creditworthiness is not necessarily a straightforward one. Although it is likely to be true that a high degree of transparency enhances creditworthiness, it is not *obviously* true. Countries with a high degree of creditworthiness will tend to be more transparent, either because they have nothing to 'hide' or because they have greater institutional capacity to meet standards and codes requirements. In that sense, transparency is a function of creditworthiness. Equally, countries with low degrees of creditworthiness and high degrees of transparency may not benefit from the transparency, particularly if all that the transparency does is to focus the market's attention on the low level of creditworthiness! If it is true that the relationship between transparency and creditworthiness is not a straightforward one, then the problem might just be that the private sector does not quite know what to do with the information coming out of the S&C process. In other words, a country that increases its transparency does not necessarily improve its creditworthiness. For this reason, the value that the private sector places on transparency may not be that high.

Another way of explaining the private sector's disregard for standards and codes is that there may be a perception that the S&C effort is somehow firing at the wrong target. In other words, that the effort itself is irrelevant to the private sector's real job of assessing risk, whether it be default risk or currency risk. If the private sector has a case for thinking that the S&C effort is essentially irrelevant to its task of assessing risk, then that would be a fairly serious indictment of standards and codes. The most notorious piece of evidence in favour of the private sector's cynicism on this issue is the 1999 Report on Codes and Standards for Argentina, which famously praised the Argentine government not only on its high degree of transparency, but also on its policy framework, particularly with respect to financial sector soundness. At this point the cynic says: 'If Argentina could win plaudits for its adherence to standards and codes eighteen months before it needed a $40-odd billion bailout, then there must be something wrong with the codes and standards.'

A more robust way of stating the problem is as follows. What the private sector really needs to do well is to assess financial vulnerability in emerging markets. Yet vulnerability does not reside primarily in the level of transparency a country chooses to adopt, nor does it lie in the quality of a country's market infrastructure or market supervision. That is not to say that these things have *no* influence on a country's vulnerability. But in the main it is possible to argue that the major source of vulnerability for emerging markets lies in the *quality of the national foreign-exchange balance sheet*. And on this critical issue the S&C effort is almost silent. Of course, a high level of transparency helps the private sector to find information about the national balance sheet. But it may be that the S&C will need to tackle balance-sheet quality issues more explicitly if financial stability is genuinely to be enhanced.

One way of summarising the emerging-markets crises since the mid-1990s is that they have all resulted from weaknesses in a country's *foreign-exchange balance sheet*: either because a country has too much short-term external debt relative to its ability to generate foreign exchange (Argentina); or because it has too much short-term external debt unhedged by foreign-exchange assets (Mexico, Asia, Russia, Brazil, Turkey).[1]

If it is true that weak balance sheets are at the heart of emerging-markets crises, then official-sector efforts to minimise the frequency of crises should aim explicitly at improving the quality of national balance sheets. As long as standards and codes fail to address explicitly these issues of balance-sheet quality in emerging markets, they might well continue to be perceived by the private sector as being an essentially irrelevant part of the international financial architecture.

The question, then, is: how can balance-sheet adequacy be embraced explicitly within the S&C debate? One possible answer is that the official sector establishes a framework whose aim is to define *acceptable levels* for a country's foreign-exchange balance sheet. We already have some internationally used 'rules of thumb' that help us to do this. The 'Guidotti rule', for example, suggests that a prudent central bank should have foreign-exchange reserves as least as large as the country's short-term external debt. The question is whether there should be a more formalised set of rules that cover emerging markets' balance sheets. Ultimately, this would involve the official sector coming up with a workable definition of 'debt sustainability' which middle-income developing countries would be expected to meet in order to qualify for official lending. The object of the exercise would be to focus both borrowers and lenders on the structure of the borrowing country's balance sheet, since a balance sheet that is at risk of being defined as 'unsustainable' ought to do two things: it should act as an incentive for the developing-country policy-maker to adjust to any imbalances rather than seek to finance them; and it should act as a disincentive for lenders to extend further credit to a country whose access to official resources may be constrained by virtue of its overindebtedness.

Although this approach may be controversial, it is not completely unprecedented. The Maastricht criteria, for example, set explicit caps on the accumulation of government debt for countries wishing to be part of the European Monetary Union. Equally, the Heavily Indebted Poor Countries (HIPC) initiative defines 'debt sustainability' for low-income countries by setting a cap on external debt in relation to exports or government revenues. What we have here are examples of where the international community has arrived at commonly accepted definitions of sustainable debt, for very rich countries (Maastricht) and for very poor countries (HIPC). What we lack is some definition of sustainable debt for middle-income developing countries that have access to international capital markets. There is already some evidence that this kind of thinking exists in the official sector. Haldane and Kruger (2001), for example, note that 'if a country's debt burden is not sustainable, then the provision of official finance risks worsening a country's financial position: the solution to the country's problem is less debt, not more'.

If this makes sense, then the remaining task is to define a 'sustainable debt burden' for middle-income developing countries. There are undoubtedly huge problems associated with this kind of exercise. While it is outside the scope of these comments to enumerate them, one noteworthy obstacle is the difficulty in dealing with the complex interaction between a country's external debt burden and its public-sector's domestic debt burden. Take Brazil, for example. The clearest way of making a case that Brazil has an unsustainable debt burden is to point to the size of Brazil's overall external debt in relation to its exports: Brazil's ratio of external debt to exports is something over 300 per cent. This may or may not be sustainable, yet any conclusions one would make about the sustainability of this debt stock would be quite different were it not for the fact that the Brazilian public sector also has a relatively large domestic debt burden, the bulk of which is linked either to the short-term interest rate or the exchange rate. The point is that the presence of this large *domestic* debt burden constrains the policy options available to the government to adjust to the *external* debt burden.

The unsurprising conclusion is that it is no simple matter to assess 'debt sustainability' for emerging-market borrowers. Yet at the same time it is true by definition that a developing country that suffers a financial crisis has, in some respect, an unsustainable debt burden. In view of this, the official sector might do well to focus more resources on the analysis of sustainable debt for middle-income developing countries. It is a concept widely in use in other parts of the international financial system, and there is no particular reason why it should not be applied to emerging-market borrowers. And if the S&C effort is to achieve its goal of minimising the risk of crisis in emerging markets, then it might be appropriate for 'debt sustainability analysis' to become a more central part of its work.

Note

1   The essential role of balance sheets in analysing vulnerability is now being acknowledged in the official sector (see Keller *et al.*, 2002).

References

Haldane, Andy and Mark Kruger (2001) 'The Resolution of International Financial Crises: Private Finance and Public Funds', *Bank of England Financial Stability Review*, December.
Keller, Christian, Cristoph Rosenberg, Nouriel Roubini and Brad Setser (2002) 'The Bottom Line', *Finance and Development*, December.

Part IV
Invited Commentary

13
International Standards and Codes – Comments on Emerging Issues

Y. V. Reddy[1]

The Overseas Development Institute is to be complimented on holding a 'Conference on International Codes and Standards: The Developing Country Perspectives' in June 2002 at the Commonwealth Secretariat in London. The objective of these comments is primarily to analyse the issues that have emerged in the process of developing, implementing, assessing and monitoring the international standards and codes (S&C), as well as the greater insights that are available now in matters relating to financial stability, while drawing heavily but not exclusively on the chapters in this book and deliberations at the conference. After outlining the background to the initiatives on S&C, the second section of this chapter focuses on the relevant policies and institutions in terms of domestic *vis-à-vis* international dimensions: the significance of S&C in crisis prevention and the role of the Bretton Woods institutions (BWIs). Next comes a discussion of the processes of formulation, implementation, monitoring and updating of S&C, followed by an explanation of the links with the private sector. The concluding section provides an agenda for further debate and research.

Background

It is useful to recognise that the international standards and codes in themselves are not new. There are, however, five important features of their development that emerged as a global initiative in 1998: namely, it is part of the reform of the international financial architecture; it represents a consolidated view of several interrelated standards and codes; it is a collaborative effort involving different groups of countries, markets and international financial institutions, and standard-setting bodies; it has elements of both external and internal assessment of degrees of compliance; and, finally, there is an assumption of a link between the implementation of standards and codes, and financial stability. It is essential to recognise that the integrated thrust towards S&C was primarily in response to the Asian crisis and because of the global concerns relating to financial stability within and across countries in an increasingly integrated financial world. Two defining events with regard to S&C were the establishment of the Financial Stability Forum (FSF) in April 1999 under the auspices of the Bank for International Settlements (BIS), and the introduction of the Financial Sector Assessment Programme (FSAP) in May 1999 by the IMF/World Bank to strengthen monitoring of the financial systems in the context of the IMF's bilateral surveillance and the World Bank's financial sector development work. Several forums, including the G-24 and the G-20, the IMFC, and the Development Committee have been involved closely in the processes, in addition to bilateral initiatives such as that by the UK Department for International Development to take the process further. At the time of writing, these initiatives have been in operation for nearly four years and it would be useful to assess the extent of this progress, relevance and usefulness, with special reference to the perspectives of developing countries. The chapters in this book, written by experts in the area of multilateral bodies, developed countries, emerging economy market participants, and academics, provide an excellent overview of developments, experiences and perceptions that reflect emerging issues. A critical examination of issues as they emerge, primarily from these chapters, should provide a useful framework for the way forward.

Chapter 2, by Benu Schneider, provides an excellent overview of the origins of S&C as well as later developments, and an exhaustive account of emerging issues with regard to S&C. In the background section she makes a telling point about the two major lessons from East Asia – namely, that the health of both internal and external balance sheets is important in all sectors of the economy, be it the central bank, the government or the private sector; and regarding the role of information in the smooth functioning of international financial markets, the lack of which often leads to contagion and herding behaviour by international investors. Unfortunately, as subsequent events have demonstrated, much of the attention and effort of the international community has been devoted to countries external balance sheets and improvements in the public sector, especially in developing countries, with the result that the dimensions of domestic debt in emerging-market countries, the behaviour of the private sector in developed countries, and the functioning of international financial markets as a whole proved to be major sources of instability. One can argue that the contagion has been contained and the resilience of economies has improved, while market participants have become more discerning, but these are events which may or may not be attributable to exercises on S&C.

A second notable point made by Schneider is that self-assessments are not collected systematically by any international organisation, and information about them is often difficult to obtain, though some is available through private initiatives. In this regard, an interesting issue to be explored is whether multilateral bodies should be mandated to recognise and encourage such self-assessments and, instead of being viewed as biased, they should be regarded as solid foundations both for the ownership of improvements/compliance and for independent domestic or external assessments. Schneider's third important point is that implementation of S&C is of interest to a country only if it intends to borrow from the private financial market, or bilateral or multilateral official sources. She also makes a reference to 'original sin', namely, developing countries are faced with exchange-risk impacts on their balance sheets because they almost always borrow in a foreign currency. It is not perhaps appropriate to link S&C too closely with external debt alone and, in any case, once a country adopts open capital accounts, it becomes difficult to distinguish the consequences of domestic-currency-denominated and foreign-currency-denominated debt, particularly if the significant holders of domestic debt are non-residents.

Finally, there should be no difficulty in concurring with Schneider's list of open questions, though they may be neither exhaustive nor of equal significance. In particular, an important but relatively under-debated open question is the case for separating the function of monitoring S&C from the lending operations of multilateral institutions, but then the additional question of such monitoring being equated with rating needs to be recognised.

Policies and institutions

Standards and codes moved to the global agenda after the East Asian crisis – a move that is related to the two explanations that dominated the literature – namely, domestic and international. Andrew Walter's explains, in Chapter 6, that initially views were polarised, but over a period there has been harmonisation of positions, the emerging consensus accepting both elements of explanation. However, we need to note that academics took time to accept the twin explanations that had been evident among practitioners. For example, on 1 May 1998, in an address on the 'The Asian Crisis: Asking the Right Questions', I described ten of the domestic and external factors (five factors for each) explaining the Asian crisis, and pointed out that 'Perhaps it is appropriate to accept that both domestic and external factors were to be blamed, though it is difficult to assign precise weights to each of these factors.'

The question of domestic versus international factors in the Asian crisis, or more generally in the approach to measures for crisis prevention, is an important issue with regard to the relevance and significance of S&C. In any event, to the extent that the diagnosis of the crisis gave more weight to domestic factors, a correspondingly greater emphasis on S&C was justified; but if the diagnosis has altered, so should the dosage of medicine. Furthermore, as the package of measures for crisis prevention contained domestic measures such as S&C, and international measures affecting the governance as well as the functioning of the international finance institutions, the progress in implementation should ideally be synchronised. It is agreed that there has been little progress in the Contingent Credit Line Facilities of the IMF, private-sector involvement and so on. Thus there is an influential view – for example, in UNTCAD – that efforts such as S&C have focused mainly on disciplining debtor countries, while the root of the problem lies in the failure to establish a stable system of exchange rates after the breakdown of the Bretton Woods arrangements. In brief, the relative weights to be attached to the domestic and international dimensions of crisis prevention as well as crisis mitigation need to be revisited in view of more recent developments, and thus proceed to redefine the role of S&C in the package of measures.

With regard to the role of S&C in crisis prevention, it needs to be recognised that the link between the two has never been argued convincingly on theoretical grounds, and has also not been established empirically, either in the context of the Asian crisis or of subsequent developments, though on first principles or intuitively the link seems to be appealing. Furthermore, the multiple causes, which may vary from country to country, or situation to situation, involve several participants. For example, with regard to the Asian crisis, there appears to be little doubt that it was caused by the failure of the private sector rather than the public sector, and the failure was related more to the financial system than to fiscal or monetary policy. Furthermore, it was a failure of global financial markets to ensure an optimal allocation of global capital. And, finally, it was also a failure of regulatory systems in developing countries, major financial centres and global institutions. Hence, actions taken with regard to one set of causes through S&C, with no corresponding action to address the other sets of causes, cannot resolve the issues of crisis prevention adequately. Moreover, the relative importance of S&C in crisis prevention must also be judged from the point of view of the relative openness of the economy's capital account and its overall external orientation. Among those which are relatively open, it has to be recognised that the level of market confidence in some countries, particularly developed countries, may have less correlation with S&C than in others. Similarly, with regard to emerging-market countries, the financial markets may tend to be pro-cyclical by their very nature and hence not closely linked to S&C.

One should not overlook the link between macroeconomic policy and transparency, and it is possible to make general observations about such a link. Good macroeconomic policy and transparency are perhaps an ideal situation for a country. Good macroeconomic policy and poor transparency, though not ideal, are perhaps not risky in themselves. Bad macroeconomic policy and good transparency have large elements of risk, and warrant a change in policy before launching into transparency. But the most risky combination, perhaps, is bad macroeconomic policy and bad transparency. In a more dynamic sense, it can be argued that transparency provides incentives to adopt good macroeconomic policies.

The major institutions for assessing, monitoring and enabling the adoption of S&C are the Bretton Woods institutions. Aziz Ali Mohammed, in Chapter 3, provides a comprehensive and insightful account of the work on S&C being done by the BWIs. In particular, the conclusions that deserve to be noted are: while developing countries have generally welcomed the role of the BWIs in S&C, the nature of the tasks makes it difficult for the BWIs to respond to a number of their concerns; while the BWIs endeavoured to avoid any coercive element in their assessment work, it became necessary, under certain circumstances, to exert a degree of pressure even when they were not always convinced of the benefits relative to costs; and finally, the desire of the BWIs to interest private market participants in their S&C work has generated apprehensions that they are seeking to impose a market discipline to supplement their own.

There are three particularly noteworthy observations in Mohammed's chapter – namely, that the BWIs in their assessment are serving conflicting audiences, such as member authorities who are expecting advice, and market participants seeking assessments; that while S&C do not strictly mean conditionality, they have already become an element of 'informing' surveillance; and that the BWIs' involvement in the AML/CFT areas continues to be contentious in terms of whether the subjects are consistent with their mandates. These are concerns which need to be addressed effectively by the BWIs, and perhaps the G-24 might play a leading role in suggesting appropriate processes.

Javier Guzmán's case study of the Mexican experience, in Chapter 5, is very apt and instructive. Specifically, the Mexican authorities' decision to ask for a FSAP in 2001 responded to a combination of objectives, mainly to capture the expertise of the Fund and the Bank for an external objective examination of the financial system to help in its series of reforms, while at the same time sending a message of transparency to the international community consistent with the commitment among the G-20 member countries to undertake a FSAP. The timing coincided with complete absorption in the banking crisis of 1994–5 and the consequent effort to reform. Guzmán confirms that the FSAP was useful because of its inputs in the financial reform measures, and the help it gave to the authorities in reviewing the strengths and weaknesses of the financial system on the basis of an international point of reference.

It is interesting to note the similarity in approach of the Mexican authorities and of India as described in Chapter 4 by T.C.A. Anant. The Indian approach to implementation of financial standards and codes is based on their efficiency-enhancing elements, and on the need to consider them as part of the process of institutional development in the country, while not ignoring their relevance to domestic as well as international financial stability. Thus they are viewed as an integral part of the process of economic reform, as appropriate to the country's needs. The emphasis is on creating awareness to promote their adoption by the relevant official agencies, self-regulating bodies and market participants rather than prescribing compliance at the instance of a central authority. The message seems to be clear; the role of S&C as reference points for the development of a country's financial system appears undeniably to be valuable, while their relevance to attaining financial stability is not free from questions.

Andrew Walter's Chapter 6, on the basis of a study of financial liberalisation and prudential regulation in East Asia in recent years, argues that a reform strategy based on formal convergence on S&C is the easy part, but the actual implementation is beset with problems of governance. More relevant to the BWIs, he contends that, despite the desire of such institutions to promote the implementation of financial governance in

East Asia, there are reasons to doubt that they have a strong interest in exposing the degree of implementation failure in the region. He further argues that this, in turn, casts doubt on their role as enforcers of S&C.

It is difficult to find evidence of the inadequate appreciation of implementation failures. However, to the extent that the BWIs encourage the formal adoption of S&C, and the markets perceive that such formal adoption is accompanied by an inadequate focus on implementation failures or governance issues, observation in Walter's chapter may be appropriate, but that the BWIs are indeed acutely conscious of the implementation issues is undeniable. This does not imply that the role of the BWIs has been less than adequate, but there is a continuing process of review by the IMF and the World Bank in an effort to improve the operationalisation of S&C.

In any event, two main messages emanate from Walter's chapter. First, there is the question of whether financial openness for some of the East Asian countries was premature and counter-productive. Second, a strong implication in Walter's comments is that domestic political and institutional factors are more important than external factors in explaining the degree of real convergence in regulatory governance.

Andrew Cornford's Appendix to the book captures comprehensively the latest developments, with regard to both the developments in financial centres and the work of the BWIs. It gives a succinct account of the latest status of work on the various S&C in a variety of forums, as well as commenting briefly on the limitations of several of these exercises. Some of the most pertinent questions Cornford raises need to be emphasised. First, to what extent have the new disclosure rules served as an effective warning system? Second, is there a danger of the IMF 'moving willy-nilly in the direction of assuming an increasing number of the functions of a global rating agency' in view of the additional work on macro-prudential analysis, as well as SDDS, FSAP and ROSCs. Third, is the work by the IMF–World Bank in a position to capture the implications of insolvency of a large firm with an extensive international network of entities?

Formulation, implementation, monitoring and updating

The contributions by Alastair Clark (Chapter 7) and Axel Nawrath (Chapter 8) display a full understanding of the processes of formulation and implementation of S&C, by virtue of their intimate association with the ongoing efforts in this regard under the auspices of the Financial Stability Forum. Clark mentions that, as far as the formulation of S&C is concerned, the two arguments of manageability and ownership tend to fall in opposite directions, but that this problem is being resolved satisfactorily. The additional issue of 'suitability' to country circumstances has been flagged up correctly in his chapter, but whether it is being resolved satisfactorily is a moot point. There is merit in pursuing this matter further. On the issue of implementation, Clark makes the significant observation that, at the level of principles, there is no difference between the developed and developing countries, while in regard to the appropriateness of different standards and problems of implementation, the latter do face challenges, including perhaps resource constraints. The issue of the trade-off for developing countries between the costs and benefits of implementing S&C ought to be addressed squarely – by both BWIs and the countries concerned.

Nawrath's insightful comments on external assessment versus self-assessment and the further updating of S&C deserve to be noted. He considers self-assessment to be an important first step, but it cannot replace external assessment by neutral parties, in particular the IMF and the World Bank. The questions that arise are: how far are the BWIs encouraging self-assessment as a first step. And is it not possible to have independent but domestic assessment rather than depend wholly on multilateral bodies? As recognised by the FSF Task Force on the Implementation of Standards, chaired by Andrew Sheng, 'A balance would need to be struck between international and domestic considerations.' It is possible to presume that external assessment will have greater awareness of, or orientation towards, the international dimension. It is also possible to presume that less-developed financial markets, or those less integrated with the rest of the world, will have more domestic orientation towards the S&C. It is against this background that a number of countries, such as India, have expressed concerns about the efforts of the international financial institutions to spearhead implementation. On the question of review, Nawrath is of the opinion that the bodies that established the S&C should review them. The question then arises as to why the respective standard-setting bodies themselves should not do the external assessment, and multilateral agencies such as the BWIs only consolidate or attempt an 'overview' or integrated view with primary inputs from the standard-setting bodies?

While significant attention has been paid to monitoring and updating the S&C by the BWIs or by standard-setting bodies, not much has been said about such arrangements at the national level. For example, the Report of the Standing Committee on International Financial Standards and Codes of India makes specific recommendations on institutional arrangements for ongoing assessment, on the basis of an initial assessment by Advisory Groups of all the core standards. It was indicated that the Reports of the Groups and the subsequent action could not be a one-off affair, nor could its implementation be turned into a strictly sequenced process. In view of this, it was felt to be desirable that some permanent mechanism be established for monitoring and evaluating follow-up, responding to new developments and co-ordinating with government, regulators, self-regulatory organisations and other market participants on a continuing basis. While the analogy of creating a domestic Financial Standards Forum would not be inappropriate, the responsibility of the proposed mechanism was to monitor both international and domestic developments in this regard and follow up with annual reports. It was suggested that, where required, non-official Advisory Groups, involving experts to assess and evaluate change, could be set up from time to time, and that, in this context, periodic reviews by independent experts would help in providing vital inputs for improved governance. An incidental benefit of such a formal structure was said to be in terms of promoting greater international awareness of efforts in these critical areas, as well as acting as a reference and pressure group for economic reform.

On the issue of prioritisation, it is agreed universally that this depends on the country concerned and the relevant circumstances. On detailing and implementing S&C, the IMF as an assessor categorises S&C into three groups: relating to (a) transparency; (b) supervision; and (c) market integrity. From the viewpoint of an assessee country, it is possible to classify the standards in a conceptual framework under three broad headings – namely, technical, policy and socio-cultural – though the dividing lines may be blurred. Standards such as Special Data Dissemination Standards (SDDS), accounting and auditing, and supervision may be classified as purely technical, and therefore, easily amenable to implementation. Standards on monetary and financial policies, fiscal transparency and securities regulation have certain policy implications and would form an integral part of the economic reform process in many developing countries. Changes in these areas depend on the timing, sequencing and complementarity in related areas, and the availability of institutional, technological and legal infrastructure. Nevertheless, while it is desirable to adopt these standards quickly, in fact it reduces to the issue of managing policy reforms in a non-disruptive fashion. Finally, standards in the areas of corporate governance, insurance, and to a certain extent insolvency and bankruptcy practices, take a socio-cultural dimension and pose challenges of design, adoption and implementation.

In view of the complexities in implementation, awareness of practical issues is critical to any meaningful assessment of, or advice on, S&C. Some of the issues already identified can be recalled here. First, while transparency and financial stability appear to be fundamentally complementary, there could be a trade-off at some point. Therefore, codes should be treated as milestones, and the exact manner and timing of the dissemination of information – including the structure of reporting – should depend not only on constitutional, legal and institutional mechanisms but also on the likely impact of that dissemination on the soundness and stability of the financial sector in a given context. Second, many codes emphasise legislative provisions in a concrete manner. Legislation provides the shield or back-up for such actions. The emphasis of codes should be on promoting a general effort to improve legislative provisions, and it is necessary to recognise that the process of legislation is time-consuming and complex.

Third, the implementation of monetary policy is centralised under a single authority, usually the central bank, while the implementation of financial policies pertaining to various sectors such as non-bank financial institutions, insurance, securities markets, and payments and settlement, may rest with different institutions. While standards and codes could be taken as an umbrella benchmark for all institutions, different aspects of implementation have to be dealt with separately for different sectors. This is necessary because the objectives of the institutions may differ fundamentally. Fourth, in implementing the codes, since there is a multiplicity of institutions or arrangements for regulating different segments of the financial sector such as insurance, banking, securities markets, and payments and settlement, the overall approach to covering different agencies in overlapping/grey areas of regulation becomes important.

Fifth, transparency practices are often addressed to financial agencies (regulatory authorities) that are not applicable to companies or other entities in the private sector. The emphasis on the implementation of standards and codes, and the accountability thereof, is still heavily concentrated in the official sector. There is some asymmetry here. An optimal balance between regulation and competitive efficiency in the financial system and in markets can be achieved only with an equal emphasis on the responsibility and accountability of the private sector. Sixth, finnancial agencies may be justified in not disclosing certain policy measures in progress, contingency plans, corrective actions, emergency lending decisions and supervisory or enforcement sections. The revelation of such information could be based upon case-by-case deliberations, and no standardisation is possible in such areas.

There may be a tendency to stress the legal aspects of standards and codes as an effective way of ensuring convergence among them, and this issue was addressed at a seminar on 'Legal and Regulatory Aspects of Financial Stability' held on 23 January 2002 at the Bank for International Settlements. One of the papers at the seminar emphasised the importance of the national law perspective, and indeed a legal framework was considered to be only one enabling factor. The complexities relating to the global financial system in the context of strong national interests continuing to dominate public policy, when viewed in the light of the Indian experience, warrant, more than a legal basis, emphasis on three aspects – namely (i) the standards may be set domestically with a recognition that they also have some international dimension; (ii) the processes of setting, prioritising, incentivising, monitoring and reorientating should be consultative and should embrace both domestic and international dimensions; and (iii) effective implementation is a complex and varied process, with the domestic legal framework being one enabling factor at this juncture.

Anant's chapter provides an overview of the process of implementation of S&C in India, and brings out clearly how the recommendations for action are not directed at mechanical compliance with the S&C but are focused on the adoption and delineation of pathways. The value of the chapter lies in distinguishing between legislative, institutional, regulatory, policy and procedural changes to illustrate the complexity of the process. Yet another point relates to interrelationships and overlaps between different S&C, as, for example, in the fiscal and monetary areas; in payments and settlement systems and the securities market; in corporate governance, banks and bankruptcy and so on. Three unexceptionable lessons are drawn from the overview: namely, there are no universally valid model codes; the accent should be on gradualism; and reform itself is a dynamic process requiring institutional support.

Links with the private sector

The involvement of the private sector in the formulation/implementation or monitoring of S&C has not been flagged up as an issue, though there have been arrangements by which some participation was ensured. While, operationally, the different information needs of the public and private sectors are recognised, and some parallel private initiatives are being taken to consolidate the assessments made, the major focus has been on the response of market participants to S&C. The chapters by Lionel Price (Chapter 9) and David Lubin (Chapter 12) are welcome contributions to the debate. Lubin argues that the private sector's 'disregard' for S&C may not be entirely caused by ignorance, but may reflect 'some underlying problems with the initiative'. One reason for the private sector's cynicism is said to be the fact that there has been a crisis in a country that was applauded for its transparency and policy framework, particularly with respect to financial sector soundness.

Second, the more telling point made is that S&C are an incorrect target, since the main source of vulnerability for emerging markets lies in the quality of the national foreign-exchange balance sheet, an issue on which S&C are silent. The argument reinforces the view that S&C have a greater developmental significance than for global stability. At a conceptual level the national balance sheet is recognised as being very useful, but at the same time its operational significance has been questioned. More importantly, with a relatively open capital account, the feasibility of computing the national foreign-exchange balance sheet and the policy instruments available to influence such a balance sheet, comes into question. The level of reserves would then perhaps be an important policy instrument.

The concept of a national balance sheet, of course, raises several tricky questions relating to private-sector foreign assets that offset liabilities, and the extent to which their foreign-exchange exposures fully capture their vulnerability. In spite of all these complexities involved in the national balance sheet approach, there is merit in exploring such an approach to provide guidance to policy relating to reserves, in terms of both adequacy and management. It is also necessary to examine whether the foreign-exchange balance sheets of various countries can be viewed in isolation. If the balance sheets of developed and emerging countries are aggregated to track the global balance sheet, there may be better scope for assessing imbalances in an objective fashion.

Third, on debt-sustainability analysis, as Lubin admits, 'it is no simple matter to assess debt-sustainability for emerging market borrowers'. Lubin concludes by arguing that, if the S&C effort is to achieve its goal of minimising the risk of crises in emerging markets, it might be appropriate for debt-sustainability analysis to become a more central part of its work. Indeed, the IMF has made debt-sustainability central to its work relating to surveillance. There is a strong message in Lubin's chapter about the link between the private sector and S&C initiatives.

Price in Chapter 9 focuses on the link between S&C and sovereign ratings. The main observations are that ratings do use SDDS and ROSCs, and some link, if not causality, can be found between transparency policies in terms of publishing ROSCs and ratings upgrades. Analytically, it is important to recognise that sovereign ratings are especially significant since regulators use them, and they are very closely related to debt. It is necessary, in analysing the link between sovereign ratings and S&C, whether or not coupled with publication, to recognise the unique features of sovereign ratings, and in particular the importance of geopolitical considerations affecting both sovereign rating and debt sustainability. As articulated by the Bank for International Settlements, sovereign rating differs from rating corporates in several ways. Sovereign ratings do not have a long track record, and the past record of sovereign defaults provides a less reliable guide to the assessment of risk than in the case of a corporate. The reasons for a corporate default are easier to discern, since there are legal structures that can seize assets and change management. There is possibly a greater element of judgement or human will in sovereign defaults, which leads to less predictability. The sovereign has the option, in extreme cases, of being able to access official sources for borrowings, but such a course of action is conditioned by non-economic factors. The responses of creditors to a potential sovereign default could also be different. While there are many common features between sovereign and corporate debt, there are three special factors in assessing the default probability of a sovereign – namely, the behaviour of the sovereign; of other official lenders; and of the creditors themselves.

Michael Bates' is perceptive in highlighting three relevant factors in Chapter 11. First, the issue of the observed 'timeliness gap' in providing assessments by the BWIs to the market participants, for which, according to him, a feasible solution 'might involve the member countries themselves undertaking self-assessment on an annual basis. These assessments could then be audited by the international financial institutions and in some cases by standard-setting bodies'. Second, there is the issue of the governance gap, on which Bates eloquently says:

> If the adoption of standards and codes is to achieve the FSF's ambition in spreading beyond governments and central banks, then the private sector must become increasingly involved. If this is to be the case then the 'governance gap' in the current operation of Standards and Codes needs to be addressed by establishing a body which engages with the private sector and standard-setting bodies on the basis not of consultation but of real partnership and trust. Such a body could receive flows of information from the private sector which may be used to augment official sector self-assessments and target technical assistance better. An international body could be

replicated at national level to provide symmetry in the new financial architecture.

Third, as regards the relative responsibility between individual countries and the others, Bates makes a highly pertinent observation. Initially, it must be individual countries that take the lead in reforming their domestic markets and governance systems out of enlightened self-interest. The secondary responsibility is to make information available in a timely way under guidance from the standard-setting bodies and the international financial institutions.

Michael Metcalfe and Avinash Persaud make a somewhat orthodox but extremely valid point on transparency in Chapter 10. While stating first that, in much of the literature on S&C, the practitioners of public policy, especially in developing countries, have been expressing reservations about the excessive emphasis on the real-time and comprehensive nature of disclosures of some information, the chapter gives a boost to such scepticism and this reviewer has no hesitation in supporting the stance it takes – namely, that some forms of disclosure might even increase financial instability. After recognising the recent shift in the crisis-prevention debate towards the importance of information, and mentioning the two possible theoretical links between information provision and crisis (the first being the skeleton in the cupboard theory, and the second that a sub-optimal information environment has a tendency to encourage herding behaviour on the part of investors), the authors take a long-run perspective on crises, say, over the past century when information has actually increased, to suggest the possibility of the market's tendency to ignore the warning signs. Furthermore, according to Metcalfe and Persaud, the delivery of clear information may add to herding behaviour. In other words, by implication, this argument seems to be that either the market ignores warning signs or, if it does treat some critical information as vital, any warning sign may lead to herding.

While there is some merit in these arguments, two important points need to be appreciated. First, there is a need to maintain, over the longer haul, a stream of official information in the public domain on a continuous basis, both for credibility and accountability, but the degree of detail as well as timing needs to recognise market sensitivities. Second, the relevance of ignoring warning signs (as in the case of ENRON, cited by Metcalfe and Persaud, is more for developed countries, while the relevance of herding behaviour may be more for emerging markets.

In this regard, another issue worth exploring relates to the differentiation between what has been described as the herding behaviour of financial markets in general, and the pro-cyclical tendency of private capital flows to emerging markets. Furthermore, there needs to be a differentiation between the role of information in enabling better allocation of capital and the actual flow of capital during the bubbles and bursts, when the warning signs initially are ignored and subsequent herding takes place, whether or not triggered by the good or bad news that true information may carry.

Finally, one cannot afford to ignore totally evidence in Chapter 10 indicating the relationship between the number of Reports on the Observation of Standards and Codes (ROSCs) and the volatility of cross-border flows, leading to the conclusion that 'at present, however, the best that can be said is that the argument that the publication of ROSCs reduces the volatility of cross border equity flows is unproven'. Similarly, one cannot ignore the reality of the link between disclosure of forex reserves and market behaviour, argued eloquently by Avinash Persaud in the context of the publication of daily reserves.

Agenda for further debate and research

The review of experience so far and an appreciation of perceptions indicate several areas for further debate and research. First, the desirable focus of S&C needs to be revisited. Their relevance to global stability in the case of emerging economies may not be as close as was originally contemplated. Further S&C effectiveness in this regard, in the absence of complementary efforts in crisis prevention, also needs reassessment. While their positioning in the evolving international financial architecture needs reassessment, the role of S&C in enhancing the institutional infrastructure for developments in the domestic context has to be appreciated. Second, the relative significance of S&C assessment as between developed and developing countries in general, and in the context of global stability, needs to be revisited. Recent developments indicate that developed financial centres may also be deficient in S&C, triggering market volatility and some elements of contagion. Similarly, the relative role of S&C in both development and stability, in developing and transition economies, is also worth exploring.

Third, experience and recent events also indicate that while strengths or deficiencies in macro-policies which have a potential for crisis may be addressed in the short run and seem to have greater weight in the eyes of markets, improvements in S&C appear to be essentially a medium-term agenda with less weight in the financial markets. Fourth, there is general recognition that S&C need to be reviewed from time to time by standard-setting bodies, but whether this is being done in a timely or adequate manner and, if so, whether such bodies are getting the benefit of reviews undertaken by the BWIs, is yet another area on which there is inadequate information in the public domain. There are a number of issues – institutional, legal and policy – of procedures concerning the implementation of S&C faced and resolved by member countries, but there are not many case studies in the public domain. Fifth, external assessments, particularly with regard to developing countries, have been completed successfully by the BWIs, but such assessments appear to be resource-intensive, warranting re-evaluation of their coverage, depth and periodicity.

Sixth, there may be a need to distinguish between some sort of destination for compliance and desirable practice. Thus a regulator may need to become involved in market development, especially in providing infrastructure. Similarly, the premature adoption of transparency relative to policy and market preparedness may have to be avoided. Seventh, in the light of the experience, the scope for self-assessment, independent but domestic assessment, peer assessments, and differentiating between initial and subsequent updates need to be considered. Furthermore, the original assumptions about the integrated nature of S&C in review and assessment may need to be revisited. Related to such an assessment of linkages would be the role of standard-setting bodies in assessments. Recognising that exercises relating to S&C should be viewed as a process more or less unique to each country in a medium-term context, there may be merit in considering domestic institutional arrangements for monitoring them, which could, incidentally, enhance ownership. Eighth, there are several ongoing exercises complementary to S&C, in particular Collective Action Clauses, the Sovereign Debt Restructuring Mechanism, the review of the IMF's Contingent Credit Facility, the parameters for debt sustainability, technical exercises relating to national balance sheets and so on, and any assessment of S&C should be considered against the backdrop of developments on the complementary front. Depending on a review of such developments, there may be a need for repackaging.

Ninth is the increasing disharmony between public policy and market behaviour, in the sense of the extent to which macro-policy or micro-institutions drive the market becoming increasingly difficult to assess. There is another serious divergence, not entirely explained by economic considerations, between the attitudes of market participants in industrialised and developing countries with regard to financial flows. Moreover, there is a divergence between a *de jure* policy of financial liberalisation and the *de facto* financial integration of a developing country. In other words, the domestic economic policy may enable an open market account but cannot by itself ensure capital flows, and this divergence may have to be explained with reference also to the attitudes of financial markets. Stated briefly, the issues of what matters for the behaviour of financial markets need to be assessed in order to appreciate the role of S&C, in the light of several critics questioning their significance for stability and for growth. In particular, the study of information and its effect on market behaviour may need deeper understanding, capturing instances where signs (reflected by S&C) were ignored; where there were reactions to signs with unintended consequences; where signs helped to bring about the expected responses; and, finally, where no signs existed because of a lack of official information.

Finally, the advocacy of S&C was based on a strong presumption that financial liberalisation and integration into global financial markets enhances growth, using the analogy of the benefits of trade liberalisation. But there could be a downside to such liberalisation in terms of crises which need to be prevented. S&C were an element of such an advocacy which necessarily involved the liberalisation of the capital account as a desirable goal, though some caution or preconditions may be warranted. There appears to be some empirical evidence to strengthen the view that capital markets are, by their very nature, procyclical with respect to emerging countries, and further that there is a disconnection between *de jure* and *de facto* financial liberalisation. More significantly, there is some empirical evidence to support the view that financial integration may not be as much of an unmixed blessing as trade liberalisation; it may not accelerate economic growth in emerging economies, and it may even add to volatility. These findings would warrant in-depth studies of the implications of global integration of developing countries in financial markets, and consequently the significance of S&C in an international context relative to a domestic but developmental context.

Note

1   These are the personal views of the author.

References

International Monetary Fund (2001) *IMF Survey*, vol. 30, no. 7, 2 April 2001, www.imf.org/imfsurvey.

International Monetary Fund (2003) *Proposals for a Sovereign Debt Restructuring Mechanism (SDRM) – A Fact Sheet*, http://www.imf.org/external/np/exr/facts/sdrm.htm.

Jalan, Bimal (2002) *India's Economy in the New Millennium*, New Delhi: UBS Publishers' Distributors.

Prasad, Eswar, Kenneth Rogoff, Shang-Jin Wei and M. Ayhan Kose (2003) *Effects of Financial Globalization on Developing Countries*, http://www.imf.org/external/np/res/docs/2003/031703.htm.

Pringle, Robert and Nick Carver (eds) (2003) *How Countries Mange Reserve Assets*, London: Central Banking Publications.

Reddy, Y. V. (2000) *Monetary and Financial Sector Reforms in India*, New Delhi: UBS Publishers' Distributors.

Reddy, Y. V. (2001) *Implementation of Financial Standards and Codes: Indian Perspective and Approach*, BIS Review, http://www.bis.org/review/r010312c.pdf.

Reddy, Y. V. (2002) *Lectures on Economic and Financial Sector Reforms in India*, New Delhi: Oxford University Press.

Reddy, Y. V. (2003) *Economic Policy in India: Managing Change*, New Delhi: UBS Publishers' Distributors.

Reserve Bank of India (2002) *Report of the Standing Committee on International Financial Standards and Codes*, Division of Reports Review and Publications, Mumbai: Reserve Bank of India.

Shailendra, J. Anjaria (2002) *IMF and Transparency – Moving Forward*, http://www.imf.org/external/np/speeches/2002/102802.htm.

United Nations Conference on Trade and Development (2001) *Trade and Development*, New York and Geneva: United Nations.

Vasudevan, A. (2003) *Central Banking for Emerging Market Economies*, New Delhi: Academic Foundation.

Appendix

Appendix:
Key Financial Standards – a Guide

Andrew Cornford[1]

Macroeconomic policy and data transparency

The codes and their rationale

Both the key financial standards on data dissemination as such, and those dealing with transparency in monetary and financial policies, and with fiscal transparency, are directed at enhanced transparency regarding major macroeconomic indicators and at procedures required for this purpose. The remit of the latter two standards extends to closely related issues such as the accountability and integrity of the institutions and the staff who are responsible for these procedures. The links between these three standards are particularly close, and their rationale has several facets. The effectiveness of monetary, financial and fiscal policies is likely to be enhanced if the objectives and instruments of policy in these areas are known to the public and if the government's commitment to these objectives is credible. Furthermore, good governance more generally requires that central banks and other financial agencies and fiscal authorities are accountable. An important aspect of the standards' rationale also concerns international lenders and investors. Here the idea is that transparency should help lenders and investors to evaluate and price risk more accurately, thus contributing to policy discipline in recipient countries. Moreover, the assessment of countries on an individual basis, made possible by the three key standards, is expected to prevent a loss of confidence in one country spreading to others simply because they belong to the same category or region – the so-called contagion effect. Finally, transparency is also capable of facilitating multilateral surveillance by organisations such as the IMF.

The *Code of Good Practices on Transparency in Monetary and Financial Policies* identifies desirably transparent practices in the conduct of monetary policy and policies towards the financial sector. These practices require: clarity with respect to the roles, responsibilities and objectives of central banks and other financial agencies with responsibility for supervising different parts of the financial sector; open processes for the formulation and reporting of decisions on monetary and financial policy; public availability of information concerning policies in both spheres; and accountability and assurances of integrity for the central bank, other financial agencies, and their staff. There is also an ongoing review by IAIS of relevant international accounting standards.

The *Code of Good Practice on Fiscal Transparency* is based on four principles. First, the roles and responsibilities of, and within, the government should be transparent, and for this purpose there should be a clear legal and administrative framework for fiscal management. Second, governments should commit themselves to public disclosure of comprehensive, reliable information on fiscal activities. Third, the process of budget preparation, execution and reporting should be open. And, fourth, fiscal information should meet accepted quality standards and be subject to public and independent scrutiny.

The *Special Data Dissemination Standard* (SDDS) was developed by the IMF in response to the recognition of widespread deficiencies regarding major categories of economic data after the Mexican crisis. It prescribes the data which countries wishing to use the world's capital markets are expected to provide publicly concerning the real, fiscal, financial and external sectors of the economy, and lays down minimum benchmarks to be met in terms of periodicity and timeliness. Since its inception, the SDDS has been strengthened by the inclusion of a requirement to disclose not only reserve assets but also reserve-related liabilities and other potential drains on reserves, such as short derivative positions and guarantees extended by the government for borrowing by the private sector in foreign currency. The SDDS is supplemented by the *General Data Dissemination Standard* (GDDS) designed to improve the quality of data disclosed by all member countries of the IMF.

Commentary and new work

While the potential of such key standards to contribute to policy credibility and improved governance is incontrovertible, none the less there are grounds for not entertaining exaggerated expectations as to what they can achieve. The new disclosure rules of the SDDS failed notably to serve as an effective early warning system in the case of the Asian crisis. And if the availability of pertinent data failed to deter capital flows associated with the build-up of eventually unsustainable external financial positions in certain Asian countries, the same applied *a fortiori* to the behaviour of international lenders and investors in Russia prior to the crisis of the summer of 1998. A more fundamental limitation of transparency's potential contribution to the prevention of financial instability is a consequence of the variation in accompanying macro-economic conditions and other features of policy regimes evident during recent financial crises. A common characteristic of the countries affected by these crises was their openness to capital flows, but there were also substantial differences in many of their macroeconomic indi-cators and other features of their economies. These differences involved external deficits, the extent of currency overvaluations, the size of budget deficits, the relative importance of consumption and investment in the booms preceding the crises, the relative size of countries' external debt owed by the public and private sectors, and the coverage and effec-tiveness of regimes of financial regulation and supervision. Finally, analysis of recent international financial crises also points to other diffi-culties as to the extent to which improved disclosure of macroeconomic variables can contribute to greater financial stability, in particular to the avoidance of contagion effects. For example, national balance sheets do not always reflect the pressures on external payments that can result from the adjustment of derivative positions which are off-balance-sheet and not always covered adequately by accounting rules, and which, even if required under these rules, are capable of blurring distinctions between different categories of exposure.

Some of the more recent work in the area of macroeconomic policy and data transparency is concerned with guidelines for implementation and for assessment as part of FSAPs and ROSCs. Other work is directed at improving the effectiveness of data dissemination and of policy man-agement in particular areas covered by the three key standards. This includes guidelines for foreign-exchange reserve management, practices of public debt management (where the IMF has been co-operating with the World Bank and there is a parallel initiative of the OECD), and guidelines for the compilation of external debt statistics (where the work involves an Inter-agency Task Force including the BIS, the OECD, the World Bank and others in addition to the IMF). Regarding macroeco-nomic financial and fiscal policies, the emphasis of the three key finan-cial standards is on disclosure, process and procedures rather than on substantive guidelines. This is understandable, since the codification of the rules for policy itself would be a much more complex task because of the variety of situations and countries that would have to be covered, and would confront more severe difficulties in obtaining a consensus. However, two other initiatives under the heading of macroeconomic policy and data transparency may eventually have the effect of increasing the substantive policy content of the three key standards, or of linking them more closely to other initiatives with such content.

One area of work that may be relevant here concerns the liberalisation of the capital account of the balance of payments. On the basis of papers submitted by the IMF and the OECD itself, the OECD is preparing a report on the forty-year liberalisation experience of its member countries. The intended political import of this report is not clear, but it bears remembering in this context that one of the original forces driving the initiative on key financial standards was belief among policy-makers in the major industrial countries in the adoption and implementation of such standards as a prerequisite for a successful push for greater liberalisation of capital transactions.

Another area of work deserving attention concerns the development of Financial Soundness Indicators (FSIs) as a part of efforts to improve the monitoring of financial vulnerabilities.[2] This is an important component of the IMF's work on macroprudential analysis – namely, the assessment and monitoring of strengths and vulnerabilities of financial systems on the basis of quantitative information and indicators which include not only FSIs but also macroeconomic indicators, information on systems' structures, and other quantitative information on the institutional and regulatory framework (including that on compliance with key financial standards). Such work can, of course, be seen as a logical extension of the inclusion of the key standards on macroeconomic policy and data transparency in FSAPs and ROSCs (and thus in the IMF's Article IV surveillance). But the work also has a potentially more controversial dimension in that macroprudential analysis bears a close resemblance to types of analysis carried out by credit-rating agencies. The IMF's current efforts in this area raise the question of whether the institution is moving, whether one likes the idea or not, in the direction of assuming an increasing number of the functions of a global rating agency.

Institutional and market infrastructure

Insolvency

Insolvency rules are generally considered to be part of corporate governance, but a part so substantial as to be treated often as subjects in their own right. There is general recognition that existing regimes for insolvency are characterised by widespread weaknesses or, for some situations and countries, by their absence. At a national level (particularly in many developing and transition economies) weaknesses are associated with problems regarding the enforcement of contracts, ineffective modalities for the netting, clearance and settlement of outstanding obligations, poorly functioning arrangements for the collateral and security of loans, and conflicts of law. Such features are capable of complicating the valuation of firms' securities and collateral, and thus of increasing financial risks. By raising uncertainties as to the value of collateral, they also pose problems for the allocation of regulatory capital for banks to cover credit risk.[3]

The lead role in developing globally acceptable rules for insolvency has been attributed to the World Bank, whose objective is to develop an 'integrated matrix' of components and criteria for such rules, highlighting existing best practice (see Group of Thirty 2000: ch. 2, sect. 1). The results are intended to be a complement to a country's legal and commercial system, with guidance provided as to how they would interact with and affect the system. Consensus is to be developed through a series of assessment exercises and international insolvency symposia.

A major outcome of this process so far is the approval by the World Bank Board of a first set of *Principles and Guidelines for Effective Insolvency and Creditor Rights Systems*, which cover the key areas of (i) creditor rights and enforcement procedures; (ii) the legal framework for corporate insolvency; (iii) the regulatory framework to implement the insolvency system; and (iv) the enabling framework for credit-risk management and informal corporate workouts. Work on more detailed guides to the implementation of these principles and guidelines, and to their inclusion in legislation, is being carried out by the World Bank and UNCITRAL (United Nations Commission on International Trade Law). It should be noted that this work on insolvency standards is directed at the framework for the insolvency of enterprises and is thus distinct from ongoing international initiatives directed at sovereign insolvency. However, major proposals under the latter heading (such as those for standstills and debt restructuring) involve measures whose implementation is likely to be facilitated by effective insolvency regimes at the national level.

In parallel with its work on insolvency in general, the World Bank has also undertaken a joint project with the IMF on bank insolvency, the objective of which is to identify an appropriate legal, institutional and regulatory framework for dealing with bank insolvencies, including those linked to systemic crises. Such work would seem naturally to be related to the issue of appropriate standards for dealing with cross-border insolvencies more generally. Such insolvencies pose difficult problems of co-ordination and conflicts of law. Here the danger is that the insolvency of a large firm with an extensive international network of entities could seriously disrupt the flows of cross-border transactions, a special threat being posed by the possibility of the failure of a large multinational bank (a subject that will presumably be addressed by the IMF–World Bank joint project).[4] Attempts to develop international rules in this area are currently concentrated mainly in other private forums (see Group of Thirty, 2000: ch. 6).

Corporate governance

Corporate governance involves the relationships between a business's management and its board of directors, its shareholders and lenders, and its other stakeholders such as employees, customers, suppliers and the community of which it is a part. The subject thus concerns the framework through which business objectives are set, and the means of attaining them and otherwise monitoring performance are determined.

The *OECD Principles of Corporate Governance* (published in 1999) covers five basic subjects: (i) protection of the rights of shareholders – a heading that includes allowing the market for corporate control to function efficiently, transparently and fairly for all shareholders; (ii) equitable treatment of shareholders, including minority and foreign shareholders, with full disclosure of material information and the prohibition of abusive self-dealing and insider trading; (iii) recognition and protection of the exercise, of the rights of stakeholders as established by law, and encouragement of co-operation between corporations and stakeholders in creating wealth, jobs and financially sound enterprises; (iv) timely and accurate disclosure and transparency with respect to matters material to company performance, ownership and governance, which should include an annual audit conducted by an independent auditor; and (v) a framework of corporate governance ensuring strategic guidance of the company and effective monitoring of its management by the board of directors as well as the board's accountability to the company and shareholders (certain key functions of the board being specified under this heading).

Corporate governance thus sets rules concerning matters where variations of approach among countries are often rooted in societal differences, with respect, for example, to the relative importance of family-owned firms as opposed to corporations, as well as to prevalent norms regarding the primacy of sometimes conflicting business objectives such as long-term sustainability, on the one hand, and value for shareholders on the other. These societal differences, in turn, generally reflect differences in national histories and in the political and social consensus that has grown out of them. The preamble to the *OECD Principles* acknowledges that there is no single model of good corporate governance, and the principles themselves are at a fairly general level and avoid rules concerning the more contentious subjects of relationships between companies and their lenders and investors, such as appropriate levels of leverage and the more detailed rules for the market for corporate control. Nevertheless, there remains a danger that the technical assistance and assessment exercises to promulgate the OECD principles and the assessment methodology for ROSCs, areas where the World Bank is also involved, will incorporate features reflecting excessive reliance on concepts linked to particular models of corporate governance, most notably those of the UK or the USA.[5]

Corporate governance is an integral part of work under several other key financial standards, through its relationship to such subjects as transparency (and thus to financial reporting), insolvency (see above), and the proper functioning of categories of enterprise (such as banks) which are also the focus of other standards. For example, a working group of the Joint Forum of the BCBS, the IAIS and IOSCO has been studying the corporate governance of financial firms and the use of internal and external auditing in supervision.

A note on the bankruptcy of ENRON

The autumn of 2001 was marked by the bankruptcy of ENRON, a US firm which combined energy development and transmission with trading businesses originally set up in connection with its other activities. On 16 October the firm announced that it was making a US$544 million after-tax charge against earnings and a reduction of US$1.2 billion in shareholders' equity related to transactions with a partnership created and managed by a senior officer of the firm. Less than a month later, ENRON announced that it was restating its financial results for the period 1997–2001 because of accounting errors related to transactions with another similar partnership, and with a further related-party entity, net income being reduced by US$508 million for the whole period and reported shareholders' equity by US$258 million in 1997, US$391 million in 1998, US$710 million in 1999, and US$754 million in 2000.

The resulting shock to market confidence led to a precipitous fall in the firm's share price, and at the beginning of December, EnROn declared bankruptcy.[6] Subsequent disclosures about EnROn have raised serious concerns about the integrity of financial reporting in the financial markets of major industrial countries – an issue that has a bearing on the effectiveness of transparency in achieving the objectives of key financial standards – lacunae in market regulation, and weaknesses in corporate governance.

At the time of writing, the main systematic source of information concerning the causes of EnROn's failure was the Powers Report of a special committee of the firm's board of directors.[7] This report discusses at length the three partnerships already mentioned. In the case of one of these (Chewco), a major business objective was to keep off EnROn's balance sheet the debt of another investment partnership. A precondition for the validity of such balance-sheet shifting was Chewco's independence from EnROn for the purposes of consolidation, a condition that required a minimum equity stake from outsiders. However, because of difficulties in the finding of such outsiders, the stake was financed largely by a bank loan secured by cash collateral from EnROn itself. The other two partnerships (LJM1) and (LJM2) were used for two categories of transaction – asset sales and hedging. The first enabled EnROn to move assets from its books. Such operations are not improper so long as they transfer the risks and rewards of ownership to the counterparty, a condition not met here in the opinion of the special investigative committee. Moreover, the hedging did not involve contracting with a counterparty prepared, at a price, to take on the risk of the position, so that, if its value declined, the counterparty would bear the loss. Rather, the entities on the other side of the hedges were to meet any losses by EnROn, with EnROn's own stock or stock options transferred to them as a source of payment for this purpose. To quote the BIS commentary, 'EnROn was in effect hedging with itself.'[8] This meant that, if the value of the positions fell at the same time as that of EnROn's stock, the hedges would fail. This is what happened in 2001 and, as the credit problems in the partnerships became insoluble, EnROn had to recognise losses hitherto concealed through them.

In addition to abuses of accounting and financial reporting, the EnROn case is notable for other failings in connection with issues usually treated under the heading of corporate governance. Particularly notable are instances of self-dealing in which senior EnROn employees, in return for often risk-free roles, were richly rewarded for their participation in the partnerships. As the Powers Report says in its summary,

> The tragic consequences of the related-party transactions and accounting errors were the result of failures at many levels and by many people: a flawed idea, self-enrichment by employees, inadequately-designed controls, poor implementation, inattentive oversight, simple (and not-so-simple) accounting mistakes, and overreaching in a culture that appears to have encouraged pushing the limits. Our review indicates that many of those consequences could and should have been avoided. (Powers *et al.*, 2002: 27–8)[9]

Accounting

Improvements in financial reporting and transparency are essential to the success of most of the initiatives on key financial standards. The standards directed at accounting and auditing aim explicitly not only to increase transparency worldwide but also to harmonise standards in this area. Through their impact on disclosure, these standards have an obvious bearing on counterparties' ability to assess the financial risks of transactions, and the need for international harmonisation is because of the growth in the cross-border business, especially lending and investment. The principal body with responsibility for promulgating international accounting standards is the International Accounting Standards Committee (IASC).[10] Much of the recent work of the IASC has been directed at reaching a compromise on a set of standards that is acceptable both to the USA and to other member countries, and which satisfies disclosure requirements for the issuance and trading of securities in the world's major financial markets. As expressed by a member of the International Accounting Standards Board (IASB), the technocratic body with responsibility for setting IASC standards, 'The objective ... is to produce one single set of high-quality global standards so that a transaction occurring in Seattle, Stuttgart, Sheffield or Sydney will be accounted for in exactly the same way' (Tweedie, 2001). Thus, many of the IASC's problems concern the reconciliation of different national accounting standards as well as of its own understandably pluralistic approach with the more specific and constraining rules of the United States' Generally Accepted Accounting Principles (GAAP).[11]

Hitherto, the objective in many countries of facilitating their firms' access to US securities markets has given that country considerable leverage in the vetting of IASC proposals in order to ensure that differences from US standards would not entail any compromise of the objectives of its accounting regime. It is not yet clear what effects weaknesses in this regime highlighted by the collapse of EnROn and by other incidents of aggressive accounting and possibly (in some cases) fraudulent financial reporting, will have on the IASC's work.

Auditing

Because of the integral links between financial reporting and auditing, the impact on transparency of international initiatives in accounting standards cannot be separated from the success of initiatives to raise auditing standards. The targets of efforts here include internal auditing (that is, the assessment of the extent and effectiveness of a firm's management and accounting controls, and of the safeguarding and efficient use of its assets) as well as external auditing (that is, the auditing of financial statements and supporting evidence to determine the conformity of the former with applicable standards). Internal auditing is now a legal requirement in several countries, and auditing committees frequently have acquired greater importance in countries where shifts in corporate governance have resulted in increased power for boards of directors in relation to senior operating executives. But it is external auditing that is the principal subject of international initiatives. Here the problems of harmonisation relate partly to differences in the accounting standards underlying financial statements, but also to divergences in the audit standard-setting processes themselves. These divergences result, for example, from the fact that in some countries auditing standards are set by the accounting profession but in others are based on requirements mandated in laws and regulations or resulting from a process involving the joint participation of both the accounting profession and the government. The body with the lead responsibility for international harmonisation of auditing standards is the International Federation of Accountants (IFAC),[12] which collaborates closely with other bodies also occupying key positions in this area, such as IOSCO and the European Union.

The IFAC-released a Code of Ethics for Accountants including Independence Rules to be followed by auditors operating under IAS. In the context of its collaboration with other standard-setting bodies, it recently completed a joint guidance paper with the BCBS on the relationship between banking supervisors and banks' external auditors.

Payments and settlement

Payment systems enable the transfer of funds between financial institutions on their own behalf and on behalf of their customers, a role which makes such systems a potential source of systemic risk. This role is evident from consideration of four key dimensions of an economy's flow-of-funds process. One dimension consists of the activities of various economic agents; the second of the markets for financial instruments, assets and liabilities; the third of the supporting infrastructure, in which an integral component is the payments system; and the fourth of economic conditions binding the markets together and ensuring that they clear. Failures at the level of any of the first three dimensions are capable of disrupting links between the markets and between economic agents whose mutual interdependence is based on several different kinds of transaction and exposure. If large, such disruptions can easily take on a systemic character.[13] Moreover, payment systems also play an essential role in foreign-exchange transactions and are thus an interface between different countries' payment systems. As a result of the links and similarities between systems of payment and settlement for fund transfers and for transactions in other financial assets, the main vehicle for international initiatives regarding payments systems, the BIS Committee on Payment and Settlement Systems (CPSS), the agency attributed the lead role for the standard in this area, has extended its purview beyond fund transfers to settlement systems for securities and foreign exchange, and to clearing arrangements for exchange-traded derivatives.

The main risks in systems for the transfer of funds are the following: credit risk – that a counterparty is unable to meet obligations within the system currently or in the future; liquidity risk (clearly closely related to credit risk, but not identical), that a counterparty has insufficient funds to meet obligations within the system, though it may be able to do so at some future time; legal risk, that an inadequate legal framework or legal uncertainties cause or exacerbate credit or liquidity risks; and operational risk, that factors such as technical malfunctions or operational mistakes cause or exacerbate credit or liquidity risks. As discussed above, any of these risks can have systemic consequences, since the inability of a counterparty or counterparties to meet its/their obligations within the system can have a domino effect on the ability of other counterparties to meet their obligations and thus ultimately threaten the stability of the financial sector as a whole.[14] These risks are the target of the CPSS's *Core Principles for Systemically Important Payment Systems*.

The first core principle is directed at legal risk and specifies the need for a robust legal basis for the payment system, a requirement that links its rules and procedures to related areas of law such as those concerning banking, contract and insolvency. The second and third principles concern the need for rules and procedures that enable participants to have a clear understanding of the system's impact on financial risks as well as defining how credit and liquidity risks are to be managed and identifying responsibilities for this purpose. A system's risks can be exacerbated by the length of time required for final settlement, or by the nature of the asset used to settle claims, so that the fourth and sixth principles specify the need for prompt settlement and for a settlement asset that is either a claim on the central bank or one carrying little or no credit risk (owing to the negligible risk of its issuer's failure). The fifth principle requires a minimum standard of robustness for multilateral netting systems.[15] The seventh principle is intended to minimise operational risk by ensuring a high degree of security and operational reliability. The eighth, ninth and tenth principles address the more general issues of the system's efficiency and practicality (including the need for explicit recognition of any trade-off between safety and efficiency), the need for objective and publicly-disclosed criteria for participation in the system permitting fair and open access, and governance arrangements that are effective, accountable and transparent. The *Core Principles* attribute to central banks a key responsibility in ensuring that payments systems comply with the Principles.

The second part of the report on the *Core Principles for Systemically Important Payment Systems* provides detail on issues such as the identification of systemically important payments systems, the modalities of system review and reform, structural, technical and institutional factors to be considered, and the kinds of co-operation necessary with participants in the system, user groups and other parties to the reform process.[16] The second part also takes up certain cross-border aspects of payment systems.

The extension of the purview of the CPSS to systems for securities settlement, mentioned above, has led to co-operation with IOSCO on the preparation of *Recommendations for Securities Settlement Systems* (a subject also pertinent to IOSCO's *Objectives and Principles of Securities Regulation*). Appended to the *Recommendations* are commentaries on the individual recommendations, key questions for the assessment of implementation, and surveys of the principal risks in securities clearance and settlement.

Market integrity, money laundering and terrorist financing

Money laundering is one of the most politically sensitive of the subjects covered by the key codes and standards. It is an area where financial supervision interfaces directly with law enforcement, including some of the latter's tougher manifestations, since the activities financed with laundered money include drug dealing and terrorism. Much of the initial attention given to money laundering reflected the political difficulties in major developed countries in dealing with the problem of drug taking. The policies adopted here have focused mainly on repression of production and consumption as opposed to alternative approaches, with the result that profits from illegal supply remain high. Money laundering is also closely connected to corrupt activities in developed and developing countries, since it is used to conceal the size, the sources and the recipients of money involved in such activities. Generally accepted estimates of the global scale of money laundering do not yet exist, but there is no doubt that it is very large.[17] Money laundering has long been an important issue in relations between OECD countries and offshore financial centres, but some recent scandals indicate that it is also a major problem in traditional financial centres.

The principal international body entrusted with the task of combating money laundering is the Financial Action Task Force on Money Laundering (FATF),[18] which was established after the G-7 summit in 1989. Its current membership consists of twenty-nine (mainly developed) countries and two international organisations, the European Commission and the Gulf Co-operation Council. In 1990 the FATF drew up a list of forty recommendations which members are expected to adopt. These were revised in 1996 to take into account experience gained in the meantime and changes in money laundering practices.[19] Among the obligations contained in the forty recommendations are the following: criminalisation of the laundering of the proceeds of serious crimes; the identification of all customers and the keeping of appropriate records; a requirement that financial institutions report suspicious transactions to the competent national authority, and that they develop programmes to counter money laundering, including comprehensive internal controls and employee training; adequate supervision of money laundering and the sharing of expertise by supervisors with other domestic judicial and law enforcement authorities; and the strengthening of international co-operation through information exchange, mutual legal assistance and bilateral and multilateral agreements. Implementation by member countries of these recommendations is monitored on the basis of a two-pronged approach: first, an annual self-assessment exercise; and, second, periodic peer reviews of a member country by teams drawn from other countries.[20]

At a meeting in Washington, DC in October 2001, in the aftermath of the terrorist attacks of the previous month, FATF agreed to an extension of its remit to cover terrorist financing. This extension is defined in eight special recommendations covering the following subjects: ratification and implementation of UN instruments;[21] criminalising the financing of terrorism; freezing and confiscating terrorist assets; reporting suspicious transactions related to terrorism; international co-operation for mutual legal assistance or information exchange; licensing and registration procedures for alternative remittance (including that involving transmission through informal money or value transfer systems or networks); tightening procedures for the identification of originators of wire transfers, and for the monitoring of such transfers; and reviewing the adequacy of legal regimes for non-profit organisations which are vulnerable to abuse for the financing of terrorism. Under the plan of action associated with these eight recommendations, FATF members agreed to comply by June 2002, inviting non-members to do the same.

In November 2001, the IMF's International Monetary and Financing Committee (IMFC) called for several specific actions to prevent the international financial system from being used to finance terrorist acts or to launder the proceeds of illegal activities (Communiqué of the IMFC, Ottawa, 17 November 2001). It also endorsed an extension of the Fund's involvement in anti-money-laundering initiatives to efforts directed at countering terrorist financing: this is to include coverage of relevant aspects of legal and institutional frameworks as part of Financial Sector Assessment Programmes (FSAPs), acceleration of Offshore Financial Centre (OFC) assessments, assistance to countries for the purpose of identifying gaps in their anti-money-laundering and anti-terrorist-financing regimes, and enhanced collaboration with FATF to develop a global standard covering the FATF recommendations.[22] Under the last heading, the IMFC in April 2002 drew attention to the need to complete a comprehensive methodology for the assessment of legal, institutional and supervisory aspects of anti-money-laundering efforts, and for combating the financing of terrorism (the AML/CFT methodology). This methodology will be used either on a stand-alone basis or in conjunction with FSAPs or OFC assessments, and its finalisation is to take place concurrently with the preparation of an assessment methodology incorporating the FATF recommendations in the framework for Reports on the Observance of Standards and Codes (ROSCs).

Draft versions of the AML/CFT methodology have been used in FSAPs and OFC assessments since the autumn of 2001.

Financial regulation and supervision

For the purposes of the key standards for financial systems, three subjects – banking supervision, securities regulation, and insurance supervision – are classified under the heading of financial regulation and supervision. It should be noted that the distinction made for this purpose between this heading and that of institutional and market infrastructure is somewhat arbitrary, since many of the topics under the latter heading – such as accounting and auditing with their links to transparency and insolvency, and systems for payment and settlement with their links to systemic financial risk – overlap in multiple ways with matters treated under financial regulation and supervision. The initial focus of the exercise on key standards under the latter heading was the separate sets of principles (described below) for regulation and supervision for the three major categories of financial service already mentioned. But recent work by institutions with lead roles in the key standards initiatives has also been concerned with issues posed by areas of convergence between the three categories, and the problems for harmonisation of regulation and supervision posed by such convergence. Thus, work on the comparison for the three categories of core principles for regulation and supervision, and on risk-management practices and regulatory capital, has been undertaken in the Joint Forum of the Basle Committee for Bank Supervision (BCBS), the International Association of Insurance Supervisors (IAIS), and the International Organisation of Securities Commissions (IOSCO). Other ongoing work bringing together the headings of financial regulation and supervision, on the one hand, and of institutional and market infrastructure on the other (and thus the lead agencies involved), includes principles and guidelines for effective insolvency and creditor-rights schemes and combating terrorist financing, a subject discussed in the previous section of this chapter and concerning which current initiatives entail contributions from the BCBS, IOSCO and the IAIS as well as FATF, the IMF and the World Bank.

Banking supervision

Weaknesses in the banking sector and inadequate banking supervision have played a central role in recent financial crises in developed as well as developing countries. Recognition of the increasing potential for domestic banking crises to have destabilising cross-border effects as a result of the internationalisation of banking business has led to initiatives since the 1970s aimed at improving international co-operation regarding banking regulation and supervision. These initiatives were directed first primarily at banks in industrial countries and offshore financial centres. However, the standards which emerged from these initiatives eventually also achieved widespread acceptance among developing economies, and the BCBS, the most important vehicle for most of these initiatives, has increasingly assumed the role of global standard-setter regarding banking regulation and supervision.[23]

A major outcome of the BCBS's extension of the focus of its activities beyond the concerns of its member countries is the *Core Principles for Effective Banking Supervision* issued in the autumn of 1997. The Principles, in the development of which the BCBS collaborated with supervisors of economies outside the Group of Ten (including several developing and transition economies), cover seven major subject areas: (i) the preconditions for effective banking supervision; (ii) the licensing and structure of banks; (iii) prudential regulations and requirements; (iv) methods of ongoing supervision; (v) information requirements; (vi) the formal powers of supervisors; and (vii) cross-border banking. In April 1998, the BCBS undertook a survey of compliance with the Core Principles in 140 countries, an effort paralleled by reviews of compliance in selected countries conducted by the IMF and the World Bank. Subsequently, a Core Principles Liaison Group (CPLG) of twenty-two countries[24] was set up to provide feedback to the BCBS on the practical implementation of the Core Principles. The reviews of compliance and the feedback from the CPLG led to the development by the BCBS of the *Core Principles Methodology* issued in October 1999.

This document is intended to provide guidance in the form of 'essential' and 'additional' criteria for the assessment of compliance by the different parties to which this task may be entrusted, such as the IMF, the World Bank, regional supervisory groups, regional development banks and consulting firms, but not the BCBS itself. In addition to the specific criteria relating to banking supervision, the assessors are also to form a view as to the presence of certain more general preconditions regarding such subjects as (i) sound, sustainable macroeconomic policies; (ii) a well-developed public infrastructure including an adequate body of law, covering, for example, contracts, bankruptcy, collateral and loan recovery as well as accounting standards approaching international best practice; (iii) market discipline based on financial transparency, effective corporate governance and the absence of government intervention in banks' commercial decisions, except in accordance with disclosed policies and guidelines; (iv) adequate supervisory procedures for dealing with problems in banks, and (v) adequate mechanisms for systemic protection, such as a lender-of-last-resort facility or deposit insurance (or both). The parts of the assessment directed more specifically at banking supervision comprise not only the procedures of supervision but also its subject-matter (which, of course, includes the standards for prudential regulation and for banks' internal controls and risk management covered in the BCBS's own documents over the years).

Thus assessment of compliance with the Core Principles requires evaluation of several related requirements, including prudential regulation and other aspects of the legal framework, supervisory guidelines, on-site examinations and off-site analysis, supervisory reporting and other aspects of public disclosure, and enforcement or its absence. Assessment is also required of the supervisory authority's skills, resources, and commitment, and of its actual implementation of the Core Principles. If evaluation of the preconditions for effective supervision (mentioned earlier) and assessment of the criteria relating to supervision itself are considered together, the exercise takes in substantial parts of a country's commercial law, its accounting and auditing standards, and to some extent the quality of its government's macroeconomic management. The assessment of relevant laws, regulations and supervisory procedures would appear to be fairly straightforward, but that of supervisory capacity and the effectiveness of implementation is more complex. Perhaps understandably, the annex to the *Core Principles Methodology*, which sets out the structure and methodology for assessment reports prepared by the IMF and the World Bank, focuses principally on the former set of subjects, and not the latter. Full assessment of supervisory capacity and the effectiveness of implementation is likely generally to be feasible only through the kind of in-depth scrutiny that will require several individual assessment exercises.

As is evident from the above description, the coverage of the *Core Principles for Effective Banking Supervision* includes the major areas of regulation and supervision. Thus subsequent statements of the BCBS on different subjects within its purview can largely be treated, *inter alia*, as providing elaboration and sometimes extension of the Core Principles. This applies, of course, most importantly to the current work on a revision of the 1988 Basle Capital Accord but also to recent statements on the relationship between banking supervisors and banks' external auditors, customer due diligence standards for banks (which include Know Your Customer Policies, an essential part of measures to control money laundering and terrorist financing), and procedures for dealing with weak banks.

Securities regulation

The *Objectives and Principles of Securities Regulation*, published by IOSCO in September 1998, sets out three major objectives: the protection of investors; ensuring that markets are fair, efficient and transparent; and the reduction of systemic risk. For their achievement, the document promulgates thirty principles covering responsibilities of the regulator; self-regulation; enforcement of securities regulation; co-operation in regulation both domestically and internationally; the responsibilities of issuers, rules and standards for collective investment schemes; requirements for market intermediaries; and rules and standards for the secondary market. The principles related explicitly to systemic risk are dealt with mainly under the last two headings, and are concerned with capital and prudential standards for market intermediaries, procedures for dealing with the failure of a market intermediary, and systems for clearing and settling securities transactions that minimise such risk. In other words, the focus of the principles for reducing systemic risk is on measures directed at firms and market infrastructure.

Unsurprisingly for a code produced by a global organisation of specialist regulators, these principles are concerned mainly with the fairness and efficient functioning of markets themselves. Connections to broader issues of macroeconomic policy and to policy towards the financial sector, both of which have been associated with systemic instability in developing and transition economies, are largely ignored. It might be argued that a more comprehensive and representative set of principles for securities markets, which included issues highlighted by recent crises in developing and transition economies, should address some aspects of policy with regard to the capital account of the balance of payments (concerning, for example, appropriate conditions for the access of foreign portfolio investors) and the commercial presence of foreign investment institutions.

As is also the case with the *Core Principles* of the BCBS, more recent work of IOSCO is likely to provide interpretative elaboration and sometimes extension of the *Objectives and Principles*. Such work includes the subjects of transparency and market fragmentation in the secondary markets for securities, enhancing information exchange among securities regulators, and management of funding and liquidity risks by security firms.

Insurance

Traditionally, insurance is not regarded as a source of financial instability or systemic risk, and in consequence the principal objectives of its regulation and supervision are client protection and the closely connected subjects of the safety and soundness of insurance companies and of proper conduct of business (an area covering such matters as disclosure, honesty, integrity and competence of firms and employees, marketing practices, and the objectivity of advice to customers). The principal grounds for playing down the systemic risks of the insurance sector are that companies' liabilities are long-term and not prone to runs, while their assets are typically liquid, and that mutual linkages among insurance companies and linkages between such companies and other financial firms are limited. However, more recently, questions have been raised as to the adequacy of this characterisation. This is in part because of the expanding role of the insurance sector in savings and investment products. Such trends have increased the possibility of contagion between insurance and other forms of financial business, and where large firms are involved, the scale of the possible adverse consequences of such contagion.

The focus of the *Insurance Core Principles* issued in October 2000 is the organisation and practice of the sector's supervision, and a series of sector-specific subjects – namely, the corporate governance of insurance companies, their internal controls, prudential rules, conduct-of-business issues, and the supervision of cross-border business. The prudential rules cover the management of an insurance company's assets, the identification and classification of liabilities, rules for capital requirements and for the use, disclosure and monitoring of derivatives and other off-balance-sheet items, and reinsurance as an instrument for risk containment. The principle covering the supervision of cross-border business operations is designed to ensure that no cross-border insurance entity escapes supervision, and that adequate arrangements are in place for consultations and information exchange between such an entity's home-country and host-country supervisors.

There is other more recent work of the IAIS which has a bearing on subjects covered by the *Insurance Core Principles*. This work includes the development of detailed supervisory standards in several areas, such as capital adequacy and solvency, evaluation of reinsurance cover and the security of reinsurers, and the exchange of information between supervisory bodies as well as anti-money-laundering guidance notes for insurance firms and supervisors.

Notes

1 This update makes extensive use of UNCTAD, 2001, Pt 2, ch. IV, reprinted in Akyüz, 2002, and of FSF, 2002.

2 FSIs are indicators designed to monitor the health and soundness of the financial sector and of financial firms' counterparties. They include aggregated information on institutions and markets as well as selected relevant macroeconomic indicators. Concerning the IMF's work on FSIs and macroprudential analysis, see Sundarajan *et al.*, 2002.

3 Under widely accepted international best practice, creditors are afforded the ability to foreclose on collateral within a period of 3–6 months. In East and South Asian countries affected by the financial crisis of 1997, the times required for foreclosure varied from three months to more than five years.

4 As the point was expressed recently in an OECD publication,

> 'The incidence of banking crises, and the costs these have imposed on countries, is quite large and the systemic consequences of the failure of a large institution are of a different order of magnitude from those associated with the failure of smaller institutions. In particular, the costs of bailing out a very big institution might be large relative to the resources of the country in which the institution resides… it is not clear that an increase in size and perhaps geographic scope of an institution makes the risk of its failure any greater than before. Accidents do happen, however, and it is likely that the systemic consequences of bank failures grow as institutions become larger and larger. The situation is also more complex in the case of internationally operating banks. (OECD, 2000)

5 Financial systems that have progressed beyond a rudimentary level incorporate mainly the same major features as building blocks. In comparisons of the financial dimensions of systems of corporate governance, the question is thus not the existence or non-existence of these features or building blocks, but their relative importance and the links between them, issues linked integrally to the power and influence of the system's different actors and institutions. To the extent that such a characterisation is meaningful (and many students of financial systems would dispute this once one's historical perspective goes back further than the last 25–30 years of the twentieth century), the so-called 'Anglo-Saxon' model attaches greater importance than others to the external discipline exercised by debt and equity markets – a discipline considered as exerting a pervasive and basically beneficent influence on the other parties to corporate governance. In this context, key features of the chapter, 'A framework for better corporate governance', of a recent major World Bank publication (Iskander and Chamlou, 2000) are of particular interest, because of the extent to which they may be reflected in the Bank's technical assistance and assessment exercises linked to the application of the *OECD Principles*. Although the publication notes that 'there is no one-size-fits-all blueprint for corporate governance', and that the different models attribute relative different weights to shareholder value and the protection of stakeholder rights (ibid., p. 21), in its prescriptions it attributes to the discipline of competitive financial markets an importance that does not seem warranted by the historical experience of economic development.

6 At the end of October, Moody's had downgraded the rating of EnROn's debt to Baa2, a rating none the less associated with a probability of default within a year of only 0.16 per cent.

7 Powers *et al.*, 2002 (whose principal findings are well summarised in BIS, 2002).

8 Ibid.

9 Powers *et al.*, 2002: 27–8.

10 The IASC was created in 1973 by major professional accounting bodies and at the time of writing includes more than 130 such bodies from more than 100 countries. The entities concerned with international accounting standards include not only professional accounting bodies, international accounting firms, transnational corporations and other international lenders and investors, but also other bodies such as international trade unions concerned with cross-border business activities.

11 In December 2001 the seven largest accounting firms issued a summary of differences between accounting standards in sixty countries and the standards of IASC (IAS), which found significant progress towards convergence in about twenty countries.

12 IFAC was established in 1977 to promulgate international standards in auditing and closely related subjects. IFAC and IASC have an agreement of 'mutual commitments' for close co-operation and mutual consultation, and membership in one automatically includes membership in the other.

13 This framework for analysing policies aimed at the stability of the financial sector is deployed frequently by William White of the BIS. See, for example, White, 1996: 23.

14 See CPSS, 2000a. The initiative to develop an internationally agreed framework of core principles for the design, operation and oversight of payment and settlement systems was a response to the conclusion in the report of an *ad hoc* working party on financial stability in emerging-market economies set up after the 1996 G-7 summit concerning the essential role of sound payments systems in the smooth operation of market economies, as well as to growing concern regarding the subject among emerging-market economies themselves. See Working Party on Financial Stability in Emerging Market Economies, 1997: ch. II.

15 In a multilateral netting arrangement, a participant nets obligations *vis-à-vis* other participants as a group throughout a specified period (typically a day), and then settles the debit or credit balance outstanding at the end of this period through the arrangement's common agent.

16 See CPSS, 2000b. Part 2 of the *Core Principles* was a response to widespread comments elicited by Part 1, that more detail on interpretation and implementation was needed.

17 The difficulties of estimating the flows involved in global money laundering are a recurring theme of the annual reports of the Financial Action Task Force on Money Laundering (FATF). For a pioneering effort at such estimation by John Walker ('Modelling global money laundering flows – some findings') see http://members.ozemail.com.au/~born1820/mlmethod.htm.

18 Various other regional or international bodies, either exclusively or as part of their work, also participate in combating money laundering. These include

the Asia/Pacific Group on Money Laundering (APG), the Caribbean Financial Action Task Force (CFATF), the PC-R-EV Committee of the Council of Europe, and the Offshore Group of Banking Supervisors.

19 FATF/GAFI, *The Forty Recommendations*, including an up-to-date version of *Interpretative Notes to the Forty Recommendations*, Paris: OECD, 1999.

20 The FATF has also conducted an exercise to identify jurisdictions deemed to be non-cooperative in the combat against money laundering. See FATF/GAFI, 2000.

21 The first of FATF's forty recommendations required immediate ratification of the 1988 UN Convention against Illicit Traffic in Narcotic Drugs and Psychotropic Substances (the Vienna Convention). The first of the new eight special recommendations also requires ratification of the 1999 UN International Convention for the Suppression of the Financing of Terrorism and of UN resolution 1373 passed by the Security Council after the terrorist attacks of September 2001. The 1999 Convention covers many matters similar to those in FATF's eight special recommendations, such as the definition of offences and offenders; obligations as to the criminalisation of certain activities and as to the imposition of penalties; seizure of funds and investigation of pertinent reports; mutual legal assistance; and procedures for the identification of customers as well as financial firms' reporting obligations. Resolution 1373 binds UN member states to seek out and prosecute terrorists and to halt funds supporting them, as well as requiring states to collaborate in criminal investigations and proceedings relating to the financing or support of terrorist acts.

22 The communiqué of the Development Committee issued on 18 November 2001 highlighted the need for both the World Bank and the IMF, as part of their increased attention to governance-related issues, to help countries to identify and address abuses such as money laundering and terrorist financing.

23 The Basle Committee on Banking Supervision comprises representatives of the central banks and supervisory authorities of Belgium, Canada, France, Germany, Italy, Japan, Luxembourg, the Netherlands, Spain, Sweden, Switzerland, the United Kingdom and the United States.

24 The members of the CPLG are from Argentina, Australia, Brazil, Chile, China, the Czech Republic, Commission Bancaire de l'Union Monétaire Ouest Africain, France, Germany, Hong Kong, India, Italy, Japan, Republic of Korea, Mexico, the Netherlands, Russia, Saudi Arabia, Singapore, South Africa, the United Kingdom and the United States. In addition, the CPLG has representatives from the European Commission, the Financial Stability Institute, the IMF and the World Bank.

References

Akyüz, Y. (ed.) (2002) *Reforming the Global Financial Architecture: Issues and Proposals*, Geneva: UNCTAD/Penang: Third World Network/London and New York: Zed Books.

BIS (2002) *BIS Quarterly Review: International Banking and Financial Market Developments*, Basle: BIS, March.

CPSS (2000a) *Core Principles for Systemically Important Payment Systems: Part 1 – The Core Principles*, Consultative Report of the Task Force on Payment System Principles and Practices, Basle: BIS, July.

CPSS (2000b) *Core Principles for Systemically Important Payment Systems: Part 2 – Implementing the Core Principles*, Consultative Report of the Task Force on Payment System Principles and Practices, Basle: BIS, July.

FATF/GAFI (2000) *Review to Identify Non-Cooperative Countries or Territories: Increasing the Worldwide Effectiveness of Anti-Money Laundering Measures*, Paris: OECD, June.

FSF (Financial Stability Forum) (2002) *Ongoing and Recent Work Relevant to Sound Financial Systems*, Basle: FSF, March.

Group of Thirty (2000) *Reducing the Risks of International Insolvency: A Compendium of Work in Progress*, Washington, DC: Group of Thirty.

Iskander, M. R. and N. Chamlou (2000) *Corporate Governance: A Framework for Implementation*, Washington, DC: The World Bank Group.

OECD (2000) 'Mergers and Acquisitions in the Financial Sector', in *Financial Market Trends*, no. 75, March.

Powers, W. C., R. S. Troubh and H. S. Winokur (2002) *Report of Investigation by the Special Investigative Committee of the Board of Directors of EnROn Corp.*, Austin, 1 February.

Sundarajan, V., C. Enoch, A. San José, P. Hilbers, R. Krueger, M. Moretti and G. Slack (2002) *Financial Soundness Indicators: Analytical Aspects and Country Practices*, IMF Occasional Paper No. 212, Washington, DC: IMF.

Tweedie, D. (2001) 'Accounting for the World', *The Financial Regulator*, vol. 6, no. 2, September.

UNCTAD (2001) *Trade and Development Report, 2001*, Geneva: UNCTAD.

White, W. R. (1996) *International Agreements in the Area of Banking and Finance: Accomplishments and Outstanding Issues*, BIS Working Paper No. 3, October, Geneva: BIS.

Working Party on Financial Stability in Emerging Market Economies (1997) *Financial Stability in Emerging Market Economies: A Strategy for the Formulation, Adoption and Implementation of Sound Principles and Practices to Strengthen Financial Systems*, Basle: BIS, April.

Index